Moving a Community College Forward

THE FUTURES SERIES ON COMMUNITY COLLEGES

The Futures Series on Community Colleges brings together the expertise, creativity, and foresight of visionaries who are reshaping the nation's community colleges. It is designed to produce and deliver books that strike at the heart of issues that will shape the future of community colleges. Futures books examine emerging models, policies, issues, and systems, and stretch prevailing assumptions about leadership and management by reaching beyond the limits of convention and tradition.

Series Editors

Richard L. Alfred, PhD, Series Founding Editor, University of Michigan
Debbie L. Sydow, PhD, Series Senior Editor, Richard Bland College of William & Mary
Kate Thirolf, PhD, Series Editor, University of Maryland Global Campus

Titles in Series

Moving a Community College Forward

My Story as an Educator, Researcher, President, and Radical

James Jacobs

BLOOMSBURY ACADEMIC
NEW YORK · LONDON · OXFORD · NEW DELHI · SYDNEY

BLOOMSBURY ACADEMIC
Bloomsbury Publishing Inc, 1359 Broadway, New York, NY 10018, USA
Bloomsbury Publishing Ireland, 29 Earlsfort Terrace, Dublin 2, D02 AY28, Ireland
Bloomsbury Publishing Plc, 50 Bedford Square, London, WC1B 3DP, UK

BLOOMSBURY, BLOOMSBURY ACADEMIC and the Diana logo are trademarks of Bloomsbury Publishing Plc

First published in the United States of America 2026

For legal purposes the Acknowledgments on p. x constitute an extension of this copyright page.

Cover design by Kathi Ha
Cover image © iStock.com/olaser

Bloomsbury Publishing Inc does not have any control over, or responsibility for, any third-party websites referred to or in this book. All internet addresses given in this book were correct at the time of going to press. The author and publisher regret any inconvenience caused if addresses have changed or sites have ceased to exist, but can accept no responsibility for any such changes.

Library of Congress Cataloging-in-Publication Data is available

ISBN: HB: 979-8-2163-7798-6
PB: 979-8-2163-7797-9
ePDF: 979-8-2163-7796-2
eBook: 979-8-2163-7795-5

Series: The Futures Series on Community Colleges

Typeset by Deanta Global Publishing Services, Chennai, India
Printed and bound in the United States of America

For product safety related questions contact productsafety@bloomsbury.com.

To find out more about our authors and books visit www.bloomsbury.com and sign up for our newsletters.

For all of us who work at community colleges
because we believe they will change America.

Contents

Figures

Table

Acknowledgments

I originally wrote a draft of *Moving a Community College Forward* for myself as an analysis of my presidency at Macomb Community College. I shared a draft with a few friends, and they encouraged me to seek a wider audience for the book. While this is a personal narrative, I hope it has some relevance both for practitioners inside community colleges seeking leadership roles and for anyone who wishes to understand the workforce development mission of community colleges. In addition, my hope is that my story will motivate young people who are interested in changing America to consider working at community colleges.

When you write a book concerning nearly sixty years of activity, there are literally thousands of people you should acknowledge. There is no way I could recall all of them, let alone specifically mention how they aided in the development of this book. So rather than risk offending someone or boring the reader with a list of names, I will cite those who were directly involved in giving me their time, energy, and advice to make this into a book. Of course, despite the efforts of everyone, I am responsible for any errors or omissions.

Steve Babson, my friend and political comrade, was instrumental in helping me frame the book as well as teaching me how to write and edit. Ron Aronson, professor emeritus from Wayne State University and another political ally, carefully read the manuscript and thoughtfully challenged me to confront issues both personal and political. I am grateful to both of them for their support. In addition, Hank Ackerman, Tom Bailey, Joe Blum, Michael Jacobs, Sue Calkins, Jack Cantrell, Christopher Brockett, Richard Fried, Arthur Ritas, Jim Varty, and David Wessel read earlier drafts and provided much-needed critique and suggestions on how to develop the manuscript. Finally, I thank my long-term support group of former Macomb teachers—the Royal Society—for providing me with positive encouragement and support during the entire process.

In addition, I was dependent on professionals in the publishing world who used their skills to fashion the manuscript into something worthy of publication. Judy Burns motivated me to place the Macomb story within the context of changes in the Detroit region and the auto industry. The editors of the Futures Series on Community Colleges at Bloomsbury, Kate Thirolf and Debbie Sydow, provided their insights, edited the chapters, even gave me a title, and shepherded the book into publication. They were willing to take a risk on this hybrid manuscript that blended personal narrative and research-based analysis for their highly regarded community college series. Kate especially helped me avoid some major errors in the draft.

While the book tried to discuss general community college workforce development issues, there is one college that plays the central role. The book could not have been written without the support of the present Macomb Community College staff who provided the photographs for the book, helped with gathering college data, and gave me access to the college's archives. I want to thank James Sawyer, president of the college, for providing invaluable college support. Macomb staff members Jeanne Nicol, Nicole McKee, April Conant, and Ann Bentson were extremely helpful in pulling together some of the material used in the book. Moreover, during this process, no one at the college ever asked me to see a draft or attempted to influence what I wrote. I hope they will think of this book as a valuable contribution to understanding the college and Macomb County.

Ideas mean nothing unless you have people who can do the work. While the book focuses on my role as president, nothing would have been accomplished without the dedication of my staff who worked with me in the President's Office at the college. I want to thank them for their efforts at implementing our activities and making me look better than I was: Patty Martz, Sharon Kowal, Gerri Pianko, Jill Little, and Nicole McKee.

Finally, as anyone who completes a book knows, none of this could be written without a supportive family. My children and their partners and my grandchildren were all helpful. Even though she knows more about English grammar and proper writing than certainly I do, my wife Gabriella had the foresight not to read a single word of the book until it was completed. Her most important contribution was her perspective of growing up outside of American culture, which kept me honest and prevented me from taking myself too seriously and believing whatever I think is so important. In this process, she has sacrificed a great deal. Without her love and support, the book would never have been written.

Introduction
Why This Book?

Education is a journey. This is the story of mine, and my transformation from student radical to college president. It's also the story of one of the most profound yet least understood transformations in higher education in the United States, namely how community colleges have evolved from an educational afterthought to an engine of personal and economic development. By sharing both stories in this book, my goal is to provide insight into how community college leaders can best lead their colleges and support their communities as we look to the future.

To prepare for the future, we must take the time to reflect on the past. Looking back, my decades-long career in community colleges was almost cut short. In the fall of 1970, when I was a social science faculty member at Macomb Community College in Michigan, I walked onto the campus and was surprised to see that the clerical workers had gone on strike. They had recently organized themselves into a union, and the administration refused to bargain their first contract. I thought of myself as a radical activist, so of course, I joined the clerical workers on the picket line. This was not the best career move for someone newly named as a full-time instructor. What I did not know at the time was that the Federal Bureau of Investigation (FBI) had alerted the college about my political activism, increasing my reputation with the administration as a troublemaker. My solidarity with the clerical workers did not go unnoticed. I was quickly fired, then reinstated when the union-negotiated arbitration process saved my job. Unquestionably, my career at Macomb Community College was off to a shaky start.

Forty years later, I walked across the same campus as president of Macomb Community College. I was headed to greet President Barack Obama, who was scheduled to announce his national agenda for community colleges, citing Macomb Community College as a model for meeting the needs of working-class students in a rapidly changing economy. When we met, Obama asked me how long I'd been president. "It's my first year," I answered. "Me too," he replied.

This book explores Macomb Community College's transition from a small two-year institution based in rented classrooms to what it is today, a multi-campus center of higher education at the center of the economic and civic life of Macomb County, Michigan. In its first year, in 1954, the college served just eighty-four students; now, it has tens of thousands enrolled in its programs. I'm happy to have played a role in its transformation.

When I retired, a local newspaper reporter who had covered the college for decades and knew me well posed this question: "How is it that you, as a self-identified radical, became successful within the current system? Didn't you change?" My immediate response was to reject that notion, noting that my beliefs and values, and my commitment to radical change, remained the same as ever.

Figure 0.1 Here I am greeting President Obama when he visited Macomb Community College to announce his national agenda for community colleges in July 2009. Image courtesy of Michael Sarnacki.

Even as those words came out of my mouth, I knew my answer was too quick and not wholly accurate: of course, the experience transformed me. I started at Macomb Community College in 1967 as a part-time instructor with no goal other than to organize working-class white people for social change. Detroit, in general, and Macomb County, specifically, seemed a good place to start. As I became part of the community, my goal shifted to developing the college and advising others who were struggling to develop their own community colleges.

The success of any college depends on how well the institution understands the community and what it needs. So, of necessity, this is not only a book about Macomb Community College, but how it responded to the pressing issues confronting the Detroit region and the US auto industry. It is also a book about how community colleges have evolved into an important new sector of American higher education.

While this book focuses on community colleges and how they can realize their true potential, a larger audience may find the personal narrative useful. This book is not an attempt to justify the choices I made or even suggest they should be a model to be followed by others facing similar issues. Instead, it tries to provide a more accurate, complete, complex, and, I believe, an optimistic answer to the question, "Did you change?"

Macomb Community College by the Numbers

Macomb Community College is in Macomb County, which borders on the northeast side of Detroit. The college has two main campuses (South and Center) and two smaller facilities: the Michigan Technological Education Center (MTEC) and the Public Safety Training Center.

In 2016, the total duplicated headcount included 22,000 credit students and 12,000 non-credit students. In addition, there were 3,100 students attending classes at the University Center.

Almost 70 percent of Macomb's students attend part-time, and over 85 percent of the students were residents of the county. In 2016, 13,000 students received $43 million in federal, state, and private scholarships.

1 **From Brooklyn to Macomb County**

Working fifty years at a community college was not something I aspired to while growing up. Nothing I can identify in my childhood influenced me to work in education, let alone spend a lifetime at a community college. Moreover, there seems to be little in common with Macomb County in Michigan, where I served as college president, and Brooklyn, New York, where I was born and raised.

Macomb County is located on the eastern border of Detroit, Michigan. Before the Second World War, this was primarily a rural area, with a few small towns surrounded by farmland. The County seat was Mt. Clemens, which was settled in the eighteenth century along the Clinton River about 20 miles from Detroit. Macomb County's growth after the Second World War was stimulated by two important trends in the Detroit region—one technical and the other social. The first trend—initiated during the War but developed during the next few decades—was a major change in the construction of automobile manufacturing facilities. Many of the original automobile factories were multi-storied buildings where part-making and assembly operations were coordinated in an intricate process by which the assembly line started at the top of the facility and moved through the levels of the building as more parts to the vehicle were added to it. But during the Second World War, as defense production had to be quickly ramped up, a more efficient process was developed to construct one-storied facilities where assembly and part production were spread along a single massive factory floor. The two benchmark plants for this new architectural model were the large Ford bomber plant located in Ypsilanti, Michigan, and the United States Army Tank Plant in 1941 in Warren, Michigan. These types of facilities needed significantly more vacant land than existed anywhere inside Detroit, so expansion into the suburbs was the logical alternative. From 1946 to 1956, domestic auto makers built twenty new plants in the Detroit area, all of them in the suburbs. The construction of the General Motors Technical facility in 1954 in Warren cemented the concentration of new post-war growth in the Detroit suburbs, not just the city—creating the potential for major economic growth in Macomb County.[1]

At the same time there was another important trend that contributed to the growth of Macomb County. In part spurred by the war effort and the domestic economic expansion that followed, the Great Migration of African Americans from the South to the Northeast and Midwest in search of employment expanded the Black population in Detroit. From 1940 to 1950, the Black population of Detroit doubled. As the Black population expanded, particularly during the war years, conflict erupted with white residents over housing and other community matters. Some of this also spilled over to labor disruption within the auto plants. In 1943, Detroit experienced a major race riot, which influenced white residents to pursue housing options outside the city after the war. By 1950, 16 percent of the population in the city was non-white, and this population would almost double in the next decade.[2] The demand of this new population for employment, housing, and commercial services served to intensify the creation of Macomb County as an industrial suburb. The interrelationship between these two trends, one technical and one social, served as the enduring context for the development of Macomb County, its community college, and my work as president.

Often the media image of the auto industry focuses on the assembly plant, where scores of workers are fashioning parts on the multi-colored vehicles rolling along a conveyor belt. This is only the final stages of producing a car. The auto industry is a vast network of research, design, part-making, and component production activities, many often performed outside of the Original Equipment Manufacturers (OEM). All of these activities can be found in Macomb County. In addition to the large "Big Three" facilities, many tool and die, machine tool builders, and software design firms located in the county created many highly skilled and highly paid manufacturing and technical jobs. In addition to this private automotive sector focus, during the Second World War, the United States Army centralized all its control, design, and a good deal of its manufacturing of armored vehicles in Macomb County, making the county the home of the fourth largest vehicle producer in the United States, the United States Army.[3]

The industrial expansion into Macomb County was soon accompanied in the early 1950s by the migration of white working-class families from Detroit. Many settled in the southern end of the county, rapidly increasing the size of these previously small towns. Warren, which was a small community of 22,146 before the Second World War, became the fourth largest city in Michigan by 1970 with a population of 179,260.[4] The population growth in the county outpaced the development of hospitals, libraries, schools, and municipal police and fire services. There was little mass transportation; mobility was entirely dependent upon the private use of the automobile. Until Macomb Community College was founded in 1954, there were no postsecondary institutions public or private operating in Macomb County. With almost no planning, the population of the county grew through the construction of suburban subdivisions, which were simply overlaid upon the previous township boundaries, often resulting in several school districts inside, each with their own set of property taxes located within one Macomb city.

The new Macomb residents were primarily young families with children moving from Detroit. They were mostly from Polish and Italian ethnic backgrounds. Most worked in the auto sector directly or in auto-related jobs. Many were unionized jobs with fringe benefits. There were very few low-income people migrating to Macomb County. Only two small Black communities existed in the county, which originated from the pre-Civil War Underground Railroad days as escaping ex-slaves thought they had reached Canada when they settled in Macomb County. The population of the county was overwhelmingly white.

During this high-growth period, the county-wide institutions were relatively marginal and insignificant to how things were changing. With the exception of implementing the water and sewage lines (which made the Drain Commissioner the most important and powerful County official), there was little intentional community development planning on the county level. There was no county executive; governance was through a 24-member Board of Supervisors elected in geographical districts to represent their local interests. This maintained the political control of the County in rural hands. Official county activities were concentrated in Mt. Clemens, far removed from the high-growth areas of Warren, Roseville, and St. Clair Shores, and as a result the County played little role in their development. County leadership before 1950 was dominated by rural Republicans, but as the population grew, many of these officials switched to the Democratic Party to remain in office. This resulted in little change in the political perspective of County leadership. Civic institutions were few and the participation of the new residents in what existed was low. Other than school districts, the newly constructed Catholic churches, and local property owners' groups concerned with taxes established in the communities, there were few Macomb County nongovernmental organizations representing the interests of the new residents in these communities.[5]

In essence, Macomb County was a model post-war working-class industrial suburb. Instead of urban centers, there were a number of smaller cities with very minuscule downtowns. Most commercial life was formed around the new retail innovation in the Detroit region, the shopping mall. The absence of poor people and the presence of unionized jobs with fringe benefits in the expanding automotive sector resulted in Macomb County residents possessing relatively high mean and median family incomes compared to other parts of the United States. Indeed, in 1970, according to the Census, Macomb County was among the top fifty counties in the United States in median family income.[6] Despite the decentralization of the communities and the absence of many public institutions, people liked living in Macomb County, in large part because it was not Detroit. They focused their lives on their work and their families. This was the local context I encountered in 1967 when I started working at Macomb Community College.

My background was considerably different. I was born and raised in a white working-class neighborhood in Brooklyn, New York, which then was unnamed, but today it is called Prospect Heights adjacent to the now gentrified Park Slope. There were no community colleges when I was growing up in Brooklyn. I came from an ethnic Greek American family, where no one had gone to college. Greeks were a marginal ethnic subgroup in a neighborhood where most of the families were Irish Catholics. I remember attending St. Patrick's Day events at the local Catholic church, St. Theresa, where speakers always named the six counties of Northern Ireland to remind people that the new Irish Republic remained incomplete.

None of my friends' families owned their homes and few possessed cars. Like my family, few of my friend's parents had gone to college, and most worked blue or lower-level white-collar jobs. My father worked as a linotype operator at a small Greek printing company owned by his sister's husband. He was born in Smyrna, Turkey (now called Izmir), and fled to Greece during what Greeks refer to as the Great Catastrophe at the end of the Greco-Turkish War. He came to America in the late 1920s. My mother was born on the Lower East Side of Manhattan a few months after her parents arrived from Greece. Her father died soon after they arrived, and the family was left without any regular source of income. She and her older sister left high school to find work, so the family would not solely depend on welfare.

I always wondered what in my upbringing propelled me from the ethnic-immigrant community I was raised in to a wider world of radical politics and higher education. It was, I think, a combination of internal and external factors. The internal factors start with my parents—my mother and father wanted me to attend college and made it clear that this was what they expected. While neither of my parents had completed high school, they were very literate. My mother's education was interrupted when she quit high school to work full-time, but she was always interested in literature and read books all the time I was growing up. In the late 1950s, she enrolled in Brooklyn College's first adult cohort program and eventually graduated. There were books in the house, a giant encyclopedia, and my parents played Scrabble regularly and worked together to complete the *New York Times* Sunday crossword puzzle. They wanted economic mobility for me, and that desire no doubt contributed to my success in school.

My parents were also politically progressive. I am not sure of the origins of their politics, but my father's skepticism about political and military elites may have followed from Greece's catastrophic intervention in Turkey's civil war, leading to defeat and his family's harrowing expulsion from Smyrna. After my parents married, they lived in the Bronx and interacted with non-Greek friends (primarily Jewish) whom they'd met in their apartment building. These people were close sympathizers, if not members, of the Communist Party. Even when my parents moved to Brooklyn, they continued to associate with these Bronx friends, and I interacted with them as a child. I am sure these associations contributed to my parents' literacy and progressive orientation. Years later, after my father died, I learned that many refugees from Smyrna, when they settled in Greece, became staunch leftists. Even today, the areas in Greece where they settled provide consistent support for left parties. I was motivated by my family to move beyond our immigrant enclave. Unlike most of our Greek relatives, my parents spoke Greek to each other but rarely to me. It was always English. Nor did they attend the Greek church, so outside of interaction with relatives at holiday gatherings or social events such as weddings, there was little expectation that I'd learn Greek or maintain ties within the Greek community.

External factors were equally important in my development. While the desire to achieve a better life was planted early, what allowed me to succeed was the presence of important public institutions and policies established in post-war New York City. I attended one of the most outstanding public high schools in the nation, Stuyvesant High School, where a substantial number of the graduating class was accepted into Ivy League schools. Almost all the graduates went to college. We lived in a rent-controlled apartment, so our housing costs were capped. We did not have a car until 1950, an ugly green Nash that resembled a tank more than a passenger vehicle. We rarely used the car, taking advantage of a functioning subway system which made it possible to go "into the city" (Manhattan) to visit museums, see plays, and develop an appreciation for things beyond our Brooklyn neighborhood.

As with many immigrant families, my parents assumed I would attend college. At Stuyvesant, which at that time only admitted boys, I was a below-average student, playing on the football team and hanging out with classmates from the poor neighborhoods close to the high school. However, I also encountered boys from all over the city—many from progressive families. They were intelligent, oriented to college, and gave me a broader vision than I experienced in my neighborhood. Some were overtly political, and in my senior year, I participated in a demonstration against the nuclear air raid drills that often were held to prepare for possible war with the Soviet Union. Before I started college, I was culturally influenced by jazz and the

Beat Generation. Even as a high school student, I was going to hear John Coltrane and other prominent jazz musicians at places like the Five Spot Café and Village Gate. This was my first introduction to any Black cultural experience, which influenced me for the rest of my life.

These formative experiences all contributed to my personal motivation. In much of the debate about what to do in the United States concerning the growing inequities of American society, conservatives have correctly focused on the need for self-responsibility and personal improvement. I grew up in a stable family, which motivated me to advance. My grades and studies were principal issues at the dinner table. There was no question that parental pressure played a significant role.

But parental intentions, while necessary, need to be backed by institutions that support, develop and extend the motivations provided by the family. I was lucky to have these growing up in New York City in the late 1950s. Public investment is necessary to develop institutions that can serve the aspirations of working-class families. This is the main reason for the significance of community colleges. They are part of a public system of institutions that promote opportunities and growth for working people.

Unfortunately, many community colleges do not promote themselves to their communities in that manner. Especially in their beginning stages, the colleges portrayed themselves as a cheap alternative to a four-year education. Even when I was president at Macomb, our media advertising often used the tagline "come to Macomb and graduate debt free." While true, it can be misconstrued to mean that because we charge lower tuition we are somehow "inferior" to the classroom experience at four-year institutions. It also allows many who want to limit the growth and influence of four-year institutions to support community colleges as a cheaper alternative to those four-year schools which they believe are too expensive and too leftist. They want college budgets kept low, and the curriculum narrowed to mid-level vocational training, so students will obtain a degree but their access to wider opportunities for employment and personal fulfillment is diminished. I learned through my experience the significance of public institutions to support the opportunities of people. Instead of increasing the equity of American society by providing access to postsecondary education, the community college is seen by many as a terminal place for students who receive an associate's degree. Instead of a door to future opportunity, it is viewed as a ceiling that cuts off growth. To this day, community colleges continue to struggle against this public perception of being a low-cost inferior alternative to the four-year institutions.

Coming of Age in New York

My interest in Students for a Democratic Society (SDS) developed during the Cuban missile crisis and the helpless feeling I had as it appeared we were headed for nuclear war. I was politically active in the civil rights and student movement at Harpur College in New York as an undergraduate. In 1965, I headed off to graduate school at Princeton University (where one of my former professors at Harpur was on the faculty). I had no career plans except to "change the world." I never saw myself as a researcher or teacher at a major university like most of my peers in graduate school. I wanted to "organize," meaning I wanted to mobilize working-class people so we could produce democratic change. In the 1960s, the term organizer was highly regarded in the student and civil rights movement. It meant you were committed to collaborating with ordinary people to produce change. You did not see yourself as a leader of these people, more a vehicle to get them started so they could voice their concerns.

During the summer of 1966, Princeton supported my enrollment in a summer program at the University of Michigan. My real reason for attending was to work on a new SDS project that was starting in Ann Arbor called the Radical Education Project (REP). The goal of REP was to provide intellectual support for SDS's activist work, and because I was already a graduate student, I gravitated toward this "intellectual" part of the student movement. REP was initiated to be a think tank that would provide SDS organizers with critiques of American society, which they could use in schools and communities.[7]

REP attracted many SDS members with degrees and professional aspirations who were also looking for ways to make a difference. In 1967, it organized a vital conference in Ann Arbor entitled "Radicals in The Professions," bringing together many SDS people who were pursuing careers in law, medicine, social work, and academia. For me, the conference was important because I interacted with SDS members grappling with the same issues I faced: how to be relevant and use what they had learned in their graduate school professions to make a difference. Soon after the conference, I read about one SDS organizer, Richard Rothstein, who became a teacher at a community college outside Chicago to organize white working-class students. His description of his work at the community college deeply moved me. It seemed like a perfect fit for my "career plans." My degrees could get me a job, and I would be "organizing" working-class people at a community college.[8] It would be easy for me to relocate from Ann Arbor to Detroit. I was ready to find Macomb Community College.

Early Days at Macomb

I ended up at Macomb Community College through a combination of chance and luck. A friend from Harpur, Susan Calkins, was taking graduate classes at the University of Michigan in the School of Social Work. One of Susan's classmates was a woman who taught at Macomb and whose husband was an administrator at the college. They wanted someone to speak about the opposition to the Vietnam War, and she told them about me.

With that invitation in July 1967, I drove from Ann Arbor to the new South Campus of Macomb to speak about SDS and the Vietnam War. The talk was well received, even by a few Vietnam veterans in the class. Later that day, I had lunch with some faculty members who were anti-war and pro-civil rights, but outside of the student movement. A few had just participated in a significant local civil rights housing struggle defending an interracial couple's right to live in Warren, Michigan. Carado and Ruby Bailey bought a house in Warren and faced right-wing protesters who burned crosses on their lawn and threatened to firebomb the house.[9] The couple who hosted the lunch, Don and Lillian Bauder, had defended the Baileys and confronted the rioters. I felt comfortable around these Macomb Community College teachers and was happy we shared many political objectives. They wanted to teach at Macomb in order to be relevant to their community; this attracted me immediately. The full-time faculty at Macomb had just formed an independent faculty union and even went on a short strike in the fall of 1967, just before I was hired. It was easy for me to say yes when Don Bauder, an administrator at the college, asked me to teach a political science class part-time in September of 1967.

While I had a general picture of Detroit being the center of the auto industry, I had not appreciated the significant role the auto industry played at the college. In the early 1960s, the domestic automobile industry—Ford, Chrysler, and General Motors, commonly known as the Big Three—was at the apex of its economic power. Ninety percent of all passenger vehicles sold in the United States came from these three companies. Thousands of workers were employed in the facilities of GM, Ford, and Chrysler in Macomb County, and many of them were now living in suburban communities adjacent to the plants. General Motors employed almost 800,000 workers and was the largest private employer in the world.[10]

Warren was one of the fastest-growing cities in the United States in the 1960s. The GM Tech Center, located in Warren only a few miles from Macomb Community College and known as "the Versailles of Industry" by *LIFE* magazine, was the largest private sector research and development center in the world. In addition, along Groesbeck Highway, hundreds of smaller auto suppliers and machine tool building plants were producing equipment and parts utilized by the Original Equipment Manufacturers. The automobile industry was at the core of the American economy, and Macomb County was an important center of that core. The people of the county firmly accepted its role as an auto center, and there was an optimistic view held by Macomb residents for its future. Even critics of the industry were accepted within the county without much concern. In my first year at Macomb, the college hosted Ralph Nader who had recently published his famous critique of the industry, *Unsafe at Any Speed*.

In stark contrast, while Macomb County flourished within the expansion of the auto industry and its growing population of working-class families with children in the early 1950s, the city of Detroit began its decline. Over 300,000 residents left the city in the next decade. In July 1967, Detroit experienced the largest urban rebellion in the 1960s, which revealed a host of serious issues that had steadily built up to confront the city since the Second World War. The overall population of the city continued its decline, as white families fled to the suburbs. Economic expansion inside the city was at a standstill. There were few new industrial or commercial facilities planned for the city, and the continued decline in city-based manufacturing jobs limited employment for city residents. Institutions such as the Detroit Public Schools by 1961 were now 46 percent non-white and were forced to cut back and eliminate programs, which curtailed opportunity for an increasing number of low-income non-white families.[11] It was only in the early 1960s that the automakers began hiring Black workers in large numbers. Before that point, most Black workers were only employed in the foundry or heat treat operations, generally considered the worst and most dangerous jobs in the auto industry. The rebellion became an excuse for the political leaders in the suburbs to distance themselves from Detroit in any way possible. These actions had widespread support among Macomb County residents.

During that period, the residents of East Detroit voted to change the name of their community to Eastpointe—a symbolic gesture reflecting their desire to separate their community from any connection with the city.

Finally, these developments were joined by an important new external issue: the increasing importance of the Vietnam War. By 1967, the United States was drafting thousands of working-class men to join the armed forces for combat in Vietnam. In addition, the first troops had completed their tours in Vietnam and were returning home. For many young families in Macomb County, the war was a new reality that did not easily fit within their perceptions of opportunity and growth, although most supported the effort. There was little understanding of why the United States was committing thousands of troops to Vietnam, especially when the Detroit rebellion indicated there were many problems in our urban centers.

For my younger students, there was always an ambivalence to work in the auto industry. Unlike their parents who accepted the authoritarian culture of the auto sector workplace and believed these were good-paying jobs, the younger students often saw these jobs as a temporary compromise that had to be made. They tolerated work in the auto plants only through significant consumption of drugs and alcohol. Absences from work on Monday and Friday were so large that the auto companies were forced to hire temporary workers to fill in these days so production could be maintained.[12] Within the industry, often little rebellions of younger workers were directed at the plant conditions. This did not mean they turned to the unions for help. For those of us organizing in the industry, our most popular leaflet passed out in the plants was titled: "My Job Sucks!" While some white workers were supportive of efforts led by Black workers to change these conditions, they believed their auto work was temporary—they would not be there for thirty years like their parents. Many were attracted to the youth culture of the 1960s, although their economic situation made it extremely difficult for them not to work somewhere.

The first classes I taught at Macomb were at night. I was just twenty-three years old. Many of my students were older than me, and some were returning Vietnam veterans and/or were working in the auto industry. They had much more experience in the wider world than I. However, their concerns and reactions to my "lectures" were always respectful. Some of the students had begun to question the war and were supportive of civil rights. Others, especially the younger students living at home with their parents, were unhappy with the isolation and blandness of Macomb suburban life. However, I also realized I could learn from them. Their willingness to work long hours, attend school, and often raise young families was impressive to me. I realized their experiences were much more the norm for most working people than my own. In many ways, attending community college has been a means to better themselves, their families, and the communities. They had a good deal to teach me. They also had significant blind spots, especially in dealing with race. While some were outright hostile to Black people, many had little or no contact with people unlike themselves. Particularly younger students who were often sympathetic to civil rights and supportive in general had almost no direct ties with Black people or the city of Detroit. Moreover, the culture of the institution was dominated by a white suburban perspective, which had little or no understanding of the role race played in their views of Detroit.

The only significant pushback occurred in the spring of 1968 when the assassination of Martin Luther King Jr. sparked protests in Detroit and across the country. My students' response was fear of the "rioters" and a rejection of any attempts to discuss how white racism drove these events. As a part-time instructor only teaching in the evening, I had little interaction with the rest of the staff or even the students outside the classroom. Nevertheless, I was convinced that teaching at Macomb was a real opportunity for me.

Getting a decent salary for meaningful political work seemed too good to be true. At the time, I considered the classroom as a place for political discussion, which would motivate some students to join SDS. I paid almost no attention to the internal workings of the college—it was an institution that attracted working people, and my goal was to radically educate them. The "real" political work was in the community or supporting auto workers. However, even then, I sensed that radicals could learn from these students' struggles. In my first year as a part-timer, I summarized my experiences at Macomb in an SDS newsletter published in January 1968:

> there is another reason for activities such as teaching at community colleges. We need the help of these people to broaden our demands; often, we have a very arrogant attitude toward workers and lower-middle-class people: these are the groups that need to be "radicalized" and brought to our viewpoint. But we must learn from their demands. We are a privileged sector of America, not used to struggling and maintaining ourselves as these people are. We can draw from their experience as well as ask them to accept our vision. Then we might have a real movement, and the term "radicals" in the professions will not make us feel so uncomfortable.[13]

Reading these words more than fifty years later is immensely satisfying. I was happy to learn how much I still believed in these words. I never regretted my choice to work at Macomb Community College.

What I Learned

From the very beginning, I was comfortable working at Macomb Community College. You cannot work at a community college and be effective unless you identify with and respect the students and staff at the institution. While there are commonalities found in all community colleges, they also are all quite different because of the communities they serve. One who seeks any position of leadership in the organization must be able "to fit in their own skin." The credibility you have with the staff, the students, and the community is based on how well you fit within the community you serve. In my case, since I wanted to be in a working-class community, I was open to learning about it through interactions with my students. Teaching was not just an appreciation of the student's perspective, but also a process of challenging their perspectives. In this process, however, I also learned that issues such as race were important to address as part of their education process. In retrospect, my attempts to learn from the students were more consistent with the founders of the college than I realized at the time. Indeed, the origins of most community colleges were based on a similar mission of wanting to reflect their community and be a core part of the community. Specifically, the founders of Macomb Community College wanted to provide the county with a local postsecondary education option, but they also wanted to shape the institution to fit the needs of their expanding new community, one that was separate and different from Detroit. As this book explores, as the community changed, so did the college.

Notes

1 Thomas A. Klug, "The Deindustrialization of Detroit," in *Detroit 1967*, ed. Joel Stone (Wayne State University Press, 2017), 68–70.

2 Thomas J. Sugrue, *The Origins of the Urban Crisis: Race and Inequality in Postwar Detroit* (Princeton University Press, 1996), 23.

3 For a discussion on the US Army Tank Command, see Kevin Thorton and Dale Prentiss, *Tanks and Industry: The Detroit Arsenal, 1940–1954* (History Office U.S. Army Tank-Automotive and Armaments Command, 1995).

4 Gerald L. Neil, *History of Warren, Michigan 1837–1970* (n.p., 1971); Center for Community Studies, *Macomb County: A County in Transition* (Macomb Community College, 2003).

5 For a discussion of the early development of suburban Macomb County, see Dave Riddle, "The Rise of the Reagan Democrats in Warren, Michigan 1964–1984," PhD dissertation (Wayne State University, 1998).

6 Jack Rosenthal, "50 Richest Counties Are in the Suburbs," *New York Times*, September 19, 1972, 35.

7 Kirkpatrick Sale, *SDS: The Rise and Development of the Students for a Democratic Society* (Vintage Books, 1974) 288–9.

8 Richie Rothstein, "Organizing in the Heart of America," *Radicals in The Professions Newsletter*, Ann Arbor, vol. 1, no. 2, December 1967, 1.

9 This incident and its aftermath were detailed in: Zack Stanton, "In 1967, a Black Man and a White Woman Bought a Home; American Politics Would Never Be the Same," *Politico*, December 2023, https://www.politico.com/news/magazine/2023/12/22/macomb-county-michigan-suburbs-american-politics-00131386.

10 For a good description of the auto industry in the late 1960s, see William Serrin, *The Company and the Union* (Alfred A. Knopf, 1973).

11 Jeffrey Mirel, *The Rise and Fall of An Urban School System: Detroit, 1907–81*, 2nd ed. (University of Michigan Press, 1999).

12 Dan Georgakas and Marvin Surkin, *Detroit: I Do Mind Dying: A Study in Urban Revolution*, 3rd ed. (Haymarket Books, 2012), 105.

13 Jim Jacobs, "Working Class Political Attitudes Through a Professor's Eyes," *Radicals in The Professions Newsletter*, Ann Arbor, vol. 1, no. 3, January 1968, 6–9.

2 Finding a Role

While my initial experience at Macomb increased my desire to remain teaching at a community college, I knew nothing about the origins of the community college or its place within the American higher education landscape. The modern "comprehensive" community college represents one of the most significant American innovations in postsecondary education. Its origins can be traced back more than a century with the establishment of the first junior college in Joliet, Illinois, in 1901. However, it was not until the post–Second World War era that modern comprehensive community colleges developed. These were institutions that were extremely different from their earlier ancestors. The modern community college is, largely, a product of the post–Second World War growth and prosperity of the United States.

Origins of Workforce Education at Community Colleges

The workforce role American community colleges play is so embedded in the conventional understanding of these institutions that many are stunned to learn that this was not the original mission of the junior college founders. Many of these two-year institutions were created by the presidents of foremost universities such as Chicago, Stanford, and the University of Michigan at the turn of the twentieth century to serve an academic role. The leaders of these universities wanted to free their faculty from teaching undergraduates and encourage them to focus on research. The junior college concept permitted the universities to relocate their undergraduate introductory college courses elsewhere. There were junior colleges initiated by local community leaders who wanted the prestige of a postsecondary institution located in their area. There were also private for-profit junior colleges established, often many affiliated with religious organizations. These early institutions reflected the diversity of the decentralized American educational system. Despite the varied reasons for their creation, almost all the new junior colleges had a common organizational structure—they were modeled after their four-year counterparts.[1]

The early leadership of the public junior colleges typically came from the K–12 system. They made curriculum decisions with the understanding that these institutions were to serve the needs of their communities, and they were responsible for securing the financial support for these new institutions. In their search for local financial support, this administrative leadership began articulating a workforce mission for these new postsecondary institutions. For these local educational administrators from the public school systems, they embraced the vocational mission to increase enrollment and develop a solid community reason for local financial support.[2]

Yet, these initial attempts to "vocationalize" the new institutions did not result in a synthesis with their original "academic" mission. Rather than merge these missions, the administrators simply laid down another track of credentials alongside the traditional junior college liberal arts degree. It was clear, however, that the dominant role of the junior colleges was an academic mission. Long before community colleges had access to federal vocational funds in the 1960s, these new institutions began developing a separate set of credentials to account for this occupational learning. By the 1920s, they had created an occupational curriculum leading to an associate degree and often distinguished it from the liberal arts associate degrees by calling them "applied" degrees. Unlike liberal arts degrees, these applied degrees were terminal degrees not intended to transfer to baccalaureate institutions.[3]

Since many of these programs were designed to prepare students for entry-level occupations, the American Association of Junior and Community Colleges was lobbying by 1937 for a revision of the 1917 Smith-Hughes Act, which prevented postsecondary institutions from accessing federal vocational funds for degrees in occupational areas. These early career programs at community colleges were focused on the middle sector of the American occupational structure. In the 1930s, these occupations were skilled trades in manufacturing, retail sales, clerical, real estate, bookkeeping, and allied health sectors. There was a strong belief that community colleges could better understand the specific occupational needs of workers in this service sector and develop appropriate postsecondary programs to meet their needs. In a 1939 report, the American Association of Community and Junior Colleges defined its vocational education mission as targeting such semi-professions. These growing occupations required more than a secondary trade school, but less than the professional education provided by four-year institutions.[4]

Increased demands for semi-professional employees during the Second World War promoted the workforce mission's growth within community colleges. Under the 1943 Bolton Act, for example, 65,000 nurses were trained by American junior colleges. Many also offered short programs to train more semi-skilled workers in manufacturing. When the war was over and national leaders began to reflect on what skills would be needed in the economy, they saw the community college as an essential institution. This was particularly important for the reintegration of the millions of American military personnel returning to civilian life.[5]

This new understanding of the community college's workforce role was highlighted in the seminal discussion of postsecondary institutions by The President's Commission on Higher Education in 1947, popularly known as the Truman Commission. This Report of the Truman Commission was the first federal attempt to recognize the importance of community colleges in aiding the national post-war economic recovery. It called for the formation of more community colleges to train "young people for employment in a series of technical and semi-professional jobs such as secretaries, medical technicians, nurses' aides, automotive technicians, real estate salesmen."[6]

The growing interest in community colleges was also sparked by skill changes in occupations such as nursing. Through the Second World War, most nurses received their "job training" in diploma programs inside their hospital workplace. An innovative approach developed at Teachers College, Columbia University, called for community colleges to provide an associate degree in nursing. This curriculum would combine academic courses with on-the-job practitioner training coordinated through the community college. In arguing for a new approach, Mildred L. Montag, a nursing professor from Teachers College, cited the Truman Commission in support of her creation of the first associate degree for nursing in 1948. Her justification for training nurses within postsecondary education was that nurses now needed "skill in the art of communicating, knowledge of the economic system, understanding of people and social institutions, [and] an appreciation of the privileges and obligations of citizen." Such knowledge was needed "if the student is to be able to function effectively as a person as well as a technician." She was among the first educators to recognize that workforce programs needed to combine technical and liberal arts skills. By the 1950s, this commitment to both technical and liberal arts missions had become a central characteristic of the modern "comprehensive community college."[7]

The recognition by the Truman Commission of the community college role in postsecondary education stimulated a significant growth of the public comprehensive community college. The Truman Commission recognized the significance of providing adults with access to postsecondary degrees as an important public goal of higher education. For the first time, there was a recognition that community college expansion was a public good worthy of expansion. Not only did this result in more community colleges being created, but they were overwhelming public institutions whose goals were to be responsible to their community for meeting their higher education priorities. In 1948, there were 650 junior colleges in the United States, of which almost half (322) were private institutions. By 1975, there were 1,203 two-year institutions, of which 981 were public and only 222 were private. In many of the larger states, such as California, New York, Ohio, Illinois, Texas, and Florida, there were public state systems of the colleges being organized to serve the needs of citizens through multiple missions, including transfer and workforce.[8]

These new institutions, created by diverse state and local public strategies, all possessed similar characteristics. They were low-cost, open-access institutions that accepted anyone who wanted to register for classes. They included liberal arts classes for students who wanted to transfer to four-year institutions, but also workforce programs for students who were seeking immediate employment. They typically had three sources of revenue: support from their states, tuition, and funding from local communities. Their curriculum and the course delivery systems were flexible to fit the needs of working adults. As public institutions, they were bonded to their communities through a governance structure typically composed of locally elected or selected trustees to ensure a community presence. Even though some colleges today maintain the name "junior college," the public comprehensive community college became the dominant organizational mode by 1980.

Increasing the significance of the workforce mission to the modern community college's role did not, however, mean integrating it directly into the transfer or liberal arts curriculum. Indeed, replicating the approach taken by most American high schools, the occupational programs were organized separately from liberal arts programs often under separate administrative structures. The apprenticeship classes for skilled trades in construction and manufacturing were often taught under a separate calendar, making it impossible for technical students to take classes in the liberal arts. Even when the technical programs required traditional academic subjects, such as mathematics, the colleges often initiated separate courses such as Shop

Math, which was taught by instructors from the Technical Division, not academic mathematics teachers.

The community college technical instructors were often former high school occupational instructors, familiar with the dual educational structure imposed in most high schools and reinforced by federal support for vocational education. The educational requirement to become a faculty member in the liberal arts areas was typically a master's degree. However, for the occupational faculty, "previous work experience" and/or "occupational credentials," such as a state nursing certification or machining apprenticeship, were the more likely acceptable prerequisite for employment.

While these occupational programs helped increase the popularity of community colleges and led to increased public local and state funding, most students at these institutions enrolled in liberal arts courses, and most surveys of student educational intentions revealed they wanted four-year degrees. These students often saw community college as an inexpensive means of acquiring college credits for the first two years of education before they transferred to a four-year institution. Working-class students, particularly those who recently graduated from high school, believed attending a four-year college would increase their employment opportunities significantly.

Despite most students wanting to eventually transfer, there were few efforts made by the faculty or administrators to integrate workforce and transfer programs. The goal of most occupational instructors was to give students technical skills for entry-level work within their specific occupational sector. There was little interest on the part of occupational administrators or instructors in seeing how some of the skills from the liberal arts might be integrated into their programs. Many occupational instructors assumed that their students were *not* going to transfer to four-year institutions, so liberal arts skills were not necessary.[9] An important exception to this trend was faculty in allied health programs, such as nursing, since those programs often had biology, comparative anatomy, and other natural science classes as prerequisites.

Another issue for many community college occupational programs was how to keep up with changes in technology. While many on the teaching staff may have been initially employed in the private sector utilizing the technology they were hired to teach in the classroom, they often lacked the ability to keep up with technological trends in their subject area. They relied upon a system of advisory boards composed of local employers to provide them with advice. The quality of these boards was mixed. Many were often composed of former students who were rarely critical of the programs and did not provide much-needed independent critical feedback. The employment prospects for the students were often based on the personal ties that instructors had with employers who were willing to hire graduates because they had confidence in the instructor. This helped create a different classroom culture in occupational programs from what prevailed in the liberal arts courses. Occupational instructors saw their role as personal coaches of the students, similar to how a journeyman viewed an apprentice at work.[10]

In many ways, the coaching style of occupational educators worked well for their students and was a refreshing change from the traditional college lecture-style education. While many liberal arts instructors were concerned with weeding out their students and eliminating those who did not fit their standards, the occupational faculty were concerned that all their students obtain employment. Their task, as they defined it, was to get students on the payroll of American business. As instructors, they not only taught through lectures and classroom discussions, but they also performed hands-on learning tasks with the students. Norton Grubb and colleagues, in their observations of community college instruction, found that occupational instructors often encouraged more active student participation in the learning process. They wrote, "In our observations, students were more attentive to lectures in occupational classes than academic courses. The lecture, in virtually every case, was followed by a workshop that applied the content of the lecture. Unlike discussions where students can hide by failing to participate. The workshop is an exposed setting where ignorance and inattention to lectures are quickly revealed."[11]

There were two significant drawbacks, however, to the approach taken in occupational instruction. First, there was little time and few resources allocated to ensure that instructors were current on how the technologies they taught were being implemented at the workplace. Most community colleges recognized the need to have knowledgeable technical faculty but rarely implemented any process to hire those with up-to-date knowledge or retrain their existing faculty in new workplace trends. The need to maintain ties with the workplace became more significant as companies' actual use of technology varied enormously based on the business strategies of the individual firm. In addition, their disregard for liberal arts courses often deprived their students of critical thinking skills that would enhance their on-the-job learning and career advancement. A second problem, and perhaps more important, was that the "coaching style" of occupational instructors often morphed into a paternalistic relationship between faculty and students. This was beneficial for students who mirrored the backgrounds of their occupational instructors. They bonded quickly, and the instructors could easily take on the mentor role. However, for students with backgrounds dissimilar to the faculty, especially women, students of color, immigrants, or other non-traditional students, these same instructors—overwhelmingly white males—were often less empathetic and sometimes hostile. As more students from diverse backgrounds enrolled in community college technical programs, the teaching style of technical faculty often became an issue.

None of these issues halted the goal of public policymakers to make the workforce mission the primary driver in the expansion of community colleges. While the origins of the community colleges were still based on local efforts, state policymakers often began utilizing these institutions for their own state economic and workforce development policies. In some states, such as North Carolina, Alabama, and Georgia, the creation of a community college system was stimulated by the state economic development strategy of "smokestack chasing," that is, luring manufacturing facilities to the state from New England and the Midwest.[12]

By the 1960s, the modern community college had emerged, still possessing a strange disconnect between its two major missions, a disconnect that confounds these institutions even today. While administrators and political leaders viewed the workforce mission as central to these institutions, most college students were drawn to the liberal arts classes and many hoped to eventually get a four-year degree. As we discuss later, it is only now that a synthesis is emerging in the form of the "guided pathways" movement, in which liberal arts and occupational training are not considered separate missions, but as complementary activities designed to support and advance the success of all students.[13]

Workforce Education in the Detroit Region

While the planning of Macomb Community College was in the hands of local educators from the county's school districts, they were reflecting critical changes in the training and education needs for the hourly workforce of the auto industry. Since its origins in Detroit, the auto industry was heavily dependent upon the work of unskilled immigrant families and individuals coming from the rural South to work in the auto plants. The ideal skills for auto workers were established by Frederick Taylor over a hundred years ago: respect for authority, ability to follow orders, show up to work regularly, and "leave your brains at the door."[14] There was also a concern that workers had the "right background." Henry Ford established the infamous "Sociological Department" in 1914. This unit monitored the activities of Ford employees to verify they met the standards for the $5 a day pay rate, including being legally married, having no criminal record, or contact with progressive organizations. The company also established a Ford English school which gave lessons to new immigrants in English to ensure that commands were understood by all workers.[15]

For any necessary technical training, the automakers developed their own internal resources. Principal among them was the Henry Ford Trade Academy established in 1916. This private academy was organized and run by the Ford Motor Company to train skilled workers and managers. The program of the school also included many non-technical subjects to help students develop skills to be successful in business. In 1926, General Motors acquired a local four-year college in Flint and created the General Motors Institute. This organization was utilized by GM to give college-level degrees in manufacturing technologies for hourly GM employees who the company selected for advancement. These activities were supplemented through apprenticeship programs, which were developed when the companies were organized by the UAW. The school component for the apprenticeship programs was typically conducted by the local school districts through their adult education services.[16]

However, the restart of the domestic auto industry after the Second World War expanded the need for education and training activities. The automakers initiated new phases of automation through the utilization of large transfer line equipment that standardized the production of engine and transmission parts and made assembly operations more efficient. However, to maintain the new equipment, as well as troubleshoot issues, there was greater demand for more skilled workers. In addition, this new production equipment spun off a whole new generation of tool and die makers, machine designers, and mold makers who were needed to service the equipment. The demand for semi-skilled and skilled workers rose and made it necessary for the automakers to adapt to other methods to find skilled workers. In the post-war period, the Big Three recruited German and British skilled workers who possessed these skills. They also poached their supplier companies for talented workers. But there was a need to develop more skilled workers, and educational institutions were sought out to play a role. In 1952, Ford closed the Henry Ford Trade School but donated the land and buildings to the Dearborn School System to initiate Henry Ford Community College. In 1954, the founders of Macomb Community College included apprenticeship programs from their first-class offerings to prepare workers for the auto industry. From their outset, these colleges had skilled trades as part of their course catalogs, in a sense taking over from the school district. Apprenticeship was always part of the college program from the beginning.

Origins of Macomb Community College

Macomb Community College was initiated in 1954 as a two-year college created by a local school district in Warren, the county's largest city. The college was designed to provide postsecondary education options for citizens who lived and worked in Macomb County. Michigan already had a few junior colleges organized in the early twentieth century, including Grand Rapids Junior College and Highland Park Junior College. These colleges were administered by their K–12 school districts. Even though Macomb Community College started as part of a secondary school district, the goal from the beginning was to develop it as an independent county-wide institution. Moreover, unlike the earlier junior colleges, Macomb was designed to serve working adults, many of them attending college with support from the GI Bill after returning from service either in the Second World War or the Korean War. These were working-class students who never had any postsecondary experience. Today they would be considered "first gen" college students. As one of the college's founders put it, the school's continuing education student "generally could not quit his job, leave home and pursue higher education at an existing four-year college or university. He could, however, go to college part-time, even on Saturday, at a local community institution."[17]

To start the college, however, the original leaders believed that it needed to emerge from local educational institutions that already had a funding base and experience with adult education. Macomb Community College was initiated, therefore, as part of the Van Dyke school district, the largest of the five school districts located in Warren. Van Dyke Schools possessed a strong continuing education program and courses for adults to complete their high school education. There was, from the start, a built-in community college market. The college was initially housed in the high school and junior high school of the Van Dyke Schools, with classes in the late afternoons, early evenings, and on weekends. In the first year, there were eighty-four students enrolled. Almost all the college's founders were former K–12 educators without administrative or teaching experience at the postsecondary level.[18] They were responding to what they saw as the need in the community for working adults to increase their skills for employment in the growing domestic auto industry.

While the college was initially housed in only one school district (no other Macomb school districts participated, citing a lack of funds), the demand for courses quickly grew throughout the county. By 1959, 1,300 students were attending the college, and in 1962 that had grown to 3,800 students, making it impossible to maintain the college within the budget of one school district. Many students were not school district residents, indicating the potential for growth as a county-wide institution. In 1962, the college leadership placed on the ballot a millage initiative to fund such an institution for twenty years. While the initial millage rate was only one mill (one dollar for every $1,000 of state tax evaluation), which was one of the lowest among Michigan educational institutions, the vast demographic, commercial, and industrial expansion of Macomb County in the next twenty years would lead to significant financial support for the institution. Industrial property taxes on these large new auto facilities in the Mound/Van Dyke industrial corridor brought considerable new revenue to the college. Admission was open to students from Detroit and elsewhere, but these non-residents paid a greater tuition rate.[19]

The curriculum for the new college reflected the dominance of the auto industry in the local metropolitan economy. Macomb Community College also had a major workforce mission from the beginning. A "Citizens Report" in 1966 recommended that, "excepting for all adult education programs offered by the K-12 school districts," Macomb County Community College should provide "all public vocational-technical education of a post-high school level in Macomb County."[20] At that time, 3,094 of the 7,183 students attending the college were enrolled in occupational courses, and of these, 624 were classified as "apprentices," 182 were in secretarial programs, and 368 were in manufacturing and design technician programs.[21] Half of all the part-time students were engaged in occupational courses. From the very beginning, Macomb Community College's organizational structure assumed the traditional difference between the transfer mission (getting students prepared for four-year institutions) and the vocational mission (preparing students for work). Even so, more than half of all students were not enrolled in occupational training programs.

The college's first campus was constructed only 2 miles from the General Motors Technical Center, symbolically linking the two institutions. In retrospect, it is significant to note how little any of the local four-year institutions, such as Wayne State University or the University of Detroit, either contributed to the founding of the college or understood the significance of their growth and development. It is also true that few of the original leaders of Macomb Community College sought any relationship with these four-year institutions.[22]

This intentional isolation aligned the college founders with the beliefs of the growing population of former residents of Detroit who wanted as little as possible to do with the city. The college became "their" postsecondary institution. For several years, many in the community, including some of the founders, assumed it would ultimately evolve into a four-year college. There was a strong push to maintain liberal arts programs for students to transfer. At the same time, in this early phase, Macomb Community College also prided itself on its occupational curriculum. By 1965 it offered over seventy-four different occupational degree programs and nine one-year certifications. Determining the balance between the workforce and the transfer mission of the institution became a long-term challenge for Macomb Community College.

Full-Time at Macomb

My full-time appointment at Macomb Community College started in September 1968 as a member of the Education and Cultural Development (ECD) program. Even though my graduate studies at Princeton had been in political science, Macomb's administration assigned me to a unit commonly referred to as Basic Education. This was not the original plan. I was scheduled to teach in the college's political science area, but because of some administrative misunderstanding, that position was eliminated. Basic Education was expanding, so I was placed in that unit. I would teach social science with a team of four instructors; the others taught humanities, English, and natural science. No one questioned my academic abilities to teach these classes, and my master's degree in political science met the criteria spelled out in the union contract. I would be a probationary instructor for two years, and if there were no concerns about my performance, I would become a permanent instructor that could only be terminated or disciplined for violation of my union contract. There were no academic ranks among the faculty; you were either a probationary instructor or a permanent instructor.

Teaching in Basic Education

Basic Education was one of the most significant educational innovations ever produced at Macomb Community College. A Macomb Community College administrator originally designed the unit as part of his graduate thesis attending Wayne State's School of Education. His main goal was to provide a structured experience for students who were unsure about what curriculum to take in college, or uncertain about their ultimate goals for a college education. While his goal was to develop a program to be successful for young people in Macomb County, much of its specific design foreshadowed the pathways model currently utilized in many community colleges.

Uncharacteristically for a community college program, Basic Education was not open to all students. The admissions criteria excluded developmental students (students who scored below college-level tests in reading and mathematics), part-time students, and students with a clear career plan or four-year postsecondary goal. Only students willing to attend full-time and take the block of courses with a team of instructors were admitted to the program. There were no occupational classes offered; the goal of the program was to prepare students for success at Macomb Community College. It was a one-year, two-semester, cohort-based program where students took sixteen credit hours full-time. There were four academic areas in the block: National Science, Communications, Social Science, and Humanities. Each class was capped at thirty students. While this limited the "student market" for Basic Education, it somewhat guaranteed the students would be generally similar in age (younger, right out of high school), sometimes veterans back from Vietnam, and young single heads of household. Most worked at least part-time. They came to school almost every day, and with the block schedule, they shared all their classes and instructors as a group. This cohort model served to mitigate a significant barrier for any successful instruction at a community college: the heterogeneity of the learners' backgrounds and the lack of student interaction outside of the classroom.

The goal of the one-year program was to get students interested in finishing their degree at Macomb as well as sharpen their abilities to make further choices in curriculum and careers. It was assumed that Basic Education faculty would work together to ensure all students in their block would complete the one-year program, go on to other classes at Macomb in their second year, and earn an associate's degree and/or transfer to a four-year institution the following year.

The team of instructors assigned to teach the Basic Education block was expected to meet and plan the semester in an integrated teaching style. We met every Friday to plan out activities and discuss the progress being made by each student. There was a commitment to have every student be successful. We also had one counselor assigned to our team. She had regular interactions with the students and met with us regularly to discuss the individual progress they were making. This counselor was responsible for dealing with the needs of the 120 students in our block—a much better student-to-counselor ratio than many community colleges today, including Macomb.[23]

The Basic Education model made me understand what makes for good teaching and learning. While my political perspective motivated me to become a teacher at a community college, I had no idea how to teach effectively, especially given the challenges working-class students face. Many of them were working full-time and attending school full-time and had little contact with any friends or family members who completed college. Moreover, most had endured not-so-positive high school experiences, so continuing their education was not a high priority. To reach them, to engage them in learning, you had to be a good teacher.

I soon learned that teaching was an essential skill that was much more than lecturing factual material or a breezy discussion of "relevant issues." Most of my undergraduate and graduate school classes were traditional lecture-discussion formats where the professor was the center of knowledge and primarily lectured to already highly motivated students. In my educational experience, my classmates read their assignments, drafted papers, and prepared for class discussions. I was initially startled when Basic Education students would come to class unprepared, or when they needed to skip class because of their work and would ask me, "Are you doing anything important today?" I soon learned I needed to persuade them that applying "academic knowledge" to the issues of everyday life was useful. When I could make this connection, my students became engaged and responded exceptionally well.

Working with a group of instructors and jointly sharing a curriculum was also new for me. The expert role of "sage on the stage" was dropped in favor of a more collaborative approach focused on getting the students interested in learning. At our Friday meetings, we fashioned our classes based on our understanding of the specific needs of the students. Our goal was not just to teach a particular subject but to show the students how to approach prominent issues—often, ones they brought up from their lives that could be analyzed from the perspective of that discipline. In many cases, it was helpful to teach the class jointly so that students could see how different approaches could be taken to the same content.

While I was entirely new to this teaching style, fortunately, the Basic Education unit attracted many talented teachers—some who mastered this pedagogy either from teaching in high schools or from work experiences in religious institutions. They served as mentors for those of us who never collectively taught. Mandatory curriculum planning also forced us to consider what was relevant and, as a team, to tackle significant issues or themes from the general perspectives of our disciplines. Sometimes we team-taught together in the same classroom, challenging the students' perception of the individual instructor as the source of all knowledge. We often used the same textbook, approaching it from various perspectives or disciplines. For example, when we read Malcolm X's autobiography, we discussed it in the English, social science, humanities, and science classes. It was a great learning experience for me, and I think the students also enjoyed this approach.

Because we all had the same students, we could shape our classes in response to current events or issues that the students found interesting. This was a flexible curriculum, and I learned to be selective in choosing topics that were of interest to the lives of young working-class people—their struggles within their families and workplaces. We encouraged students to bring in outside speakers, and this could be significant for all of us. I remember when we were reading *The Algiers Motel Incident* (a book describing the police murder of four young Black men during the 1967 Detroit rebellion), Walter, an African American student, brought into class a brother of one of the victims. Later that semester, the same student brought in a dead rat from his neighborhood, a dramatic evocation of the living conditions in some neighborhoods in Detroit. Another student who worked in a meat processing plant secured a tour of that facility that complemented our reading of *The Jungle* by Upton Sinclair. Most importantly, the goal of the instructor was to engage the students and make all of them successful.

Especially important for me was that I learned that to be effective as a radical teacher I could not ignore other teachers' politics and teaching styles. While I was the only committed "organizer" working in Basic Education, most of the other teachers were progressives who supported civil rights, opposed the Vietnam War, and believed in student activism. I learned how to aggregate their views with mine, and this collaboration would reinforce what the students assimilated. To be successful, however, we did align our themes with what was developing in the Detroit region, which was undergoing some significant changes.

The Detroit Region

Until the late 1960s, the Detroit region was composed of an expanding auto industry and a decaying urban center. The domestic market for automobiles continued to grow as the number of American families with two cars as opposed to one increased from 7 percent in 1950 to 29 percent in 1970.[24] In addition, automakers' profits were increasing with several comfort "add-on" options, such as air-conditioning, power steering, stereos, and automatic transmissions.[25] These add-ons increased profits for the auto companies but contributed little to the reliability and efficiency of the vehicle. Despite the oil energy crisis of 1973, the domestic auto companies assumed the consumer market was for these options and chose not to focus on producing more fuel-efficient automobiles.

In contrast to this optimistic perspective of their future taken by the domestic automakers, the city of Detroit continued its economic decline. Manufacturing job loss of the 1950s was now matched by a loss of retail establishments. From 1954 to 1977, Detroit lost 59,700 retail jobs, as the number of city retail stores declined by over 11,000. The number of corporations filing Detroit income tax dropped by one-third in the decade from 1970 to 1980.[26] These changes were decreasing the employment opportunities for Detroiters significantly. In addition, this steady decline was intensified by two events that further shifted the white population into the suburbs. First, in 1971, was the finding by a federal court that the Detroit schools had for years practiced a policy of racism in their construction of schools and enrollment of students. While this was hardly news, the court ordered cross-district busing of city and suburban districts as the remedy. This produced an instant reaction in the suburbs. In Macomb County in the fall of 1971, a large demonstration against court-ordered busing was held. Petitions were circulated to recall the Democratic Senator Phil Hart. It also spurred the rapid development of new suburban residential housing intentionally constructed outside of the proposed communities covered by the court-ordered busing plan. The result was even greater suburban sprawl, as new communities were rapidly drawing residents from the older suburban areas closer to Detroit. While the Supreme Court in 1975 declared the plan unconstitutional, the damage to city-suburban relations was already accomplished.[27]

The tone of the white response to the Roth decision was not just racism opposing educational integration, but outrage directed at any governmental activity that "forced" citizens to attend schools which they did not want to attend. This initiated a fear of any government intervention in "social matters" as anti-democratic—a trend which continues today. Students came to Macomb, often critical of government overreach and not recognizing the college was part of the government. The other event adding to the fears of white suburbanites was the election of Coleman Young as the first Black mayor of Detroit in 1973. Young, a progressive with roots in the civil rights and trade union community, did little to curtail the continued outward migration of white residents to the suburbs. In 1969, there were 891,000 white people living within the city. By 1976, three years after Young's election, that number was reduced to 543,000.[28]

During this period, the population of Macomb County continued to grow, and the number of retail and commercial operations business units increased. The development of the Lakeside shopping mall in Sterling Heights in 1973 was an example of the shift occurring. My students from suburban families coming to Macomb were unlikely to return to the city for shopping, resulting in the department store Hudson's closing its downtown flagship facility by 1982. Even sports teams disinvested in Detroit. The Detroit Lions built their new stadium in suburban Pontiac, Michigan. The original definition used by many urban planners of a suburb comprised people who live in private homes but work, shop, and attend entertainment and sports events in the urban center. That definition was upended in the Detroit region. The region's new suburbanites wanted nothing to do with the city.

These developments influenced the classroom discussions of race relations. Right after the Detroit rebellion, most of the class discussions focused on what could be done to solve the unequal conditions that brought about these activities. While there were racist attitudes in the response to the rebellion, in general, many of my students recognized there were social and economic factors that needed to be addressed in the Black community. Especially after the Roth busing decision, I noticed the attitudes toward the condition of Black people underwent a significant change. Instead of a discussion of what could be done to aid in the advancement of Black citizens, the concern was to ensure that any remedies did not harm conditions for whites. Macomb students articulated a fear that the government would do something that would directly harm the interests of white people. Issues of racial inequality suddenly became a zero-sum game where any public actions might harm Macomb residents. The government was perceived to be not "on their side." So, to many of my students, it was logical to be against anything that would be supportive of Black people or cities because, ultimately, it would be harmful to those who live in the suburbs. The discussions in class were less about what can be done to eliminate discrimination and racism and more about what can be done to make sure these bad things from the city do not harm residents in the suburbs.[29] Fifty years later, these views are an essential component of white working-class support for Trump.

Basic Education and Macomb Students

My teaching experience in Basic Education stayed with me for the rest of my life. It helped me always ground my work for change within a perspective emphasizing respect and understanding for the ordinary struggles working people face when attempting to get an education. While I did not share the students' specific backgrounds and aspirations, such as home ownership or an interest in new automobiles (many were shocked I never had owned a car until I was in my early twenties), my experience from a working-class immigrant family allowed me to see some of myself in them. This made me a better instructor and began a critical process that was fundamental to my later career. I learned not to be arrogant in my political beliefs and to listen to understand what motivated the views of others.

Through our classroom discussions, I also learned a good deal about the lives of these predominantly white community college students. They lived a tripartite life around their families, work, and school. Despite going to school full-time, almost all of them worked. Their family life was often significantly disrupted by financial and health issues. Many cared for dependents, whether children or grandparents. At the same time, they were influenced by the youth movements of the 1960s, which questioned the conventional definitions of success and family authority. Their rebellion was expressed through long hair, drug use, and music, all alien and frightening to their working-class parents, who believed they had escaped Detroit to join conventional suburban life as depicted on television. Some had joined the military and their experience in Vietnam made them question American society. In addition, many women were going through painful divorces and trying to survive and raise children as single heads of households. Part of getting an education for them was removing themselves from traditional relationships within their communities, while at the same time not leaving Macomb or metropolitan Detroit.

In the struggle of these students to form new relationships between themselves and their communities, I began to appreciate the potential role a community college could play in not only helping them but providing a means for changing their environment for the better. The team-teaching approach allowed students to see the usefulness of different approaches to their lives, and many gravitated to change. I also learned the power of peer support for myself. While my colleagues were not self-defined "radicals," they were also influenced by civil rights and anti-war movements. The team-teaching approach bonded me with the instructors in the program. We worked together, got to know each other's families, and developed long-term respect and trust. It also provided us with a strong peer group that could withstand outside pressure from the administration to tone down our selection of materials or issues to discuss. To this day, the teachers I met in the Basic Education Division are some of my closest friends. Even though Basic Education ended fifty years ago, and we are all retired and scattered all over America, we continue our interactions through weekly Zoom calls.

Unfortunately, many of the other faculty did not appreciate our innovative unit. The Basic Education program was considered controversial because of the collaborative teaching approach and its mandated integration of courses. This approach defied the conventional understanding of college education being the mastery of specific academic subject matters, with the instructor being the sole determinant of knowledge. Many faculty were opposed to team teaching. They thought it was a "watered down curriculum," contradicting their academic discipline's commitment. Some faculty referred to the ECD program not as the "Education and Cultural Development" program but as "Educating College Dummies." They remained committed to the traditional style of college instruction, designed to "weed out" those students who should not be attending college. Only the talented few would advance. For us in Basic Education, student dropouts were a program failure, while for other faculty, they often viewed students dropping out as a sign of a high-quality rigorous program.

Our critics overlooked or didn't seem to care that Basic Education students had higher retention rates, meaning that a higher percentage of our students remained in college and stayed enrolled into the next year. This statistic is a major measurement utilized by community colleges today to determine the effectiveness of a program and institution. Basic Education students were also more likely to continue their education at four-year institutions than other Macomb students. Perhaps most consequential to faculty outside of Basic Education, since the students were locked in a full-time class schedule, many liberal arts faculty saw Basic Education as a potential competitor draining students away from their classes. The technical faculty were also not supportive because they could not understand why students would waste time with all these requirements before getting to their classes. Even though the program was designed as one year, which gave these students an opportunity to take on other courses and programs, we were still considered a threat. Ultimately, it was this issue that eventually pressured the faculty union to express concerns about the program.

In addition to the faculty's opposition to our pedagogy, there was concern among the administration that the program was a hotbed for student activism. The Basic Education students were on campus full-time, and they often reflected the values of the critical inquiry we taught. They became leaders of the student government, writers for the student newspaper, and organizers of political events. The Basic Education structure developed their self-esteem and metacognitive abilities, and they quickly gravitated toward activism and questioning authority.

They, along with other students, were fertile ground for my efforts at organizing an SDS presence on campus. I was the faculty advisor for an SDS chapter in 1968, my first semester, and we developed substantial civil rights and anti-war activities on campus. The chapter attracted cultural rebels (also known as "hippies") but also Vietnam veterans fresh out of the military, making this SDS chapter more than a collection of alienated youth. Some of the African American veterans had ties with the Detroit Black Panther Party and the League of Revolutionary Black Workers, and representatives from these groups spoke on South Campus. Other students worked in auto plants and were familiar with the Dodge Revolutionary Union Movement, a Black worker organization at the Chrysler Dodge Main plant in Hamtramck. The SDS chapter also attracted high school students from some of the local school districts. When SDS collapsed as a national organization after 1969, the group recast itself as the Macomb Liberation Front. The ease with which community college students were able to integrate political work in the high schools, the community, or the plants became a strategic political calculus for my organizing within a community college.[30]

The Macomb administration was not happy with the development of an SDS chapter. At first, I was denied the right to form one. However, the administration relented when the faculty union supported my right to form the organization as a free speech issue. I needed to be careful because I was still a probationary teacher and could be terminated without explanation. After two years, I would become a permanent instructor. During that period, my students often received calls from the Campus Police asking about what I was discussing in the classroom, looking for an excuse to terminate me. When the students told me about the calls, I exposed this activity, and they probably backed off firing me. I became a permanent teacher shortly thereafter, but the administration was still looking for an opportunity to fire me.

The administration finally got their chance during the clerical strike of 1970. During the strike, I also knew from previous encounters with the administration that it would be wise for me to avoid any activity that was not legally protected. I kept on the picket lines, talked with the strikers and students, but engaged in no confrontations or made any threats. Even so, a few days after the settlement, the administration decided to punish those faculty who had refused to cross the picket lines by docking their pay, claiming that taking personal days (under our contract we were allowed to take days off from work) to walk picket lines violated the contract. In my case, however, they simply fired me. I was given a letter before one of my classes asserting that I was fired for physically assaulting students, which prevented them from attending class, dismissing my classes early so students could not learn, and disrupting campus life! Because I was protected by my union contract, I could remain teaching and was entitled to an arbitration hearing. I was not surprised that the institution wanted to terminate me. Since at the time I saw myself as an organizer, I assumed that if I lost the job (as some of my political associates were losing jobs in other work settings), I would simply move on to new employment. Fighting to maintain my job was not a significant consideration for me, since I was young and single with no family. If my firing made people angry and more political, I thought that would be a good outcome.

Fortunately, I had a great mentor who challenged my ambivalence about resisting the firing. Saul Wellman was a former trade union organizer, Spanish Civil War and Second World War veteran, and Communist Party leader. Saul left the party in the 1950s but maintained close ties with young radicals in the Detroit area. He placed my firing in broader political terms as an outrage, not only against me but also for the future success of the Macomb College community. He saw me as an asset to the college and argued I should fight my firing because I was needed. For Saul, participation within the system while at the same time holding your vision enhanced your significance and influence. My place, he argued, should be at the community college, and if I fought the firing, I would obtain local support.[31]

The reaction of the staff at Macomb to my firing was exactly as Saul had predicted. The administration's gambit backfired. When the administration singled me out for firing, many people in the college—faculty, clericals, and students—correctly saw it as an attempt to use the strike as a pretext for getting rid of me. I became a symbolic leader at the college, strengthened, not marginalized by the administration's actions. This backing translated into significant support for my case. I now had "good friends in low places," with clerical workers supplying me with all the administration's meeting notes as they prepared for my case. We knew their arguments, and in April 1971, the arbitrator ruled there were no grounds for dismissal. The arbitrator saw that the college was using my strike support as a pretext for eliminating me and discrediting my political views.[32]

What I Learned

I was now part of the college, fused to the institution. The staff who had opposed my firing expected me to stay as a "college leader." From then on, I became not an individual radical organizer embedded within the institution, but I became convinced of the long-term significance of the institution to the future of America. I believed good community colleges would help change America for the better. I had no desire to leave Macomb; it had become part of my life. Of course, this decision confronted me with new political questions for the rest of my working life. How was I to operate on a tightrope of being within an institution while, at the same time, trying to change it? This would require me to develop a long-term perspective which meant embedding my vision into the relevant issues facing the college. Indeed, community colleges were still relatively new institutions, and there were few examples to follow for anyone. I needed to develop this strategy not only for myself, but for all of us within community colleges. How do you induce change within an institution while remaining a leader within it? You cannot easily disrupt it without harming the important functions it maintains.

This task raised the second and related question: To lead within the community college, you were continually faced with challenges on how to make the institution better for the students, staff, and the community, not just in the future, but now. What are the issues you should concentrate on that can make effective change? If you are promoting change, what are the activities that would indicate to people within the institution that you could improve their lives as well as the institution? Saying no is not a program for change. How could activities be proposed that would be fused with a radical perspective? These were the issues I would face for the rest of my time at Macomb.

I also learned what makes for good instruction at a community college. My experience in Basic Education taught me that my job was to make sure all students succeed, and that process was often a collective one. Good instruction was based on understanding the needs of your students and developing ways of engaging them. You taught students academic concepts by starting with the issues they face and bringing in your academic knowledge to assist them in understanding them. Not all students fall into this category, but many community college students had less-than-positive experiences in their formal education, so they still had to be convinced that classroom learning was useful for them. What you teach and how you teach should always be tied to a strategy that will convince them that education is worthwhile, not just in a narrow economic sense (i.e., more wages and better jobs), but within their lives for themselves, their families, and the community. When you experience their engagement in the classroom, you are on the right track.

Finally, being an instructor at a community college is a very good learning experience for those who seek to be administrators. Experiencing the students and appreciating their situations helped immeasurably for me when I considered all the macro issues of running an institution. It aids my understanding not only of the students and their concerns but also of how important other community college workers are to the institution. Those community college presidents that I have considered most effective leaders were always the ones who had direct experience as a faculty member.

Of course, my commitment to Macomb did not change my political ambition to organize the students or the staff. In April 1971, the largest political demonstration in the county's history took place. The anti-war demonstration started at Macomb College and proceeded to the Chrysler Tank Plant, the Second World War defense facility that still produced armored vehicles for the United States Army. This action was led by a group of Vietnam War veterans, some wearing their old military uniforms. It was joined by high school students who spontaneously left their classes. By the time we reached the plant, over 7,000 people had taken over the street in front of the plant, alarming the local management sufficiently that they shut down the facility. Most of the participants had never been to a demonstration before. As a participant in many demonstrations, I can tell the difference between a rally that draws all the regular suspects (people already committed to activism) and one that brings out individuals who have never or rarely participated. The Tank Plant March was an example of the latter, demonstrating that the opposition to the war was deepening within working-class America, white and Black.

Notes

1   W. Norton Grubb and Marvin Lazerson, *The Education Gospel: The Economic Power of Schooling* (Harvard University Press, 2004), 85.

2   Ibid., 85–6.

3   Terry O'Banion, *Bread and Roses: Helping Students Make a Good Living and Live a Good Life* (League for Innovation, 2016), 21–22.

4   Michael Brick, *The American Association of Junior Colleges: Forum and Focus*, Doctoral Dissertation (Teachers College, Columbia University, 1963), 163.

5   Ibid., 200.

6   Grubb and Lazerson, 87.

7   Martin S. Quigley and Thomas R. Bailey, *Community College Movement in Perspective: Teachers College Responds to the Truman Commission* (Scarecrow Press, 2003), 22.

8   Arthur M. Cohen and Florence B. Brawer, *The American Community College* 3rd ed. (Jossey-Bass, 1996), 14.

9   W. Norton Grubb, *Honored But Invisible: An Inside Look at Teaching in Community Colleges* (Routledge, 1999), 98–9.

10   Ibid., 116–17.

11   Ibid., 106.

12   Stuart A. Rosenfeld, *Competitive Manufacturing: New Strategies for Regional Development* (Rutgers University Press, 1992), 257–9.

13   For an excellent summary of the major issues involving the split between liberal arts and career and technical education, see Thomas R. Bailey and Clive R. Belfield, "The False Dichotomy between Academic Learning and Occupational Skills," *Daedalus* 148, no. 4 (2019): 164–78.

14   David Fasenfest and James Jacobs, "An Anatomy of Change and Transition: The Automobile Industry of Southeast Michigan," *Small Business Economics* 21, no. 2 (2003): 156.

15   "Ford Motor Company Sociological Department & English School," The Henry Ford Museum of American Innovation, accessed June 5, 2025, https://www.thehenryford.org/collections-and -research/digital-resources/popular-topics/sociological-department/.

16   Fasenfest and Jacobs, 261–2.

17   Walter Bradley, "The Origins and Development of Macomb Community College 1952-1975" (unpublished manuscript), 2. Bradley was a co-founder of the college and had started his educational career as a teacher in a one-room schoolhouse. He later became a high school continuing education administrator before becoming the first dean of Macomb Community College. To my knowledge, his 100-page unpublished paper is the only written history of the early years of the college.

18   Ibid., 8–15.

19   Ibid., 18–23.

20   Macomb Association of School Administrators, "A Citizens Report: Macomb Occupational Education Survey," Michigan Department of Education, Division of Vocational Education (1966), 3.

21   Ibid., 175.

22 A book issued at the 70th Anniversary of Macomb Community College mentions that curricula from Wayne State, Michigan State, and the University of Michigan were shared with the new faculty of the college. And many individuals who served on MCC's faculty and administration were graduates of these institutions. But an examination of the advisory boards and professional groups that contributed to the beginning of the college indicates no presence of four-year college administrators. See Macomb Community College, *Transforming Lives and Communities: Macomb Community College at 70* (2024), 8.

23 "A Citizens Report," 17.

24 Emma Rothschild, *Paradise Lost: The Decline of the Auto-Industrial Age* (Random House, 1973), 44.

25 James P. Womack, Daniel T. Jones, and Daniel Roos, *The Machine That Changed the World* (Macmillan Books, 1990), 46.

26 Jeanie Wylie, *Poletown: Community Betrayed* (University of Illinois Press, 1990), 30.

27 Mirel, 348.

28 Heather Ann Thompson, *Whose Detroit? Politics, Labor, and Race in a Modern American City* (Cornell University Press, 2001), 206.

29 To give a sense of the stark racial divisions, in 1970 the percentage of white residents living in Warren was 99.53 percent. Of the 179,260 residents living in Warren, 132 were Black. There were 28 Black households, 23 of them residing on US military property. More details in Zack Stanton, "The Battle for Buster Drive," *Politico*, December 22, 2023, https://www.politico.com/news/magazine /2023/12/22/macomb-county-michigan-suburbs-american-politics-00131386.

30 For a discussion of the political situation in Detroit, see Dan Georgakas and Marvin Surkin, *Detroit I Do Mind Dying: A Study in Urban Revolution* (St. Martin's Press, 1975); James A. Geschwender, *Class, Race, & Worker Insurgency: The League of Revolutionary Black Workers* (Cambridge University Press, 1977); and Michael Hamlin, *A Black Revolutionary's Life in Labor: Black Workers Power in Detroit* (Tide Books, 2012).

31 For a short description of Saul Wellman, read this biography of him: Daniel Gorelik, "NYC's Spanish Civil War Volunteers: Biographies/Saul Wellman," accessed June 5, 2025, https://scwnyc.stuy.edu/ archive/Saul%20Wellman.html.

32 The arbitrator much later shared his view about my case: "I have been practicing law a long time. If asked whether I made a difference somewhere, I think back on one case I arbitrated in which a young community college professor in Michigan was terminated for leading a protest many years ago. I put him back to work. Several years ago, he became president of that community college of 25,000 students. He is an outstanding president. His college, in my opinion, is probably the finest community college in Michigan. I made a difference in his life and the life of the community and county that his college serves." George T. Roumell, Jr., "'You Will Make a Difference': George T. Roumell Jr.'s Fall 2015 Commencement Address to the MSU College of Law," *Michigan Bar Journal*, July 2016, 36.

3 America Discovers Community Colleges

As I was making my transition to become more engaged with the institution of Macomb Community College, the community college sector was undergoing its own significant changes. By the mid-1970s, the comprehensive community college model of an open-access institution that developed programs to serve their communities was being recognized as an important new part of the American postsecondary landscape. These were not simply a few "junior colleges" covering the first two years of postsecondary college, but a potential network of publicly funded institutions with a strong presence in the local areas they served. The ability of over 1,000 local institutions to offer programs that fit the needs of their communities was being recognized and appreciated as an innovative new sector of American higher education. Their significant growth in the 1960s and 1970s triggered the first discussions of how these institutions might serve as a national network to promote workforce development. Macomb Community College, under its new president, would play a key role within these discussions.

Branding a Workforce Provider

From its beginnings at the Van Dyke school district, Macomb Community College always maintained workforce programs. However, they were not considered a part of the institution's principal curriculum but offered as an alternative separate from liberal arts degree programs. The original leaders of the college assumed that both were distinct separate parts of the comprehensive institution. In the case of Macomb, there may have been a greater interest in the liberal arts programs, both on the part of students who enrolled as well as some county leaders who wanted the college to eventually evolve into a four-year institution. However, by the late 1970s, Macomb Community College was shifting its institutional image in the community as a workforce educator provider.[1]

While there were local factors that played a role in the growing attention to the workforce mission, the evolution of workforce programs at the college was heavily influenced by important national economic trends. By the 1970s, the international economic supremacy of the United States after the Second World War was rapidly diminishing. American manufacturers were facing significant challenges from competitors in both Asia and Europe. This new competition challenged the United States' manufacturing post-war dominance in steel, auto, machine tools, and electrical appliances. New competitor companies, emerging in nations such as Japan, Germany, Korea, and Italy, were challenging the ability of American manufacturers to produce both consumer and capital goods, resulting in a significant loss of jobs within the United States. In addition, as a strategy to meet this competition, major American companies were downsizing their domestic operations and moving them overseas into these nations, adding to the job loss. The "deindustrialization" of America was particularly pronounced in the Great Lakes States, especially Michigan, Ohio, Indiana, Wisconsin, and Pennsylvania. From 1979 to 1982, over 43 million jobs were eliminated through plant closings, layoffs, and corporate downsizing.[2]

A great deal of the new international competition directly challenged the domestic auto makers. In the 1970s, while the domestic auto industry was profiting from the expansion of its domestic markets and ignoring the impact of the higher fuel costs, American consumers discovered the strength of imported cars. European car makers, such as Volkswagen, had emphasized new technological advances such as front-wheel drive, disc brakes, and fuel injection and were producing small fuel-efficient vehicles that domestic makers had not considered significant.[3] They were quickly followed by the Japanese imports, which not only produced similar technological innovations, but with their new systems of lean production were able to produce cars and transport them to the United States at a significantly lower price than many domestic car makers. Moreover, the Japanese cars were of considerably better quality (i.e., fewer defects) and more reliable than their American counterparts. For these reasons, the imported share of the US market grew considerably from 1970 to 1980. By 1980, 28 percent of the American auto market was Japanese products. Then in 1982, the Japanese began to operate assembly facilities in the United States with the opening of the Honda plant in Marysville, Ohio.

The loss of market share to imported vehicles resulted in a decline in the auto industry employment all over Michigan. The domestic automakers lost over 350,000 jobs by 1985.[4] To respond to the new competitors, the industry implemented a dual strategy of (a) rapid introduction of computer-based technologies and (b) raising the skill levels of the remaining workers. Both strategies resulted in an increased demand for community college occupation programs. The introduction of new technologies in the production of automobiles increased the need for both technical training (i.e., knowledge of the equipment, how to troubleshoot, etc.), but also the need for workers to communicate with each other regarding the performance of the equipment and its impact on quality. The emphasis on worker education focused on how well workers were knowledgeable about measuring quality and what steps they should take when they believed there were issues with part production. Much of the industry was implementing Statistical Process Control and needed a means by which large numbers of workers could be quickly trained in the fundamentals of this technology.

In 1984, the industry negotiated with the UAW the development of joint-funded education and training funds. These funds were created as independent entities controlled by a joint board appointed by the union and the management to create training and educational opportunities for UAW members. The fund was paid for by a portion of the wage increase (originally five cents for every hour worked) diverted into the fund. This formula produced an extraordinarily large amount of money that could be utilized to develop education and technical training programs. While the funds were administered jointly, since the origins of the money came from the wages of union workers, the corporate leaders in the funds generally acceded to whatever the union wanted to spend the money on. In some cases, community colleges were able to win contracts from the funds to create courses or programs that were implemented in all the plants of a company. General Motors used Macomb Community College to develop a program on financial literacy for UAW members which was offered through its facilities.[5]

The changes within the auto industry were also reflected at the national level, resulting in more attention focused on American community colleges. An emerging policy consensus argued that the reason for the loss of American jobs was not only because of low wages in other countries, but many of the new competitors also had significant advantages in the skills of their hourly workers and the organization of the production process. To confront these new realities, national policy experts argued that far more attention paid to the skill acquisition of the United States manufacturing hourly workforce. These same individuals believed that community colleges were better positioned to deal with the retraining of manufacturing workers than other potential national workforce options. First, there was a federal workforce development system maintained by the United States Department of Labor. At the time, it was called the Job Training Partnership Act (JTPA). The JTPA was administered by locally appointed boards within the state to provide training for unemployed and displaced workers. The funds were awarded on a contract basis to a few for-profit trade schools and some community non-profit agencies that focused on obtaining entry-level work for their clients. It was widely distrusted by employers, and few utilized this agency to fill anything but unskilled entry-level jobs.[6]

The second viable option was the federally supported K–12 vocational education system. While some of these federal funds were provided to community colleges, most funds were directed by state plans to high school-based programs to gain students' entry-level work. Within the K–12 system, the vocational courses and curriculum were considered a dumping ground for non-college-bound youth and given little priority or local resources. While in some rural areas the vocational education system had employer support, the large manufacturing corporations rarely utilized these programs for hiring entry-level workers.[7] Moreover, both systems focused on getting jobs for unemployed individuals. They did not have much experience with incumbent worker training, which was assumed to be a priority for the individual firms that employed the workers. In addition, neither of these systems had access to specialized instructors, sophisticated equipment, or advanced curriculum to produce a more skilled workforce.

In contrast to these options, the strengths of the American community colleges emerged. Community colleges were strategically located in every metropolitan area, within proximity to most major employment sites. They had a reputation for flexibility in course offerings and a rapid response to meeting the workforce needs of the communities they served. Finally, they had expertise in educating adults, not just eighteen-year-olds fresh from high school. For many policymakers, these characteristics made them the logical choice for any public programs on upgrading the skills of incumbent workers.

While community colleges had a previous history of attracting adults, they had less experience meeting the needs of companies for incumbent worker training. How could community colleges take on projects where large numbers of adults could be rapidly trained with the skills useful to maintain their jobs? Most existing technical programs were credit degree programs organized within traditional postsecondary structures that stressed degree completion, full-time enrollment, and long semesters, which discouraged many adults from attending and completing programs.

While there was a growing national consensus that community college workforce efforts could be important in dealing with the issues of skill development, the worker retraining programs were initiated on the state level. In response to the economic crisis, many states instituted new funding programs to provide community colleges with the ability to serve local businesses and industry in retraining their current workforce. For example, in Illinois, the Department of Commerce and Community Affairs allocated grants to all community colleges for incumbent worker training. It established a Prairie State Fund for competitive grants for companies that utilized corporate training, developed the Employment Training Panel, and began to provide funds to community colleges to undertake that training. A similar funding structure in North Carolina entitled New and Expanding Industries was established with state monies to be passed on to community colleges to perform workforce education. In Pennsylvania, the state legislature provided new funds to community colleges for the development of centers to aid new business and industry formation.[8]

These initiatives often reflected the different state economic development strategies. However, they had a common theme that their community colleges should concentrate programs on the growing number of middle ground occupations that required more than a high school degree but less than a four-year college degree. Increasingly, they defined the main mission of their public community colleges as less of a launching pad for students who wanted four-year degrees, and more as technical education and training for the skills needs of their communities. In 1964, the American Association of Community and Junior Colleges argued that "the two-year college offers unparalleled promise for expanding educational opportunity through the provision of comprehensive programs embracing job training as well as traditional liberal arts and general education."[9]

To respond to these new demands by their states for incumbent worker training, the community colleges often place these programs in the continuing education area. The mission of these units was to provide non-credit educational activities to adults, and because they were not tied to the academic or vocational mission of the institutions, they were often at the periphery of the community college. They offered personal enrichment courses, such as small engine repair programs, floral management, investing strategies, or interior design, that attracted adults who wanted to learn subjects for their personal interests unrelated to degrees or their workplace. In many states, the continuing education area offered programs where adults who never finished high school could obtain a General Education Development degree (GED). None of these classes were taught for college credit and most of the instructors were part-time practitioners without any academic qualifications. This area of a community college was often called the broadest of all community college functions. The former president of the American Association of Junior and Community Colleges, Edmund J. Glazer, Jr., was a significant proponent of community education. He argued in 1980: "The community college is uniquely qualified to become the nexus of a community learning system, relating organizations with educational functions into a complex [that is] sufficient to respond to the population's learning needs."[10]

Continuing education staff were often very skilled at discovering the local needs of their communities and quickly responding with relevant programs. In addition, since these programs were not for academic credit, their programs were excluded from traditional sources of college support and often expected to obtain their operating activities through revenue raised by their programs. This forced them to be more entrepreneurial than any other community college unit. Even though these units were staffed with individuals who knew little about technical training, they often became an ideal place for locating the corporate or state-contracted training programs. They were experienced with short-term programs, pay-for-services, and supporting programs off traditional campus sites. Some community college leaders believed that these units might become new profit centers for their institutions, providing needed revenue for the rest of the institution. Thus, these continuing education units, not the traditional vocational deans or technical instructors, became the centers for delivering the technical and organizational training sought by companies.

The first visible signs of the national impact of community college customized training occurred during the recovery from the 1980–2 recession. This recession was particularly severe in the auto, steel, machine tools, and electrical equipment manufacturing segments. In many states of the Great Lakes region, including Ohio, Michigan, Indiana, Wisconsin, and Illinois, governors began to develop state-funded programs with the community colleges to retrain incumbent workers. A typical example was Michigan's program to train hourly auto workers in statistical process control (SPC), a process invented in the United States but widely used in Japan to avoid production defects. Many auto industry executives believed great attention to quality would lead to more competitive auto products and help the sector rebound. Other states utilized their funds to develop educational programs training in computer-based technologies such as computer numerical control (CNC) machining or computer-aided design (CAD).[11]

To aid in the retraining of the industrial workforce, many states created Advanced Technology Centers on the campuses of community colleges. These facilities were often marketed specifically to employers and maintained labs with the latest computer-based manufacturing equipment, which could give incumbent workers a "hands-on experience" with new technologies. In the early 1980s, the state of Ohio established these Advanced Technology Centers at Lorain, Sinclair, and Cuyahoga community colleges. Both Illinois and Michigan also established major centers in Grand Rapids, Moraine Valley, and Rockford. Many southern states, including North Carolina and Alabama, initiated these centers as a means of attracting manufacturers to relocate their facilities from the Midwest to the South. While located on the campus, these centers were often stand-alone units intentionally separate from the traditional for-credit technical classes.[12]

The employer market for these state-initiated programs was small and medium-sized establishments often essential to local community economic growth. Economic development specialists assumed that these firms would be most at risk through international competition and the least likely to possess the resources and technical capacity to transition to the new technologies and quality initiatives. Small- and medium-sized firms were primarily locally owned and mostly had a positive image of their local community college. Many of the owners already had relationships with the community colleges, either through hiring their students or by themselves attending the institution. For these reasons, many state agencies formed direct relationships with community colleges and these local businesses.[13]

The Michigan Modernization Service (MMS) created in 1987 was among the first such state-organized agencies. MMS organized teams of technical experts in manufacturing with community college administrators to conduct on-site visits to firms. The purpose of these visits was for the technical expert to recommend new advanced manufacturing technologies in their production processes and for the community college representative to develop worker training to successfully implement these changes at the firm. Through the work of MMS, several Michigan community colleges increased their technical assistance programs to aid local firms. This was the first time Michigan community colleges directly worked with firms on technical and training issues under a state-initiated activity.[14]

Larger companies were utilizing community colleges to deliver programs for their workforces. In many of these relationships, the curriculum design was created by the company, but the delivery of the training was contracted to the community college. In some instances, when large companies downsized their operations, entire units or facilities groups were offered retraining and counseling through community colleges.

These initiatives posed new challenges for the colleges. The programs conducted for large companies required technical specializations that often were far more sophisticated than the regular instructional offerings of the colleges. In some cases, the companies mandated that the classes be offered at their locations, so they were only accessible to incumbent workers. Many times, in their contracts with the colleges, the companies demanded counseling and other auxiliary learning resources which were far more generous than what the college provided to their credit students. To handle these customized training activities, the colleges developed new units of business and industry outreach centers. College leadership supported these activities because of the new revenue brought into the institution, in addition to the positive branding the college received within the community and among state political leaders as responsive to the economic needs of their communities.[15]

These new initiatives were not universally supported within many community colleges. The traditional technical career units viewed these non-credit and contractual programs with suspicion because they believed these were competitors to their programs. Since most of the customized training never administered any tests of student learning, the college faculty questioned if there was any real learning taking place. There were also important policy issues. Since much of the actual classroom work was conducted on-site at the employer's facilities, there were issues of public access to the curriculum and student records which were often unresolved. How could a public institution funded by taxpayers restrict public access to its activities? There was also concern among businesses in the community that did not have access to these programs. The response of local business was particularly hostile when the training was provided free to companies by a state grant as a reward for their relocating in the state, but unavailable to the existing firms in the community.[16]

There were critical policy issues regarding how public institutions working closely with specific firms were utilizing their resources at the expense of educating those enrolled at the institution. Some community college educators argued this activity diverted the community colleges from their most essential tasks, the education of first-generation college students so they could obtain employment and sustainable wages. In response, the colleges argued these activities were part of their economic development and community mission. Helping their communities grow and providing jobs for the citizens increased the prospect for jobs and created additional tax revenue, contributing to the community overall.

In 1988, the American Association of Community and Junior Colleges (this name was simplified to American Association of Community Colleges in 1992) issued a new vision statement entitled "Building Communities." This document defined community "not as a region to be served but also as a climate to be created."[17] One essential relationship in this definition of community was "the collaborations with employers, industries, businesses, public employers, and organized labor groups—for the training of the workforce and the economic development in the community college movement."[18] This put forth a new role for the workforce development mission and set the stage for the future development of significant initiatives. It also made clear that one of the functions of the community college was the creation of community—a concept which included company concerns but placed them within a wider context.

Thus, the image of American community colleges evolved in policy circles because of their workforce activities. The emphasis of occupational education included not just the general preparation of students for entry-level jobs, but often very specialized programs to support skills acquisition of incumbent workers. The logic for efforts directed at companies, as opposed to individual students, was that saving and supporting firms in the long run was essential to the future opportunities of students. The emphasis on occupational education and training did increase student enrollments in credit technical programs. In 1926, they represented about 20 percent of the enrollment. By 1975, they were 35 percent of the enrollment. Community colleges became part of a national perspective to refocus their occupation programs upon the needs of employers.[19]

The increased emphasis on workforce activities did little to integrate them with the transfer or liberal arts mission of the institutions. Despite the evidence that the technical skills needed to implement many of the new computer-based technologies required critical thinking, communication, and group dynamics skills, there was little attempt by the community colleges to merge or combine courses from liberal arts with technical programs. The bifurcated distinction remained significant and became even more complex as some community college leaders began to increase their non-credit offerings to meet the needs for incumbent worker training, which was even further removed from the transfer mission. The organization of the colleges then reflected a tri-partite relationship where there were liberal arts and transfer programs, technical programs, and non-credit short-term training all existing independently from each other. How colleges develop strategic mixtures of these three areas was an important factor in determining their success for the future.

Macomb Follows National Trends

By the late 1970s, Macomb Community College had already developed a vibrant community service mission. The focus on community needs had its origins on two interconnected factors. First, since Macomb was the only postsecondary institution in the county and was established to meet the growing needs of an industrial suburban area, there was a strong sense that the college should relate closely to the county's growing employer needs. Second, many of the Macomb administrators, some with a religious background, brought to the college a strong sense of service to the needs of the community. They believed classroom instruction was only one part of the functions of the college. They established college units to aid specific student constituencies, such as the Women's Resource Center, the Veterans Center, the Performing Arts Center, and the Program Learning Center for students who needed developmental education. None of these efforts involved traditional classroom instructional activities. These were initiated to serve what the original college leaders determined as the needs of the community. Since Macomb County had few indigenous social or community institutions, the college became a logical place to play a major role in the community.

This focus on the community needs contributed to the enrollment growth of the college. College enrollment increased by 70 percent from 1970 to 1979. Part of this increase can be attributed to thousands of returning Vietnam War veterans who were utilizing their veterans benefits as they transitioned back to civilian life. In 1975, there were 5,700 veterans enrolled in credit classes at the college. In 1979, the college welcomed a new president—Albert L. Lorenzo. Lorenzo started his administrative career within the college as a Business Officer. He was not a postsecondary academic or a K–12 educator but started his career as an accountant. However, he believed the main mission of community colleges was to meet the needs of the community. Unlike many other community college leaders of the time, he relied on empirical evidence, not anecdotal stories, to understand the community needs. He believed in conducting research to identify these community needs and have Macomb respond with specific activities. To perform this continual monitoring of the community, he initiated two units that were not typically found within community colleges: a Center for Community Studies in 1982 and then a Center for Future Studies in 1987. These organizations published materials that not only aided programming at Macomb Community College but provided a model for other community colleges that were attempting to understand their local communities. With these efforts, he was recognized as one of the few community college presidents who developed the capacity of their institution to perform relevant research on the community's needs. These activities also served to place the college as an important "border scout" for economic and social trends in Macomb County.[20]

Lorenzo's knowledge of the local economic landscape made him recognize the importance of the college playing a major role in the auto industry workforce development efforts. The auto industry was the dominant provider of economic opportunity for Macomb County. The introduction of computer-based technology was creating the demand for more skills in the industry, and the community college was the likely institution to meet these needs. As the union-management joint funds were developing, the college could position itself to create and offer courses that could meet the needs of UAW members. In addition, he saw the significance of flexibility in the delivery of program offerings. The college could offer credit and non-credit courses within the auto plants that might be tailored to the specific needs of that facility. For the first time, Macomb launched programs within the auto facilities within the county.

The college created a new internal network to launch more direct work with the auto industry. While these efforts were initiated by Lorenzo from the President's Office, the programmatic workforce activities were implemented by a college administrator named Jim Varty. Under Varty's leadership, one area of distinction was Macomb's activities with the new union-management education organizations that were created as a result of the 1982 auto negotiations. In the initial design of the programs, individuals called Life Education Advisors (LEAs) were assigned to each plant to help initiate education and training activities. Varty developed close ties with these individuals in all the Big Three plants located in the county. They promoted Macomb Community College classes and, in some plants, arranged for the delivery of in-plant classes conducted by college staff.[21]

Macomb initiated many of these activities as a means by which the College could open a new revenue source for the institution. Thus, the newly launched Center for Workforce Development became an auxiliary enterprise like the Center for the Performing Arts or the Campus Bookstore. The goal for these units was to at least break even, which meant earning enough revenue to pay for administration and marketing costs. This gave their work a good deal of freedom for these non-credit activities to offer education and training programs, provided they earned contracts to cover their costs. There was also an expectation that this growth could generate profits for the college, which could be channeled into other parts of the college.

Al Lorenzo also expanded the reach of the college beyond Macomb County through a new organization of community colleges. In 1984, he created with presidents from other large midwestern community colleges a new organization committed to workforce training and economic development named the Mid-America Training Group. While most community colleges maintained relations with each other within their states, the Mid-America Training Group was one of the first collaborations between colleges from many states organized around their capacity to perform workforce training. Lorenzo promoted this alliance by placing an ad in the *Wall Street Journal* indicating that the Mid-America Training Group was prepared to offer training for auto and steel companies that had multiple facilities in Midwest communities. This was one of the first times a consortium of community colleges from different states offered their collaborative services to major companies. The launching of the Mid-America Training Group brought national recognition to the college as an innovator in the workforce development arena. When Michigan Governor James Blanchard initiated the Industrial Technology Institute (ITI) to promote advanced manufacturing technologies in Michigan manufacturers, he appointed Lorenzo as a founding board member.[22]

My Own Transition

During this period as Macomb Community College was intentionally increasing its workforce development efforts, I was undergoing my own political journey. Even though I won my dismissal case and organized the Warren Tank Plant March, my political activity remained outside of the college. I wrote a weekly column for a local community newspaper chain, *The East Side Shopper*. I visited China in 1972, and in 1975 became a plaintiff in a lawsuit filed by the National Lawyers Guild against the Detroit Police and the Michigan State Police political intelligence units. The result of the lawsuit was the release of thousands of files on individuals and organizations. These activities gave me some visibility in the community as a radical but didn't have much impact on my standing at the college.

Working-Class Political Attitudes

At the same time, I was involved with these activities, many of my activist friends were still enmeshed inside a small group political culture. They believed we needed more disciplined political organization that had the "correct political perspective." From my experience at Macomb, I knew this was a wrong approach. People did not support my activities because of "my correct line" on what was needed—they trusted me because of my past experiences as a teacher and my interactions with them. I was not an "organizer" from the outside, but now one of them. I remember very vividly the day after the killing of the four students at Kent State in 1970. A colleague, who earlier in his life as a high school teacher organized one of the first public teacher unions in Michigan, came into my office and said, "We must do something about Kent State." He came to me not because he agreed with my politics—indeed, he was not even a radical. He came because he knew I could be counted on for something when we all needed to face a crisis. He was reacting to the horrors of the incident with the need for solidarity: "We are in this together, and we need to collaborate."

Personal Changes

If I was going to be committed to working at Macomb, I realized my involvement in a small political collective was not going to be of much help. In addition, I was faced with a personal loss. My father died unexpectedly in the fall of 1974. His funeral reconnected me with many family members I had not seen since high school. These interactions made me realize how little I acknowledged or understood my own background as a Greek American. When two of my Macomb teacher friends proposed a trip to Greece in May 1975, I was eager to join them. It would give me a chance to meet some relatives of my father who remained in Greece, travel to the village where my grandmother grew up, as well as explore some aspects of Greek culture which I experienced but never understood. What I was totally unprepared for is that I met my future wife, Gabriella Gabrilaki, when I went on a hike on the amazing island of Crete. I should also note that my relationship with Gabriella was not the conventional love story of an American marrying a poor immigrant and assimilating her into American life. Gabriella's family was part of Crete's established bourgeoisie, meaning they were reasonably well off and respected in their community. She agreed to come live in America, but only if we would regularly visit her family and friends in Greece. In retrospect, our "grand bargain" enriched me more than Gabriella. It provided a context for me to integrate my personal and political life for the first time. Viewing the United States from a Greek perspective gave me a distinct view of both the strengths and weaknesses of America. I gained much more than just my ethnic identity; I developed a new and better understanding of my own country. My marriage provided another perspective on my work at the community college.

Completing the Degree

Gabriella and I were married in Crete in January 1976. When we returned to the United States, I was confronted with an immediate decision regarding my own education. I left Princeton in 1967 without completing my doctoral dissertation. My thesis advisor at Princeton, H. H. Wilson (who was one of the few progressive faculty at Princeton), announced in 1977 he would retire. This was my last opportunity to finish my doctorate, and while completing the degree would have no immediate impact on my teaching work, I instinctively knew I should get the degree. I did my dissertation on the Detroit Red Squad case. In the fall of 1976, I secured a sabbatical leave from Macomb and completed my dissertation, including my thesis defense, in time for June 1977 graduation.[23] I am sure some of the faculty members on my committee wondered why a student they barely remembered selected this esoteric topic, but they remained silent during the entire process. Completing the degree was almost a capstone ending to my transition. I now had the credential to play a different role at Macomb Community College.

What I Learned

The longer I remained at the college, the clearer I saw the need for students to have both liberal arts and technical skills if they were to be successful. Critical thinking skills could be applied to the world of work, including in a manufacturing-dominated local economy. Yet, the college was divided organizationally into two camps: the transfer and the vocational. I realized that I did not fit in either camp, and if I was going to remain at Macomb, I would need to synthesize the two strands. In addition, if I was going to be successful at the college, I needed to develop my leadership skills and break out of the view that a small collective of political people was going to provide me with support for the future. In this long-term goal to promote change, I needed to complete my degree. Finally, finding a long-term partner was important for me to understand my own heritage and gave me a perspective to see both myself and the college through a new lens. While I was assembling my skill set, so were community colleges focusing on areas where they could demonstrate value not only in higher education but also in American society. As the workforce issue became more critical to America's economic future, community colleges began to mold their efforts around this mission. Their distinctive competence in the workforce area provided them with an important "brand" among higher education institutions and also empowered them to offer a distinctive value to their communities.

Notes

1 In the first Macomb Community College course catalog, all the occupational classes are listed separately from the credit classes and with a different financial charge. (Macomb Community College, *College Catalogue*, 1954.)

2 The New York Times, *The Downsizing of America* (Random House, 1996), 4.

3 Womack, 46.

4 Center for Automotive Research, *Beyond the Big Leave: The Future of U.S. Automotive Human Resources* (Center for Automotive Research, 2007), 1–8.

5 Allen L. Phelps, Dale C. Brandenburg, and James Jacobs, *The UAW Joint Funds: Opportunities and Dilemmas for Postsecondary Vocational Education* (National Center for Research in Vocational Education, 1990), 28–30. In addition, Macomb coordinated UAW-Ford relocation and retraining efforts, as well as a career development initiative for UAW-Chrysler.

6 For a discussion of JPTA, see Grubb and Lazerson, 107–28.

7 Grubb and Lazerson, 184–212.

8 Norton Grubb, Norena Badway, and Denise Bell, *Workforce, Economic and Community Development: The Changing Landscape of the Entrepreneurial Community College* (National Center for Research in Vocational Education, 1997), 25–9. Some of these efforts were also based around the assumption that short-term customized training would lead workers to consider enrolling in the career and technical credit programs to earn degrees.

9 National Advisory Committee on the Junior College, *A National Resource for Occupational Education* (Association of American Junior Colleges, 1964) as quoted in Terry O'Banion, "Bread and Roses: Helping Students Make a Good Living and Live a Good Life" (League for Innovation in the Community College and the Roueche Graduate Center at National American University, 2016), 21–2.

10 Edward J. Gleazer, Jr. *The Community College: Values, Vision, and Vitality* (American Association of Community and Junior Colleges, 1980), 10. As quoted in Cohen and Brawer, 276.

11 Grubb et al.

12 For a discussion of Advanced Technology Centers, see Stuart A. Rosenfeld, *New Technologies and New Skills: Two-Year Colleges at the Vanguard of Modernization* (Regional Technology Strategies, 1995).

13   James Jacobs, "Training the Workforce of the Future," *Technology Review*, August-September 1989, 66–72.

14   The Report of the Modernization Skills Commission, "Skills for Industrial Modernization," *The Modernization Forum*, 1993.

15   Jacobs, "Training the Workforce of the Future," 69–72.

16   F. L. Pincus, "The False Promises of Community Colleges: Class Conflict and Vocational Education," *Harvard Educational Review* 50, no. 3 (1980): 30.

17   American Association of Community and Junior Colleges, *Building Communities: A Vision for a New Century* (AACJC, 1988), 3.

18   Ibid., 3.

19   Cohen and Brawer, 226.

20   Lorenzo discusses his perspective in *Transforming Lives and Communities* on page 17.

21   Grubb et al., 4–18.

22   Jacobs, "Training the Workforce of the Future," 72. For a brief review of guiding principles of the Mid-America Group with the names of the colleges, see Albert L. Lorenzo and James J. Blanzy, *Mid-America Group: A Foundation for Renewal* (Macomb Community College, January 1988).

23   James Jacobs, "The Conduct of Local Political Intelligence" (PhD diss., Princeton University, 1977). Unfortunately, Wilson died a few months after his retirement.

4 Becoming a Workforce Development Expert

From 1985 through 2000 was the Golden Age for community college workforce development activities. For the first time, a national consensus was emerging that community colleges should play a major role in meeting the workforce training needs of America. Most colleges experienced a significant growth in customized training, workforce development programs, and other forms of non-credit instruction and technical assistance related to skills acquisition in their communities. Many of these efforts were funded through state and sometimes federal public initiatives. Attention was also focused on the traditional credit Career and Technical Education programs, especially as there was a renewed interest in making sure high school students not interested in a four-year degree were prepared to make the transition from school to work. In addition to this public attention to community college efforts, for the first time, major national foundations were making investments in community college workforce efforts. Finally, the community college model was attracting international interest as many nations wanted to increase their postsecondary based workforce development efforts. The community college model was viewed as an inexpensive, flexible alternative to the rigid university system which many nations possessed as their only postsecondary institutions.

Changing Conditions for Community Colleges

There were multiple reasons for the emergence of the community college as a national workforce system. The broadest explanation focused on the changing skill needs at the workplace. The implementation of computer-based technologies in many sectors of the economy did eliminate many jobs. But for those occupations that remained, there was an increased need for both greater technical and critical thinking skills. Even for most entry-level occupations, there was a need for skills beyond the traditional high school degree, but less than what a four-year degree could bring.[1]

The presence of community college workforce programs could help create a restructuring of American manufacturing, which would retain employment in the manufacturing sector. In 1984, Charles Sabel and Michael Piore published a very influential book, *The Second Industrial Divide*, which argued that computer-based technologies would create the possibilities of a new system of "flexible specialization," where small manufacturers with highly skilled workers could produce consumer and capital goods quickly and competitively. Their model was based on their observations of a network of clothing and shoe making firms in the Emilia-Romagna region of Italy. Many of these firms worked collaboratively using computer-based technologies to produce products quicker, cheaper, and with better quality than the traditional mass production firms. The owners of these businesses originally started as skilled craftsmen who wanted their firms to remain in the region and create sustainable jobs for the local citizens. Sabel and Piore argued these arrangements could succeed the "Fordist" mass production industries, eliminate major loss of manufacturing work to overseas producers, and provide a new basis for sustainable manufacturing in the United States.[2]

There was an important role for community colleges, the authors argued, in the implementation of this framework within the United States. The initial education and training of the skills needed for these small firms to flourish could be found at the colleges. Since the colleges were rooted in their communities, they could serve as local anchors for the firms in their transition to flexible specialization. This would provide the focus of the colleges upon the needs of small- and medium-sized manufacturing firms and create an opportunity for increased federal and state support for community college workforce development opportunities.[3]

There was widespread support for greater community college efforts in workforce development in more conventional arenas. In 1990, under the Republican administration of George H. W. Bush, a critical report was produced by the United States Department of Labor Secretary's Commission on Achieving Necessary Skills (SCANS): *America's Choice High Skill or Low Wages*. This Commission assumed that unskilled mass production work was destined to be performed in less developed nations. Rather than compete for low-wage jobs, American education and training institutions should focus on creating the skills necessary for high-wage jobs. The SCANS report argued that these important skills were a combination of technical and "basic skills" of reading, writing, and the ability to work in teams. For the first time, the federal government indicated that mastery of technical skills was necessary but insufficient to ensure the success of American industry in the era of international competition. These skills could be acquired by the current workforce through the community colleges. Reports such as the SCANS commission reinforced the belief among policy analysts that community colleges are the institutions which could integrate technical and essential workplace skills.[4]

As computer-based technologies penetrated all sectors of the economy, an additional perspective developed that viewed the need for a new occupational group of individuals with skills necessary to design, build, program, maintain, and troubleshoot these new computer-based technologies. The skills needed by this group of technicians could be applied to most of the key sectors of the American economy. These technicians needed postsecondary experience, an associate degree, and perhaps a pathway into four-year science and technology programs. In 1992, under the Clinton administration, the National Science Foundation created an Advanced Technology Program to fund community colleges and their four-year partners to establish programs that prepared these new technicians in the new emerging sectors of the American economy. These programs were not part of the traditional activities initiated by the Department of Labor or the Department of Education, and they were often housed within the credit career and technical programs within the community colleges. The NSF funding also gave colleges access to resources from another federal agency, and served to elevate their role as the solution to the skills acquisition process for the United States. Known as the Advanced Technological Education (ATE) program, it resulted in an upscaling of community college career and technical programs, many of which in the past were considered terminal programs ending in a certificate or associate's degree. They would now be a pathway to four-year technical degrees. That a prestigious federal agency such as the National Science Foundation considered it important to create a program designed for community colleges was a significant indication of the changing federal view toward these once junior colleges.[5]

This new attention on community colleges by government and businesses had a programmatic impact on the operation of community colleges. While the traditional credit side of the institutions remained, the significant interest for more intense participation in local economic development activities resulted in what some observers called "The Shadow College" or "The Entrepreneurial College." These were units independent from the traditional credit programs, and often separated from continuing education, that worked directly with either companies or local and state economic developers to increase the workforce skills in communities. In some cases, they provided technical assistance to firms and space on their campuses to house small business incubators designed to stimulate local economic development. While there was very little educational data collected on state or federal levels regarding the size or impact of these non-credit activities, some researchers suggested between 15 and 20 percent of the students were involved in non-credit contract training activities with business and industry. This figure did not include many of the non-instructional economic development activities, such as business incubators or small business assistance centers, which were performed by the colleges.[6]

Traditional occupational credit programs were also changing. They refocused their efforts to become more compatible with public school secondary vocational programs. For the first time, there was a national attempt to promote intentional relationships between the occupational programs of the colleges and the high school occupational programs. In the past, high school and community college occupational programs were organized as separate silos within their institutions with little regard for potential collaborations. They often clashed over the distribution of federal vocational funds. However, in late 1988, a private foundation authored an influential study entitled *The Forgotten Half* which focused on the economic needs of young people (eighteen to twenty-four years old) who did not enroll in a four-year college after graduating from high school. This report argued that their economic future and those of their families were substantially diminished without some form of career education beyond high school.[7]

The report called for substantial federal efforts to extend educational and training benefits for these individuals. As a response to these findings, the president of the American Association of Community Colleges, Dale Parnell, helped initiate a new movement called Tech Prep, which linked technical programs at high school with technical community college programs. It was designed to give the "forgotten half" a rigorous technical perspective so their lives would improve—even if they did not complete a four-year degree program. While the original design of Tech Prep called for a voluntary partnership between school districts and community colleges, the concept was embedded in new federal funding of career-technical education by 1990, and many states mandated the development of Tech Prep programs in their state plans for federal dollars. The number of Tech Prep consortiums grew substantially as a result. A program review found that over 88 percent of the secondary school districts participated, with over 750,000 students enrolled in these programs.[8]

Tech Prep was the first national effort to integrate technical education at the secondary and postsecondary levels. The emphasis on the development of a new systemic relationship between high schools and community colleges often bypassed some existing work-related systems such as apprenticeship. Since both community colleges and school districts were local institutions, there was no common national definition of Tech Prep programs or curriculum. The actual delivery of courses and programs within this initiative was extremely heterogeneous—depending upon a number of factors such as the size of the institutions involved, the number of secondary districts associated with community colleges, and the collective-bargaining agreements governing the instructors at both institutions. In addition, while the Tech Prep concept originated among community college leaders, there was less participation among community college liberal arts faculty, depriving the programs of courses that mastered critical thinking skills crucial, with many of the new computer-based technologies. However, the initial relationships created within Tech Prep became a foundation for future activities between high schools and community colleges which would continue to unfold.

Finally, during this period, some of the larger national philanthropic organizations such as Kellogg, Ford, Mott, and Kresge Foundations initiated investments in community college workforce programs. They believed community colleges could play a role in obtaining sustainable-wage jobs for low-income students and their families. One of the first such investments was the "Bridges to Opportunity" grant program from the Ford Foundation, which created projects in six states to bring together community college workforce programs with community-based organizations that served low-income students. The Mott Foundation supported community college efforts to enhance traditional adult education programs with workforce preparation by combining adult primary education and workforce programs. The new interest in community colleges expressed by these foundations encouraged some colleges to initiate efforts designed to support their work with low-income students.[9]

These trends were challenging the ability of the community colleges to respond by increasing their activities, stretching their capacities, and causing them to search for more resources to support this growth. Despite the new interest in their activities, the traditional sources of state and local funding for the colleges were not keeping pace with these new initiatives. In some instances, the increase in federal initiatives and foundations allowed some states to decrease their support for their community colleges, assuming these new sources of revenue could handle the increased need. Even when there were increases made by the states, in contrast to other public postsecondary institutions, they were not particularly sizable. While community colleges dealt with the most challenging postsecondary students to teach and counsel, which required significantly more resources than their four-year counterparts, state legislators rarely recognized these additional factors in their calculations for financial support for postsecondary education. For example, in 2010, the entire credit headcount for the 28 community colleges in Michigan was over 275,000 students. Nevertheless, the combined annual state support from the Michigan legislature for all these institutions was less than what was given to one institution, the University of Michigan, with an enrollment of 35,000 students.[10] The president of Miami Dade College at that time, Eduardo J. Padrón, summarized what many community college leaders believed when he said, "All the state leaders say how much they love community colleges. I wished they loved us a little less and gave us more money."

Workforce Development in Detroit

Perhaps no other sector in the American economy was affected more by the skills changes than the auto industry. The introduction of computer-based technologies by the automakers changed skill levels across all aspects of auto production, motivating the development of new forms of education and training. In 1984, the domestic automakers and the UAW negotiated the established "training funds" managed jointly by union and management and funded through a portion of the negotiated wage settlement diverted from the workers' paychecks into these separate entities. For the first time, technical training was supplemented by courses and programs designed to give all hourly workers a primer on the growth of the auto industry and contemporary trends. The funds also provided all hourly workers with tuition assistance and career counseling. For laid-off workers, over $5,000 per worker was allotted annually for vocational courses that might improve their skills. Community colleges were often utilized for much of these programs because of their ability to deliver instruction at flexible times that could cover all shifts. The faculty from the colleges had previous experience in the education of adults, which helped hourly workers feel secure within the program. Many had direct experience within the auto industry. The classes were held at the plants or in the regional centers of the UAW. In addition, the funds supported Life Education Advisors (LEAs) in all major facilities, many of whom were former community college staff members who were advising workers about their options. Some of the LEAs were former staff from local community colleges.[11]

A second major development that focused on the auto industry expansion was the significant training funds available through the states, particularly when a new start-up plant was announced. In Michigan, the legislature established the Michigan Job Training and Re-Investment Fund (JTRIF), which funded technical training for companies that would be matched by funds from the community colleges. This permitted the colleges to purchase up-to-date computer equipment to provide training to local auto plants. In the Detroit area, these monies were used by General Motors in the start-up for the training of the new Poletown plant, the revitalization of the Chrysler Jefferson Assembly plant, and the Ford Romeo engine plant in Macomb County. For the first time, the state was actively involved in the technical training of incumbent auto workers.[12]

In 1984, General Motors created a whole new car division—Saturn—which was based on the experience of the company working with Toyota in a joint run production facility in Fremont, California. Saturn was utilizing Japanese production and training techniques. Not only did it introduce new technologies in auto production using new technologies, such as aluminum casting engine blocks, but it created a production process based on work teams that focused on continuous product development. The traditional foreman first line supervision was eliminated using these teams. Every worker in the Saturn division was expected to have an annual training and education plan, which was supported through company funds. General Motors' intention was to spread the lessons learned with Saturn to all its other car divisions.[13]

In addition to the growth of increased training of hourly workers within the auto industry, the companies also pursued two other strategies to raise the skill levels of new workers entering the industry. The OEMs hired HR firms to screen workers through interviews and performance testing to determine their suitability for hiring. In some cases, prospective workers were put into teams and given "projects" to work together to resolve. The goal was to determine whether new hires possess the appropriate foundation and social skills to work in the new auto plants. In some instances, an associate's degree or other postsecondary experience was determined to be necessary.[14]

A second part of the strategy for a future workforce was to encourage educational institutions to produce more capable students for the industry. Instead of creating their own schools, the companies developed partnerships with Michigan public schools. In 1997, the Ford Motor Company, in partnership with the Wayne County Regional School District, initiated a Henry Ford Academy, which was located next to their technical training facilities in Dearborn, Michigan. In 1999, Chrysler Corporation, in an alliance with Oakland County Regional School District and Oakland Community College, founded the Chrysler Academy for Manufacturing close to their new corporate headquarters in Auburn Hills, Michigan. Macomb Community College initiated the Design and Manufacturing Alliance to develop a pathway from high school programs into college programs that would prepare students for automobile-related employment.[15]

One other new development within the auto sector served to promote greater education and training in the Detroit region. To combat the growing penetration of imported vehicles into the American market, the domestic auto makers began utilizing non-union auto suppliers, not only for parts but for the development of new product innovations. Whereas in the past, suppliers were utilized only to make parts at the cheapest possible prices, the OEMs were turning to suppliers to develop entirely new product lines in key auto components, such as seats and information systems. This resulted in a different type of auto supplier who had to have technical expertise in product development as well as production capacity. It also meant that supplier companies had to remain close to their customer base. These trends resulted in new technical training centers in the Detroit region. By 1990, twenty-six of the thirty largest auto suppliers had located their own research and development facilities in southeast Michigan. These suppliers did not have the resources to develop internal education and training abilities, and as a result, they became heavily dependent upon community college programs to provide the technicians in their centers.[16]

This new emphasis on education and training was raising many important pedagogical issues for both the companies and the community colleges. How should adults, many of whom have been out of school for twenty years, be educated and trained in the new technologies? What was the correct mixture of technical and foundational skills? What was the role literacy played in some of the new training? How much should be done through computer-assisted job aids versus classroom training? The new corporate emphasis on education and training was stimulating some important changes in the practices of adult education.

Macomb Community College Expands Its Auto-Related Activities

During this period, Macomb Community College expanded its workforce education activities to meet the challenges of the 1982 recession, which had a significant impact on the auto industry. The college took advantage of its well-established ties within the automobile industry to intensify relations with all the domestic OEMs (GM, Chrysler, and Ford). This included training incumbent workers within the plants, participating in the Joint Training Funds, and responding to OEM downsizing with retraining programs for staff who were permanently laid off. There were also significant numbers of auto workers attending the college under one of the paid tuition plans offered to employees by their companies. Many of these individuals were attending credit classes on their own time to earn degrees that would allow them mobility into technical or supervisory jobs.

When General Motors decided to eliminate all its plant protection employees and subcontract the work to an outside vendor, the corporation hired Macomb Community College to provide a one-year skills enhancement program that gave these terminated workers skills to find other work. This program not only included specific occupational courses designed for these employees, but a designated ratio of counselors to students/employees had to be maintained by the college. Many of the requested activities General Motors demanded, such as the ratio of counselors to employees in the program, exceeded what the college offered its regular credit students. This form of comprehensive programming designed by the industry and implemented by the college often was utilized by other auto industry partners.[17]

Unlike many other colleges that did not place an emphasis on apprenticeships, Macomb maintained strong work-based learning programs. The apprenticeship program between Macomb and General Motors, Ford, and Chrysler continued to expand, with over 70 percent of all apprentices at the Chrysler Corporation taking their classroom education at the college. In addition, many small- and medium-sized manufacturing firms that were not unionized contracted with the college to provide classroom instruction synchronized with their on-the-job training activities. Since these firms were non-unionized, they did not qualify as formal Department of Labor registered apprentices, but the curriculum designed and delivered by the college was similar. These agreements were called an Employee in Training (EIT) model. Many firms in the Detroit area took advantage of these apprenticeship and EIT programs.[18]

The college also developed a strong program with another form of postsecondary work-based learning called cooperative education. Cooperative education was originally developed in four-year colleges to give students a work-based experience, often without compensation, to help sort out their future career plans. Traditionally, the four-year cooperative education programs occurred during the regular semester or in the summer alongside classroom instruction. In contrast, the Macomb co-op program was focused on obtaining full-time employment for participating students. The Macomb co-op program was based on an alternative assignment model where a student spent one semester in class and the next semester working full-time with compensation at an employer in a job related to their technical major. While they worked full-time at their placement, once a week these students attended a class at Macomb to discuss what they were learning at the workplace. Over 80 percent of these students were eventually hired by the companies where they served their original co-op positions. In the 1980s, many Macomb cooperative education students became the first women and the first non-white individuals to enter white-collar and technical areas within the auto industry. By being associated with the college through the co-op program, the traditional hesitancy and sometimes opposition by companies in hiring these "non-traditional" students was reduced.[19]

In many of these efforts, a critical ally of Macomb Community College in these workforce activities was the local workforce development board. The director of the Macomb-St. Clair Workforce Development Board responded to the needs of local small- and medium-sized manufacturers who provided machine parts, tools, and fixtures, and designs for the auto industry. The workforce board created a Machinist Training Center, which was turned over to the college to administer.

There were also major new workforce initiatives in the credit technical programs. One significant specialized sector of the auto industry concentrated in Macomb County was the design and styling of new vehicles called auto body design. This activity was formerly done almost entirely by hand with rulers and protractors on large drafting tables. Now it was transformed by the introduction of computer-aided design (CAD). Not only could vehicles be designed more accurately, but the process was much quicker, permitting the auto makers to produce more new vehicles in the marketplace. This, of course, added to the numbers of CAD designers needed by the industry. There were both opportunities to train new autobody designers with this technology and retrain some incumbent workers already in the trade with computer skills. Since each of the OEMs utilized different software applications for their activities, workers in the smaller contract design firms had to be proficient in more than one autobody design program.

To respond to these increased needs, Macomb developed one of the nation's most extensive postsecondary autobody design programs. At one time, over 1,000 Macomb Community College students enrolled in credit and non-credit autobody design classes. General Motors utilized the Macomb autobody design associate degree as a condition for hiring designers. In some instances, the company mandated its suppliers to hire individuals who completed the Macomb autobody design program. For several years, overseas auto design firms, such as the British company Hawtal Whiting, sent many of their employees to the Macomb program. To increase the talent pipeline in 1988, General Motors design staff members initiated a Project Design in Macomb County high schools, which started high school students in courses that would lead to an associate degree at the college.[20]

Macomb Community College also played a major role in the state of Michigan initiative to aid small- and medium-sized manufacturing firms, known as the Michigan Modernization Service (MMS). Macomb staff, while remaining at the college, became training specialists for MMS and participated in site visits which resulted in training programs designed and implemented at the college. Typically, these courses were taught by college faculty. These activities brought a large amount of contract work to the college.

The Macomb staff in both credit and non-credit technical areas grew steadily. By 2000, the College had two vice presidents for Workforce Education: one responsible for credit workforce programs and another for customized training and non-credit programs. Often there was conflict between the two areas, as the full-time credit faculty believed the non-credit workforce programs were drawing students away from their courses. The credit faculty were also critical of the faculty selection process utilized in the non-credit programs. They wanted the first right to teach these classes even if they had little direct experience with recent manufacturing applications. The increased demand for contract training resulted in the college hiring more non-credit adjunct faculty who had recent experience working with these new technologies.

The college was also very active in a new federal initiative under the Clinton administration with high schools called School to Work. While the original Tech Prep programs focused on meshing occupational programs at the secondary and postsecondary level, this federal initiative added the dimension of the workplace to these activities. The Advisory Board of the Macomb School to Work initiative was designed to include the active participation of the major auto companies, the UAW, building trades, and local financial institutions. These organizations aided high school students in finding employment while they were making the transition into community college. School to Work activities were developed in Macomb County's thirty-two high schools with articulation agreements signed between the high schools and community colleges. These agreements gave high school students college credits for courses they took at their high schools in several specific areas, such as Auto Body Design, Machining, and Automotive Repair Technology. New coalitions developed between employers, school districts, and the college to create a career pathway from high school into college. In addition, for the first time, the college provided on-site instruction in Detroit high schools, expanding the School to Work efforts beyond the borders of Macomb County. These activities were time-consuming to coordinate with the school districts, but this initial work established a culture of collaboration between these institutions, which would provide the basis for new activities in the near future.[21]

The increased use of computer technologies and the reorganization of manufacturing indicated that an industrial certificate or even an associate degree might be insufficient to obtain entry-level employment or many new technical jobs in the auto industry. In addition, for those who were already employed in manufacturing, advancement would require more postsecondary education. This demand for advanced skills in manufacturing was especially important in Macomb County because the county was rapidly becoming the hub for vehicle research and development centers established by auto part suppliers.

In addition to these activities in the private sector, the United States Army Tank-Automotive and Armaments Command (TACOM) was expanding its research facilities, attracting major defense companies to locate their technical centers in the county. These activities increased local demand for skilled technicians who often needed more than an associate's degree. Finally, these skill changes were affecting many occupations in the health-care industry. There were increasing demands for nurses and other skilled health-care workers to have four-year degrees. The associate degree in nursing remained sufficient to find entry-level employment, but advancement in the field required a four-year degree.[22]

Macomb University Center

These employment trends encouraged the college to reexamine its relationship with four-year programs. Macomb County never had an indigenous four-year institution, and there was a widely held belief among residents that the college should play a role in either transitioning to a four-year institution or aiding in the development of a new one. In response to these concerns, Al Lorenzo created a new process for how community colleges could relate to four-year institutions, which many other community colleges were quick to adopt. The "University Center" model created a facility located on one of Macomb's campuses but solely devoted to four-year "partner" institutions offering baccalaureate and master's degree programs. They were provided classroom, laboratory, and office facilities at little cost, providing that their programs did not directly compete with Macomb curriculum offerings. To ensure the permanence of this concept, the construction of the University Center and maintenance had to be approved by the voters through a special millage in 1988. These four-year institutional partners would offer programs that would be synchronized with Macomb's associate degree programs enabling students to easily transition from their Macomb College associate degree into a four-year institution.

This innovative approach provided Macomb residents with a local pathway to four-year postsecondary education on the existing community college campus utilizing college library facilities, parking, and other administrative services. Once established, the University Center grew to a complex of four buildings housing over 2,000 students enrolled in courses offered by ten different partner colleges. The offerings of the four-year institutions were directed at both liberal arts and the four-year professional and technical occupations, such as education, social work, engineering, and accounting.[23]

Developing an Alternative View

The new national attention given to community colleges' workforce activities provided me with the opportunity to develop a fresh perspective. Until that point, I had regarded the community college primarily as a strategic space to interact with working-class people to encourage them for political change. If I was going to be serious about working at a community college, I needed to advance a perspective that could justify my time and effort. Could a strategy be developed that articulated the contribution of these institutions to change?

The conventional critique of community colleges made by many higher education academics who studied community colleges was that they served as "cooling out" institutions where the desires of working-class people for a four-year college opportunity were diverted into a preparation for relatively modest occupations that did not require a four-year degree. Instead of being transformational for students, the critics claimed community colleges tended to lower student goals and ambitions. In addition, the colleges were criticized for emphasizing vocational programs to aid local business and insufficiently preparing students with critical thinking skills that might advance them into the four-year colleges and universities. Assumed in this position was that any vocational preparation was tracking students away from real opportunity found in the four-year institutions.[24] Even many progressives working within the community colleges, primarily in the academic subjects, accepted this view. They focused their efforts less on the administration of the institutions but more on the development of innovative classroom teaching methods for their liberal arts classes which could serve to advance working-class students. Their goal was to have their students succeed and transfer to four-year colleges. For them, occupational education was something for students to avoid, because it tracked them into employment as opposed to more college.[25]

However, by the late 1980s, there were signs this conventional critique of the community colleges was inadequate in explaining the reality unfolding within these institutions. Increasingly, many working-class students were attracted to community colleges because they viewed them as institutions that would increase their opportunity for a better life. Instead of being diverted from their desires for enrollment in four-year institutions, these students were attracted to them precisely because they offered an opportunity to rapidly develop skills for a better-paying job. Many were uninterested in enrolling in four-year institutions and did not necessarily see them as helpful for achieving their goals for economic stability. In addition, the conventional critique that divided technical and critical thinking skills was being undermined by the growing implementation of new computer-based technologies in all occupations. To master the technical skills necessary to function in the workplace, students needed to cultivate the ability to think critically and develop more communication and mathematical skills, the same skills needed for transfer to four-year programs. The American community college was not channeling students away from a four year degree but becoming a staging ground to launch a working-class student who wanted a four-year degree.

Perhaps most importantly, the academic critique of community colleges also underestimated the agency of the community college students. Those of us working inside the community colleges were often struck by how little the traditional critique understood what we saw in our classes. Our students were not simply pawns being manipulated away from attending four-year colleges. They were selecting community colleges because they were close to home, allowed them to work and go to school, and gave them skills to increase their participation in the labor market. This was especially true for place-bound adults (i.e., those with families, those caring for seniors, and/or those with some form of physical disabilities). For a single head of household, completing the nursing program at a community college was an immediate life-changing event, not just for the student, but for their family. Few liberal arts programs at a four-year institution could produce this quick boost of income and employment security for working families. The economic data that suggested a four-year degree led to greater earnings over a lifetime was unconvincing to a single mother who needed an immediate and urgent income boost, so her children could enjoy the opportunities brought to them by a stable high-paying job.

If the conventional academic view of the community college was inaccurate, could a new perspective be created? Instead of community colleges being seen as limiting students, could they be seen as offering a gateway to opportunity in ways totally ignored by most four-year institutions? Learning a combination of technical and liberal arts skills would not only get students work but would empower them to help change America.

In addition to these concerns, an alternative perspective needed to capture the impact of these institutions upon the needs of the community. Often, both the proponents of a transfer agenda and a vocational agenda omitted a consideration of how these institutions served their communities. Unlike most four-year institutions, the mission of a community college is to improve the lives of residents in a specifically designed district or service area. When community colleges initiate programs to educate and train first responders (such as emergency medical technicians, police, or firefighters), which always lose money, their motivation is that these occupations are necessary for any viable community. Just as important, communities need citizens with critical thinking skills for them to remain successful in times of economic dislocation. Finally, the ability to aid in attracting and generating new economic enterprises is an important consideration in any community. As public institutions, the community colleges need to play a role within their communities—and the programs and course offerings of these institutions need to reflect that reality.

While I would like to say this perspective motivated me to transition from being a community college teacher to an administrator, the reality was less linear and less intentional. My pathway emerged as a logical choice based on my personal and political situation. I really enjoyed working at a community college; this was my life's work. I felt close to the people who worked in the institution. I moved toward a strategy of changing the institution in part because it allowed me to continue doing what I felt was comfortable and personally satisfying. Through some political work supporting a local Detroit council member, I had learned a great deal about community-based research.

Community research was also an important part of Al Lorenzo's strategic planning process. Since the county had no four-year institution, he recognized that Macomb Community College could play an essential role in the community through research. I was asked to work on projects for the newly created Center for Community Studies. In the early 1980s, to help a new mayor of Warren, we developed a new economic development organization called the Warren Organization for Research and Development (WORD). For the first time, I began working with people from the local Chamber of Commerce and the Macomb County Planning Department on economic development projects. As a result of this work, I became a "local expert" on Macomb County and was asked to speak at community and business events in the county. These original presentations morphed into an annual Economic Forecast for Macomb County sponsored by the local Chamber of Commerce. Looking back at this period, I was filling in a local void. Because of the lack of any local four-year institution or major civic organization, Macomb Community College was the only institution with the capabilities to help steer the county forward. In the process, I was also fashioning a new career for myself, which would allow me to grow within the college.

As this work evolved, I saw new opportunities for Macomb Community College to play a greater role in the intersection of local workforce development and economic development issues. This would be important for students and also the community. I also needed to understand

Figure 4.1 One of many billboards we displayed featuring our career-focused programs. Our Fire Service program was one of those programs that were critical for the community. Image courtesy of Macomb Community College.

more about some of the specific challenges with the implementation of new computer-based technologies. My opportunity came in 1984 when Governor Blanchard established the Industrial Technology Institute (ITI) in Ann Arbor. ITI was an example of a new public-private partnership initiated by the state but funded by foundations and private contributions. It was designed to provide Michigan manufacturers with a greater understanding of the new computer-based technologies. Since Al Lorenzo was on the board, when I asked if I could broaden my research role at the college, he suggested I could perform many of these activities by being "on loan" from Macomb to ITI.

I started my new role at ITI in the winter of 1985 with the very fancy title of Visiting Scholar. ITI was reimbursing the college for my salary, and technically I was still on the college payroll, collecting my faculty salary and accumulating my years of service in the pension plan. At the time, I didn't recognize the significance of this relationship that Al Lorenzo created, but it proved both personally and financially helpful. Because I was still on the payroll of the college, I knew if my relationship at ITI did not work out, I could return to the college.

ITI's mission was to both help Michigan manufacturers make the transition to computer-based technologies and, based on these experiences, to appropriate state economic development and workforce development policies. Most of the projects were a combination of research and practical implementation—very different from standard academic research. Many of the technical staff were engineers and computer scientists with significant work experience in manufacturing. There was a small sub-unit of policy researchers who studied social and economic factors involved with technology implementation, to which I was assigned. Michigan was one of the first states to establish an organization specifically designed to help retain and even grow its manufacturing base.[26]

My knowledge of computer-based manufacturing technologies was superficial at best. However, I did have a strong understanding of the importance of manufacturing work to the Michigan economy. Also, my experience at a community college made me sensitive to training and education issues affecting frontline manufacturing workers and their employers. So, while I lacked substantive technical knowledge, my research into the auto industry and its relevance to Michigan made my transition into the organization relatively easy.

My six-year experience at ITI was a rich growing period for me. It exposed me to the practical issues related to developing skills in new manufacturing. Many of our research projects were conducted on-site within the manufacturing plants, so I got to understand the real-life issues in manufacturing. My initial study—funded in part by the state of Michigan—was to look at the training needs of Michigan auto suppliers, leading me to small manufacturing plants all over the state. It aided me in understanding much more in-depth the role of manufacturing and the specific issues affecting smaller manufacturing companies.[27]

This work also altered my somewhat one-dimensional view of the owners of these companies. In my interactions with owners of these small manufacturing firms, I found them not just as greedy bosses dedicated to extracting profits off the backs of workers. Many of the owners were often former skilled workers whose education and social backgrounds were not very different from many of the workers they employed. Their formal education was often less important to their success than their experiences at the workplace. Their companies were often dominated by the demands of the OEMs, and they had little control over the products they made or often the price they charged. They were rooted in their communities and, despite their reactionary political views, I was beginning to empathize with the issues they confronted in an environment dominated by large multinational companies. I began to realize that no transition in an economic system could occur without the skills and energies of many of these people.

In addition, I was impressed with their decision-making skills. They were forced to act quickly, not able to wait for all the evidence to emerge, and often made decisions based on their experience accumulated in the industry. In many respects, they made choices based on the best information and knowledge they had at the time, always taking a calculated risk. However, they were also very quick to make rapid adjustments or cancel their decisions when they made an error or a miscalculation was made. While no doubt their decision-making was always driven by profit expectation, their willingness to experiment and learn by doing was a refreshing contrast to an academic environment, which often studied issues continuously without coming to any conclusions.

Many Michigan community colleges were interested in learning from ITI, so they too could develop programs in these new technologies. Under a grant provided by Jim Folkening from the Michigan Department of Education, I was able to establish an ITI Michigan Community College Liaison Office that linked the activities of the ITI with the colleges. The grant allowed me to play a role as a "border scout" and bring to the Michigan community colleges the research and practical knowledge from ITI to aid in shaping their training and education agendas.[28]

While ITI was focused on the state of Michigan, given the significance of the auto industry to American manufacturing, in our project work we often interacted with national experts. I was exposed to the world of D.C. "policy wonks" or "beltway bandits," as they are often called. I had not encountered these people before, and I was amazed at their work style. They earned their impressive salaries from their ability to win research contracts from foundations or federal governmental units. Then, through their publications (often slick, well-designed reports), they were able to exert their ideas and policy suggestions in the federal government, major corporations, and the media. Depending upon which party was in power, some of these individuals took administrative jobs within federal government agencies. Even though few had concrete experience in the areas they often studied, they were sought out by the media as experts. For example, as community colleges became a national topic in discussions of workforce skills, few of these individuals had any specific experience with these institutions. They often called upon me to help formulate what steps community colleges should take to increase the skills of American workers. They used me in their reports and moved to another contract. It was often difficult to understand what they actually cared about, except maintaining their salaries and their positions, which gave them the ability to influence policies. However, through this process, I was interacting with some of the first national discussions of community colleges and workforce issues.

At the time, many of my teaching friends at the college were amazed that I was willing to trade a teaching job for much longer work hours and a daily commute to Ann Arbor. Sometimes I questioned this as well. However, being away from Macomb kept me out of many of the internal institutional squabbles inside the college. In addition, my presence at ITI enhanced Macomb's standing as a leader in the workforce area.

The ITI-Community College Liaison Office gave me the opportunity to interact with the senior leadership of other community colleges in Michigan. This work deepened my understanding of the potential that community colleges could play in providing workforce training in communities entirely different from Macomb County. In the process, I also learned how to collaborate with many career and technical Michigan community college people, often with backgrounds considerably different from mine. Until then, I had little real experience with the conditions faced by my colleagues in rural community colleges.[29]

The work at ITI did shift my perspective from being a faculty member at Macomb Community College looking to radicalize students to an advocate for community colleges in their workforce mission. It forced me to confront many important policy issues concerning technology and employment. What were the appropriate activities for public organizations, such as community colleges, in aiding local private companies? What was the impact of implementing new computer-based technologies on workers' jobs? Were workers being deskilled during this process? How should labor unions deal with the impact of these technologies upon their members? What was the specific impact of these new technologies upon urban centers and the non-white workforce living in cities? My political life shifted from organizing students or people in the community to trying to develop and implement a progressive strategy for community in workforce training and education.

Wayne County Community College

My first opportunity to handle some of these issues concretely did not happen at Macomb Community College. In 1988, I was asked by an administrator and a faculty union leader at Wayne County Community College (WCCC) to become a candidate for their Board of Trustees. WCCC served the city of Detroit and the suburbs located in Wayne County. Unlike any other Michigan community college, WCCC was originally created without pre-existing local financial support. The college was formed by local government, business, and community leaders in reaction to the Detroit rebellion in 1967. Given these origins, it was not surprising that public support for the college, especially in the white suburban communities, was tepid at best. Since there were two other community colleges located in Wayne County, this new college was always faced with significant competition for students. At the time, Henry Ford Community College, whose operating district was the city of Dearborn, was drawing two-thirds of its students from Detroit. WCCC had five campuses stretching over Wayne County, three in Detroit and two in the suburban western Wayne County.

The unique origins of the college created an institutional culture of divisiveness. While Detroit was the dominant city within Wayne County, the racial polarization between it and the many Wayne County suburbs was as intense as Macomb County's relationship to Detroit. The college governance structure, which included elected board members from specific districts, only contributed to these differences. This served a perspective of board members representing "their district" as opposed to considering issues from what was good for the college. Especially when construction issues, staff organization, or hiring of new employees were involved, board members often confronted each other as representatives for their constituents within their districts.

What drew me to run for the Board of Trustees was a belief that, as an institution created to deal with urban issues, Wayne County had the potential of becoming a major hub for providing the area workforce with the new manufacturing skills of the future. My experience at ITI made it clear that without more education and training, people from Detroit especially would find it difficult to obtain sustainable-wage work. Institutions such as WCCC could become a critical resource for the economic recovery of these communities. But the institution needed the leadership to develop these programs, leadership that I thought I could provide. Also, as a white board member who was willing to collaborate with my fellow Black members, we would be able to take on the racial issues that were creating internal divisions within the institution. Finally, since I was unopposed in the election, I was not faced with the traditional dilemma of an elected official owing their loyalty to particular groups inside or outside of the college. While still working at ITI, this elected position seemed like a good use of my time and talents.[30]

But with this very promising context, I failed miserably. I was never able to influence the curriculum at the college or build any new workforce programs, nor be effective inside the institution. I failed to bond with the Black board members who were suspicious of my efforts. I could not get the unions to accept the need for change in their teaching and learning strategies. I was marginalized quickly by my fellow board members, who were interested more in the construction and staffing issues than educational policy. It was a particularly galling learning experience for me that I failed to come even close to meeting any of my goals.[31]

What did I learn from my experience? First, and probably most important, I learned how little influence a board member has over the institution's direction. Unless there is a group of board members who can work closely and proactively with senior leadership, the chances of getting major changes accomplished are slim. A typical board member's experience is to react to the existing issues, brought with little preparation and often requiring rapid decisions. Even when the administration involves the board in the strategic planning retreats, typically it was expected that the board would support the priorities of the administration, not provide input on whether these fit the mission of the institution.

Wayne County Community College Board Meetings

One example might shed light on the typical challenges we faced at Wayne County Community College. A financial audit discovered that an employee received a double paycheck for seven years. She never told anyone at the college, kept collecting both paychecks, and when she was fired, she contested the action. Under her union contract, she was able to appeal her firing directly to the board to plead her case. At this special board meeting called on a cold November Friday evening, the employee came to the meeting with her minister who requested she not be dismissed, saying she would never do it again. Her minister asked us to forgive this oversight on her part! Fortunately, there was a board member who had been a single mother struggling on welfare assistance for several years before she finally found stable employment. She tore into this woman and her minister. She told them her behavior was criminal and an affront to all those who struggled to make a living. Watching her response alone was almost worth the wasted evening. However, the time spent dealing with organizational failures such as this made it difficult to articulate a vision for the institution.

Rarely were the needs of students discussed at the board meetings. I cannot recall any time that students presented any activity for Board consideration. During this instability, there were extraordinary individuals at WCCC who worked tirelessly to help students succeed. They often understood the significance of the institution to the community and were appalled at the scandals and personal infighting that continued to plague the institution. However, they were often overwhelmed and marginalized at the college and could only focus on their students. As one single trustee, I could do little to support their work other than provide verbal encouragement.

My inability to make a difference within the institution came to a head in 1992 during my reelection campaign. The college was also seeking its first local millage vote. Despite my concern about the effectiveness of the institution, I believed financial stability might lessen some internal college issues. I was one of the few white trustees who actively supported the college to win the millage. I lost the election, but the millage passed. This brought financial stability to WCCC, resulting in some positive changes. Curtis L. Ivery, the present Chancellor, has considerably improved the situation at the college. My electoral defeat forced me to reassess how I should refocus my political work. If I wanted to change a community college, I would need to be more involved in the administration of the institutions, not as a trustee. The experience at Wayne County was a "good" failure—it taught me what I should not be doing.

Back at Macomb

At the same time, my electoral career was nearing its end, I was brought back from ITI to Macomb Community College. Even though I remained a faculty member, I was being given non-instructional assignments to coordinate the College's Tech Prep and School to Work efforts. This decision produced a response from the administrators' union, who correctly argued that this was work within their bargaining unit. So, I was formally offered a role as an administrator. In the past, I would never have considered "moving over to the dark side." However, given my failed electoral experience at Wayne County Community College, I thought this was a step I should take. My fears of being co-opted as an administrator were exaggerated, and if I wanted to change a community college, I had to be in an administrative position to be taken seriously. In addition, the administrators at Macomb had recently formed their own "independent union," which meant they had a collective-bargaining agreement and a grievance procedure.

Because of my work at ITI, I was also given additional college assignments, which kept me in touch with manufacturing workforce issues. I became a staff coordinator for the Mid-America Training Group. This position allowed me to learn about the activities of other important midwestern community colleges. I also got to work with many of the community college presidents, which allowed me to see how well my skills matched theirs. While the Mid-America Group never landed a major project, it did develop into a significant peer learning experience for the colleges involved. The colleges reported on their workforce development activities and learned from the practices of each other. In addition, we met with individuals from some of the major manufacturers in the auto industry, and I learned more about how they perceived community colleges. Later, as president, I used this experience to resurrect the group, which continues today as—the Community College Workforce Consortium.[32]

Machinist Training Center

As an administrator, I was also asked to supervise the Machinist Training Center, a project initiated by the local workforce board to train entry-level machinists for many small manufacturing firms in Macomb County. The Center occupied a separate building in an industrial complex across the street from the college. It had two instructors, both ex-machinists who were paid from the grant funds supplied by the local workforce agency. In addition, a group of retired machinists was paid an hourly wage to "coach" the students, which really meant giving them a sense of the working conditions they would face at a small manufacturing firm. This was a nine-month program, 40 hours a week. Most of the training was hands-on with older manual machining equipment rarely found in a modern machine shop, but it provided the students with the foundation of machining skills that they could then enhance at the workplace.

There was also a significant mathematic underpinning to the curriculum at the Center. Math was critical for machinists to master, yet at the Center, these concepts were never referred to as "mathematics." It was simply part of becoming a machinist. Few of the students complained that they couldn't do mathematics, and most mastered the necessary mathematical concepts, including trigonometry. I am sure most of them would have scored very low in any formal mathematics test and would have much more trouble assimilating and utilizing these concepts if they were presented in a traditional unit of mathematics. I was very impressed with how these ex-machinist instructors could teach basic technical and foundational skills simultaneously. As former machinists, they had a good understanding of what their students needed to know to be successful in the workplace, and their goal was to get all the students through the program and into a job.

While the Center was successful in serving the needs of local manufacturing firms, I wanted our work to align with a new national skills standards initiative. Our center was one of the first community colleges to earn a Level One certification from the National Tool and Machining Association (NTMA). To achieve this certification, we had to undergo a site visit from a team of NTMA experts. The site visit produced an amusing example of why substantive knowledge cannot be easily faked. Even though I was the administrator of the Center, I had never been a machinist or ever claimed anything but a superficial understanding of specific machining procedures. I deferred to the staff on any curriculum suggestions or equipment needs issues. However, I recognized that the site visit would include discussions with the visiting team about the curriculum and the equipment utilized in the instructional program. So, with the help of the instructors, I mastered some fundamentals of the machining process and memorized the names of the different machines and lathes in the Center. I felt confident I could "fake it" during the site visit. As part of their visit protocol, the committee came in with a checklist of equipment and procedures the Center must have to win certification. After being grilled about whether our Center had some specific machines, which I correctly answered, I was then asked if we had a "tornado drill?" I hesitated to answer, thinking about all our equipment and wondering how I missed this machine. Soon the staff and some of the investigative team began laughing. Of course, they asked whether we had weather procedures for dealing with a tornado. After earning our certification, the staff presented me with a wonderful steel made replica of a "tornado drill." I displayed that in my office when I became president to remind me about the importance of competency instead of superficial book knowledge.[33]

International Workforce Development

Macomb Community College was a major educator of the Chrysler workforce. This was not surprising; at the time Chrysler was the largest employer in Macomb County. The majority of its production and assembly operations were in the county. When Chrysler was purchased by Daimler-Benz in 1998, I thought it important for the college to initiate direct ties with the new owners. A few years before, when General Motors purchased Saab, the Swedish car company, Macomb had served as a trainer for Swedish college students coming to learn the design systems GM was implementing at Saab. To establish this program with the University of Trollhättan, we visited Sweden a few times, and I was somewhat familiar with the issues involved in launching an international partnership with a different education system. My goal was to have Macomb recognized by Daimler as a potential partner. In addition, I knew about the heavy reliance the Germans placed on their apprenticeship system and wanted to utilize a relationship with Daimler to learn more about it.

Through our ties with the Chrysler staff, I received an invitation to speak at a training meeting that Daimler was organizing in Berlin and then to travel to their headquarters in Stuttgart for discussions concerning potential future activities. We organized a Macomb delegation from our School to Work group. Also included in our group was a reporter, David Wessel from the *Wall Street Journal*. In my national community college activities, I had met David previously. He had recently completed a book about community college workforce efforts, and he asked to join our delegation and perhaps write a story of the trip. He was very supportive of community colleges, related well to our delegation members, and gave our little group more prominence in the eyes of Daimler staff.

While our trip never achieved the goal of a partnership with Daimler, we did learn a great deal about the strengths and weaknesses of the German dual system. It made me realize how much training and education systems are embedded within the national culture. There were some specific parts of the German apprentice system (called the dual system) we could align and adapt in the United States, but to wholly implement another nation's approach was not only impossible but undesirable. The Germans were curious about our short-term training efforts but had little interest in adopting our workforce training processes. Nor did Daimler management want to export the "dual system" into the Chrysler facilities, so the development of an actual partnership was not an option. As a result of the trip, David Wessel wrote an article about the trip which appeared on the front page of the *Wall Street Journal* and increased the image of Macomb and me as leaders in the field of workforce development.[34]

Community College Research Center

My activities with School to Work, the Machinist Training Institute, and our trip to Germany led me to the Community College Research Center (CCRC). The origins of CCRC were directly related to the recognition of community colleges as an essential national resource. The Sloan Foundation, a national foundation that supported research into important parts of the American economy, believed that community colleges had to be examined as a distinct sector of American higher education, not simply an appendage of the four-year college system. In 1998, they gave Tom Bailey (a professor of economics and education at Teachers College, Columbia University) a significant grant to initiate a research center to study community colleges. One condition of the grant was that the center had to employ someone who worked in the community college sector. Tom asked me if I would like to participate in the new organization. He had a long-term interest in workforce development issues, and I admired his ability to focus on root causes of critical issues instead of following the various education fads. While he was a faculty member, he was proficient at seeking grants for research centers and knew how to develop relationships with funders. CCRC was run almost as a stand-alone enterprise at Teachers College. Tom developed a small staff and a very humane and decent work environment.[35]

Tom negotiated an agreement with Al Lorenzo where I would remain working at Macomb, but CCRC would pay my salary somewhat like my former arrangement at ITI. Although this meant commuting to New York and spending much more time away from home, for me, it gave me a national perch for my work. Going to CCRC was probably the first natural "career choice" I made after over 30 years of working at Macomb. I thought the transition would be easy; I had already had a similar experience with ITI a decade earlier.

However, this transition would not be as simple as I thought. By the late 1990s, when I became an administrator, I also became president of our administrators' union, the Macomb Community College Administrative Personnel Union (MCCAP). After a difficult set of contract negotiations, we realized that as a small independent union we lacked knowledge about medical issues, pension plans, and other critical benefit areas. As the union president, I argued we needed to affiliate with a national union that could provide us with the technical assistance to deal with administration attempts to change our benefits in upcoming negotiations. Much to my surprise, the membership generally supported this idea.

Through my contacts, I arranged a meeting between our executive board and one of the UAW National vice presidents. As hourly automotive employment fell in the last two decades, the UAW had developed a new niche in higher education, primarily among postsecondary colleges and universities. The union had experienced technicians who could help us understand medical, pension, and other issues, which was very attractive to our board. But when the UAW Vice President told our group there would be no dues collected until the UAW won its first contract, our board responded as if they had been offered valet parking in a snowstorm. Not only would we have access to the technical support and experienced bargainers, but it would cost us nothing until a contract was ratified. This offer won overwhelming support from our executive board (which included conservative Republicans and born-again Christians, I thought an unlikely group to join the UAW). To join, however, we needed a membership vote to decertify our present independent union and vote to become UAW members. While this was through a secret ballot, we knew Lorenzo would resist it, and many of our members feared retaliation if we changed our status. I was not sure how the membership would react, but I felt it was worth taking a chance, so we initiated the campaign to decertify our present union.

These events were unfolding just as I was preparing to join the CCRC staff. So, to pressure our members not to vote for the UAW, Al Lorenzo told me I could not accept the CCRC position unless I left the union and became an at-will employee. He knew severing me from the union would be a setback for our efforts to join the UAW just as well as it could lead to termination of my employment at Macomb. I was very conflicted by this sudden change but decided to accept the offer of becoming an at-will employee. However, much to my surprise, the MCCAP

Executive board intervened and refused to allow me to leave the union. They argued I was being forced out of the union and filed an unfair labor practice against the college. This raised the stakes for me significantly. I did want to take the CCRC position, but because I was one of the initiators of the drive to affiliate with the UAW, and especially now that my union was fighting to keep me as a member, I could not abandon them. It now was impossible to drop out of something I started and exposed others to some danger, just to fulfill my career plans.

I declined Lorenzo's offer, and he did not oppose the agreement made for me working at CCRC. Fortunately, the union election was held right before I was to join CCRC, and even though there was some internal opposition, we did win the vote. I became the first president of the new UAW Local for a few days before leaving the executive board to become associate director of CCRC.

I often wondered why Al Lorenzo backed off in the final confrontation over this issue until a friend who was a college president offered this explanation: "If you were forced to stay at Macomb, you could be a potential threat to his leadership. It was far better to have you off campus at CCRC bringing prestige to the institution and not threatening his control of the college." I don't know if this was true, but I did not realize how beneficial his decision was for me. When I became a presidential candidate eight years later, the administrator's union became my key ally in my bid for the presidency.

Again, as in 1971, when I won my teaching job back, winning the union election was another example of how important it is that you are perceived as honest and capable by others, not that you have all the answers. Most of the membership were conservatives and they knew my politics, yet they trusted my leadership in selecting the UAW and they voted for the union. They took this step, despite the pressure from the college's top leadership, who monitored our meetings through spies within our union. The victory reinforced my belief that when you have a track record of being honest with people and the timing is right, people are willing to trust your leadership and take risks, even if they don't agree with your political perspective.

What I Learned

During this period, my activities provided me with experiences that would help me when I became president. My work at ITI provided me with firsthand knowledge of how manufacturing firms considered their skills needs. This was a perspective not often found, even among technical faculty. Obtaining this perspective from the private sector would be extremely useful for me when considering issues of workforce development at Macomb Community College. In addition, administering the Laison Office for Michigan community colleges deepened my understanding of how other community colleges operated and considered issues. Until that point, my only real experience was at Macomb. I was able to bring this knowledge back to the college. In addition, experience at Wayne County Community College taught me how difficult it was for trustees to support meaningful change in any institution. At best, the trustees could work with internal staff to support staff, but they were limited in providing any administrative leadership. This experience motivated me to join the administration at Macomb.

Even as a new administrator, I was able to use these skills to lead a successful unionization effort at the institution. I always believed unions could play a positive role within community colleges. Although I was not considering being a president of a community college, these activities helped prepare me to become a leader. What I was lacking was a broad overview of community colleges and understanding the role that research could play in helping these efforts. The comprehensive community college has enjoyed years of experience in many aspects of workforce practice. It was time to assess what works and sharpen the focus of these new institutions. In particular, this meant strengthening the connection and collaboration between community colleges and employers. My invitation to join the Community College Research Center was going to provide me with some of that knowledge to make that possible.

Notes

1   For a discussion of the relationship between education and technology change, see chapter 3 of Claudia Goldin and Lawrence F. Katz, *The Race Between Education and Technology* (Harvard University Press, 2008).

2   Michael J. Piore and Charles F. Sabel, *The Second Industrial Divide* (Basic Books, 1984).

3   James Jacobs, *Final Report: Training and Public Policy* (Industrial Technology Institute, 1987).

4   Secretary's Commission on Achieving Necessary Skills (SCANS), *What Work Requires of Schools: A SCANS Report for America 2000* (Department of Labor, 1991).

5   Elizabeth J. Teles, "Curriculum and Teaching Strategies for STEM Technicians: The NSF Advanced Technological Education Program," in *Career Pathways for STEM Technicians,* ed. Dan Hull (CORD Publications, 2012).

6   James Jacobs and Roberta C. Teahen, "Shadow Colleges and NCA Accreditation: A Conceptual Framework," in *A Collection of Paper on Self-Study and Institutional Improvement* (North Central Association of Colleges and Schools, 1997): 13–19; Grubb et al., 16–17.

7   Samuel Halperin, *The Forgotten Half: American Youth and Young Families* (American Youth Policy Forum, 1998).

8   For Tech Prep origins and development, see Dale Parnell and Dan Hull, *Tech-Prep Associate Degree: A Win/Win Experience* (Center for Occupational Research and Development, 1991). For a discussion on high school and community college enrollment growth, see Robert Schwartz and Kerry McKittrick, "From Margins to Mainstream: Bringing Career-Connected Learning to Scale," *American Educator* 48 (2024): 4–11.

9   "Evaluation of the Community College Bridges to Opportunity Initiative," Community College Research Center, accessed October 6, 2024, https://ccrc.tc.columbia.edu/research-project/bridges -to-opportunity.html; Marty Liebowitz and Judith Combes Taylor, *Breaking Through: Helping Low-Skilled Adults Enter and Succeed in College and Careers* (Jobs For the Future, 2004); "Achieving the Dream: Community Colleges Count," Community College Research Center, https://ccrc.tc.columbia .edu/research-project/achieving-the-dream.html.

10   Compiled from 2010 State of Michigan financial records by the author.

11   Phelps et al., 4.

12   Ibid., 28.

13 Barry Bluestone and Irving Bluestone, *Negotiating the Future: A Labor Perspective on American Business* (Harper Collins, 1992), 189–201.

14 David Fasenfest and James Jacobs, "Revival and Change in the Automobile Industry of Southeast Michigan" (conference paper, Uddevalla Symposium 2000: Entrepreneurship, Firm Growth and Regional Development in the New Economic Geography, Trollhättan, Sweden, June 15–17), 263.

15 Ibid., 265.

16 Detroit Regional Chamber of Commerce, *Michigan Is Auto: Assets of the Motor State* (Regional Chamber, 2013), 12.

17 Kevin J. Doughtery and Marianne F. Bakia, *The New Economic Development Role of the Community College* (Columbia University, Teachers College, Community College Research Center, 1999). Macomb Community College (1999) 1998 Occupational Program Overview. Planning and Development, January 1998.

18 James Varty and James Jacobs, "The Role of a Technical Institute/Community College in Supporting Economic Development," *Proceedings of the Third International Conference on Cooperative Education*, Melbourne, Australia, 1983.

19 Ibid.

20 Phelps et al.

21 James Jacobs and George Harrison, *School-to-Work in Macomb* (Temple University, 2000).

22 *70th Anniversary*, 48–50.

23 Albert L. Lorenzo, "The University Center: A Collaborative Approach to Baccalaureate degrees," in *The Community College Baccalaureate: Emerging Trends and Policy Issues,* ed. D.L. Floyd, M.L. Skolnik, and K.P. Walker (Stylus Publishing, 2005), 73–93.

24 The most important of these works is Steven Brint and Jerome Karabel, *The Diverted Dream: Community Colleges and the Promise of Educational Opportunity in America, 1900–1985* (Oxford University Press, 1989).

25 Ira Shore, *Critical Thinking and Everyday Life* (South End Press, 1980), 84.

26 Industrial Technology Institute, *An Investment in the Future of Manufacturing* (Industrial Technology Institute, 1984).

27 Jacobs, *Final Report*.

28 Industrial Technology Institute, *Liaison Office Newsletter*, Vol. 1–4 (Industrial Technology Institute, 1987).

29 This work produced the development of the Customized Training Institute to train community college staff to work with business and industry. See Industrial Technology Institute, 1987.

30 For a discussion of my views when I was elected, see John Minnis, "New WCCC Trustees have the Right Stuff for Business, Students," *Grosse Pointe News*, November 17, 1988, 30A.

31 For a critical review of my efforts see James Jacobs, "The Role of Trustees in the Governance Process," in *Handbook of Community College Administration: A Human Resources Perspective,* ed. A. Hoffman (College and University Personnel Association Perspective, 1994).

32 The Mid-America Training Group met with business leaders and other community college presidents, something I coordinated when I returned to Macomb.

33 James Jacobs, "Community Colleges and the Workforce Investment Act: Promises and Problems of the New Vocationalism," in *The New Vocationalism in Community Colleges,* ed. Debra Bragg (Jossey-Bass, 2002).

34 David Wessel, "A Community College Hopes to Answer Call of the Global Economy," *Wall Street Journal*, May 28, 1999, 1.

35 For more about CCRC, see "Our History," Community College Research Center, Teachers College, Columbia University, https://ccrc.tc.columbia.edu/ccrc-history.html.

5 Community College Research Center and Considering the Presidency

The specific agreement struck between the Community College Research Center (CCRC) and Macomb was very advantageous for my future. CCRC paid my salary, but I remained employed at Macomb. If the CCRC position did not work out, I could always return to Macomb. One significant downside, however, was the weekly commute. While there were many daily flights from Detroit to New York making it relatively easy and accessible, I would be away from home a great deal during the week, putting significant strain on Gabriella.

At first, I thought my commute to New York would be a unique experience. However, I soon began seeing the same individuals on the flights I was taking. We would leave on Monday morning and come back on Thursday evening; we were like a small army of nomads making this passage. We saw each other at the Delta Sky Club at LaGuardia Airport, regularly enduring the numerous weather delays, and became acquaintances.

I never thought my work at CCRC would lead me, paradoxically, back to Macomb, let alone to becoming the president of the college. I began to think that being in a large research institution like Teachers College, far away from these petty college institutional squabbles, seemed a better alternative for me. I would contribute nationally to the evolution of community colleges, and maybe, if things went well, consider relocating to New York.

Community Colleges Mature

This was a particularly good time to engage in national community college research and practice. While many policymakers recognized the importance of community colleges in workforce issues almost two decades before, by 2000, their significance was now understood by the general public. Given their popularity with the electorate, the colleges had also attained bipartisan support.[1] For Democrats, community colleges represented agile response institutions that could promote skills to keep America competitive. They fit well into their agenda to promote and invest in social and economic opportunity for all Americans. However, even as supporters of these institutions, the Clinton administration did not develop a specific federal approach to working with community colleges, preferring to leave policy activities up to the states. The Bush administration supported more community college involvement in national workforce programs, in large part because of a traditional Republican aversion to anything originating in the Department of Labor, which they assumed was more sympathetic to organized labor and the Democratic Party. Most Republicans believed community colleges were part of the local postsecondary landscape they could trust. They were not institutions controlled by the liberal elite or left-leaning progressives who dominated the four-year institutions. In many red states, the governing boards of the community colleges were often appointed by their governors, and these institutions reflected their political ideology. Many workforce programs initiated by the Bush administration in 2000 were explicitly designed to leverage the strengths of community colleges as local institutions. During the decade from 2000 to 2010, community colleges emerged as the de facto national workforce development system.

The development of a federal perspective to support community colleges was continued and broadened by the Obama administration. The Obama administration connected the colleges with a broader agenda to utilize postsecondary completion as a means of supporting economic opportunity and reducing the growing income inequities of American society. For the first time, the administration sought to establish national numerical goals for individuals achieving a postsecondary credential. Finally, during this period, the philanthropic community began to focus their investments on community colleges to provide solutions to issues of equity and advancement for individuals and families out of poverty.[2]

It was not just political and philanthropic leaders that recognized the importance of community colleges. There was widespread public support for these institutions. A national survey conducted in 2003 by a public relations firm found a new understanding of community colleges not as "junior colleges" (suggesting they are somehow inferior to the "real" four-year colleges), but as fresh separate institutions where individuals could obtain relevant skills for sustainable-wage jobs close to home. In addition, compared to K–12 and four-year educational institutions, the public gave community colleges higher approval ratings. Unlike the public K–12 schools, which Americans considered inferior and troubled institutions, or four-year colleges that the public saw as institutions where wealthy kids engaged in many non-productive activities other than taking classes, community colleges were considered more accountable and mission-driven to provide people skills for work.[3]

The increased national attention to community colleges also brought more focus to their shortcomings. Most significantly, while these colleges were attracting significant enrollments, the student completion degrees or certificates were extremely low. According to the Integrated Postsecondary Educational Data Systems (IPEDS) data, only 28 percent of students who were attending college for the first time and who were enrolled full-time completed a degree within three years. Community colleges enroll many students who are not attending college for the first time and who enroll part-time, but this metric suggested community colleges needed to do better, much better. What's more, the completion results for students of color, low-income students, and students from families with no college experience were often significantly lower. Many dropped out without ever earning any credit hours. If community colleges were going to fulfill their broad mission as being a place for opportunity and equity in higher education, they needed to improve the numbers of students completing their programs.[4]

In 2004, some national foundations, led by the Lumina Foundation, initiated a national organization dedicated to increasing student success named Achieving the Dream. This organization called for a systematic reform of course structure, curriculum counseling, and student services at community colleges to raise completion rates and credentials for low-income students and students of color. Achieving the Dream focused on major reforms that aided liberal arts and transfer students. The emphasis was not on industry certifications or employment credentials but on degrees and transfer to four-year institutions. It was assumed more degrees in postsecondary institutions would result in more success.[5]

Shifting Borders Between K–12 and Four-Year Sectors

Community colleges were now fixtures in the public American education system. How these institutions fit with the two major sectors of American public education—the K–12 system and four-year colleges and universities—became an important national educational issue. The School to Work initiatives of the Clinton years increased efforts for traditional career and technical programs at the high school and community colleges to be closely connected. The competitive relationship between Career and Technical Education (CTE) programs at the community colleges and high schools was rapidly giving way to a new consensus which believed that most occupational programs initiated in the secondary school systems should be linked to similar programs at the community colleges. In the first decade of the twenty-first century, these connections were advanced with the creation of "dual enrollment programs" where high school students could take community college classes when they attended high school. Originally developed as a process by which high achieving high school seniors could begin their four-year college programs by taking courses at their local community college, dual enrollment programs rapidly expanded to include all high school students.[6]

The expansion of dual enrollment programs was supported by both parents and state legislators. Parents saw these programs as a means of cutting their four-year college costs by allowing their students to accumulate college credits for little or no cost at their local community college. In some states, the legislators seized upon the concept as a benefit for middle-class parents confronted with the growing cost of four-year college tuition. For community college practitioners and policy experts, dual enrollment was considered an important strategy to attract students from low-income families who believed that a postsecondary education was too expensive or too remote to consider. In addition, dual enrollment opened for the colleges a new student market and provided a stable revenue source with state reimbursement for classes taken by these students. By 2009, there were over 1.2 million high school students taking credit classes at American community colleges representing almost 15 percent of the community college credit enrollment.[7]

Dual enrollment programs that engaged high school CTE students produced positive results. For example, research indicated that career-technical high school students who participated in dual enrollment were more likely to enroll in college, achieve better grade point averages, and accumulate more credit than similar career-technical students who did not take dual enrollment courses. Many community colleges initiated a combination of rigorous career-technical education and introduction to college programs. For the first time, some CTE programs contained a comprehensive secondary and postsecondary curriculum component.

This changed the focus of CTE from being exclusively a terminal system primarily designed to achieve entry employment for high school graduates to an alternative learning system by which students learned through an emphasis on hands-on activities. These students were encouraged to continue their education in postsecondary institutions. Some of these changes were motivated by the changing skill requirements for occupations which once only required a high school degree. Even in entry-level occupations, earning a community college degree provided a platform for greater employment opportunities and better pay than just taking a few courses.[8]

Despite widespread public support for dual enrollment programs, there were some problems implementing them in rural areas. Rural high school students are commonly spread across many smaller communities that are often long distances from the nearest community college campuses. In these cases, the rural school districts worked out arrangements with their local community colleges to have college-level classes taught at the high school by high school teachers. This form of dual enrollment, called concurrent enrollment, was highly controversial inside both community college and four-year institutions. Providing community college instruction taught by local high school teachers at their high school, critics argued, did not produce the same benefits for high school students who engaged in college classes with other students at a college campus.

On the other hand, some rural colleges claimed there was no alternative to provide high school students college courses. If done with appropriate supervision, they could produce students who would be successful when they transferred into postsecondary education. Given the significant population decline in many rural communities, community colleges serving these areas saw dual enrollment as a crucial component of their enrollment future.[9]

Another area of change in the relationship between high school and community colleges (and a more contentious one) was the efforts to attract adult workers to their institutions. Traditionally, the credential for entry-level employment was the high school degree. For many adults who did not possess that diploma, the federal government provided funding to K–12 school districts and some community-based organizations to offer adults an opportunity for what was called a General Education Development (GED) diploma. This was based on a national test which would be taken by adults to obtain this credential.

For most of the post–Second World War period, the assumption was that a high school diploma would provide access to entry-level sustainable-wage jobs. For those adults who did not possess a high school diploma, high school districts, community organizations, and local governments would offer adult education programs that led to a GED high school degree. However, over time, the GED alone became insufficient for most adults to obtain an entry-level sustainable-wage job. More technical skills were needed, which K–12 school districts were unable to provide. Moreover, since most people without a high school degree had dropped out of a K–12 school district, it would be unlikely they would become successful returning to the same institutions they left without earning a high school degree.

For these reasons, policymakers turned to community colleges as a source for adult education. It seemed logical to combine adult primary education and community college workforce development. Combining these two areas recognized the growing labor market irrelevance of the GED as a credential. Moreover, the belief was that most adults who wanted to return to school to complete their GED were interested in obtaining a better job. One model was in Washington State called the Integrated Basic Education and Skills Training (I-BEST) program. I-BEST utilized two instructors in each classroom: a GED educator and an occupational instructor. Students received both skills to pass the GED as well as occupational training. Utilizing two instructors made the I-BEST program expensive to operate, but it was very successful in getting adults sustainable-wage jobs.[10]

During this period, the relationships between community colleges and four-year institutions were also changing. Where in the past there was a clear demarcation between the institutions offering an associate and baccalaureate degrees, the lines between the two institutions began to become less certain. In the past, without any opposition or concern among educators, there were some four-year technical colleges that offered an associate's degree as an option. Now some community colleges were petitioning their legislatures to offer four-year degrees. This was causing significant conflict between two- and four-year institutions as well as raising an issue for community colleges as to their role in the American higher education system.[11]

While many factors influence this development, one of the major changes was the increased demand for skills in many occupations. These occupational changes were producing new challenges and opportunities for the traditional occupational credit programs at the community college. While some community colleges sought specific articulation agreements with four-year schools so their occupational courses could transfer, others began developing applied baccalaureate degrees in specific technical fields where the local employers needed these skills for entry-level workers. The institutional lines between the two- and four-year colleges began to blur as community colleges began asking their legislatures for authorization to offer these four-year degrees.

There was considerable opposition from four-year institutions, but in some states such as Florida, where the rapid population growth had overwhelmed the existing four-year public colleges, the legislature granted the community college system the ability to offer four-year degrees in many technical and public service areas. In 2003, the Florida legislature allowed Florida community colleges to offer four-year degrees in some specific areas. This was the first time a state permitted community colleges to offer an "applied bachelor's degree" in specialized subjects where there were no four-year degree equivalents. These were often in occupational areas such as nuclear power operators, correctional administration, fire science, and precision agriculture production.

The Florida model provided a roadmap for other community colleges to follow. Community colleges had to gain support from local state legislatures and accreditation agencies to obtain permission to offer these degrees. This was not very easy to accomplish. Unlike dual enrollment, there was no widespread demand for these programs by either the public or employers. Moreover, there was extreme opposition from public four-year institutions that were willing to use their greater political clout with their state legislatures and were able to block efforts. However, in several states, including Florida, Washington, California, and Texas, community colleges fought hard and were able to win the right to offer four-year degrees. These states had significant population growth, a relatively short supply of public four-year institutions, and political leadership looking for a quick, cost-effective strategy for increasing the numbers of people with four-year credentials.[12]

The four-year institutions were almost uniformly opposed to the community colleges granting any degrees beyond the associate degree. However, the most contentious struggle between the two- and four-year programs was focused in the nursing programs. As mentioned in a previous chapter, the Associate Degree of Nursing was an innovation created in the post–Second World War era. By 1980, the Associate Degree of Nursing (ADN) was the source for the majority of entry-level nurses in American hospitals. These degrees rapidly replaced the diploma nursing programs that were maintained by the hospitals. The ADN programs eliminated the expensive diploma programs from hospital budgets and provided them with nurses who possessed some basic foundation skills in communication and mathematics. However, there were many nursing faculty at four-year institutions who argued the ADN programs were inferior, not only to the BSN degree but also insufficient for entry-level nursing employment. As nursing became more specialized (surgical nursing, pediatric nursing, etc.), many research hospitals in urban centers began to require a bachelor's in science with nursing specialization (BSN) as an entry point for their workers.

This enflamed the already existing competition at the four- and two-year nursing programs, and many community colleges believed their programs were endangered. Instead of attempting to develop collaboration between the two sectors, one strategy advanced by some community colleges was to obtain authorization from their states to offer their own BSN programs. Their argument for this approach was based on two factors. First, their curriculum taught the same hands-on nursing courses as many of the four-year schools. Second, their emphasis on the work-based learning (almost all community college nursing programs contain an in-hospital practicum, and many four-year programs were all school based) resulted in their graduates being more work ready, often scoring higher than their four-year counterparts in the critical National Council Licensure Examination (NCLEX) tests, which are used by all states to grant nursing licenses. The four-year programs countered with research that indicated hospitals with more four-year nursing students had better medical outcomes measured by lower hospital death rates than those staffed primarily by students with community college degrees. While the debates between the two- and four-year programs focused on entry-level nursing employment, it was clear that for advancement in the nursing field a four-year degree was becoming the emerging requirement.[13]

Changes in the Auto Industry

Macomb Community College continued to evolve its workforce programs as the auto industry entered a new phase in the Detroit region. Despite the implementation of new manufacturing technologies and the reorganization and downsizing of the domestic automakers, their domestic market share continued to decline. By 2007, the domestic three automakers controlled only 50 percent of the market of automobiles sold in the United States. In the prior decade, the domestic manufacturers had closed 69 plants and trimmed their employment by 148,000 workers. Much of the competition they faced was not imported vehicles but European and Japanese transplant operations in the United States. Many of these new facilities were concentrated in rural southern states, and most were not unionized. Their wages and especially fringe benefits were considerably lower than the domestic automakers, but in comparison to southern rural labor markets they were higher than what could be earned for similar work in their region. Moreover, these new facilities were hiring younger workers, and with no retirees, their medical and retirement costs per worker were considerably lower than the domestic OEMs.[14]

This long, steady decline of the domestic auto industry had a significant influence on the entire Detroit region. By 2006, the domestic automakers, which had employed over one million workers in the 1970s, were reduced to a domestic workforce of 295,600 employes.[15] Unlike earlier downturns, which had primarily affected older Detroit facilities, the shrinkage of the domestic auto industry was felt across the entire Detroit metropolitan area. The auto design and machine tool supplier plants in Macomb County were now experiencing significant loss of auto-related business. The one growth area in manufacturing was the defense sector, which was expanding both its production and research and development activities in Macomb County. Many Macomb manufacturers were securing work in the defense industry through TACOM (US Army Tank-automotive and Armaments Command) and TARDEC (Tank Automotive Research, Development and Engineering Center) ties.

As the automakers downsized their managers and professional workforces, these were primarily concentrated in the metropolitan area. While some of the auto suppliers were able to refocus their business to the transplants, the elimination of workers in the industry was considerable. For hourly UAW workers, there were contract provisions in place that permitted them to use their seniority to transfer to other facilities of their company. This produced thousands of "gypsy workers" who relocated sometimes hundreds of miles away from their homes, commuting back to Detroit to see their families. Few could relocate permanently to their new work locations because they were unable to sell their homes in a depressed Detroit region housing market.

The significant decline of the domestic auto industry was felt most strongly in Detroit. The population within the city declined by 25 percent from 2000 to 2010. For the first time, many working-class Black residents were also leaving the city in significant numbers to relocate to the suburbs. This left Detroit with significant numbers of people without stable work and large numbers of elderly citizens, resulting in a 55 percent loss of income tax revenue during the decade. By 2008, the local tax revenue from the three Detroit gambling casinos exceeded revenues from local income tax. One of the only positive population gains was the increase of new immigrants from the Middle East, particularly escaping the conflicts in Iraq and Syria. By 2007, the population growth from international migration in the Detroit region exceeded the annual number of newborns from local residents.[16]

During this decade, there was a consensus among local regional leadership that raising the education levels of the young people would be crucial for any revitalization of the region. All the automakers assumed that their skills needs would increase with the rapid adoption of new information technology within the automobile. There was also great interest in the development of information technology applications that could be used to develop autonomous vehicles. Detroit auto companies were having a difficult time recruiting information technology workers from Silicon Valley to migrate to southeast Michigan, so their revised goal was to grow local talent. This was not an easy task. Many of the best young people seeing the shrinkage of the auto industry were leaving the region for jobs in other areas. For policymakers, there was a belief that urban K–12 public education was often unable to respond adequately to the region's educational needs. Thus, in the 1990s, the state of Michigan passed legislation that permitted charter schools as alternatives to public education. As a result, the Detroit Public School District lost significant numbers of students as about half of the Detroit school-age population started attending charter schools or enrolling in suburban public school districts.

These developments, coupled with the increasing number of Black people living in the suburbs, were changing the city-suburban dynamic. The impact of the gambling casinos (all located in downtown Detroit) and new sports stadiums brought more suburban residents to the central city for entertainment and professional sports. Detroit became more of a hollowed shell and less important in the region as a population or major production center. In addition, as the economic difficulties in the suburbs intensified, suburban politicians could not easily accuse the city of Detroit as the cause of all local problems. A new consensus was emerging—the entire region was suffering.[17]

Macomb Community College Response

Macomb Community College responded to these trends by establishing closer ties with firms that were transitioning to defense production. The college opened an office to help companies secure defense contracts, which was a very different process than working as a supplier in the defense industry. In addition, as TACOM expanded, there were technical positions opening, and the college was able to place students within these operations. Furthermore, Macomb began applications for the National Science Foundation program that would provide funds to develop the college's capacity to offer programs in both electric vehicles (EV) and autonomous vehicles (AV). The future for the auto industry was much more reliant on the applications of information technology skills and less on the metal bending skills that determined the past strength of the sector.

In the late 1990s, Macomb Community College experienced the first enrollment decline in the history of the college. The major reasons for this enrollment decline were the leveling off of the school-age population in the county and the fading of Vietnam veteran enrollment. In addition, as the domestic economy recovered, the number of adults looking for skills that would get them employed was also diminishing. For the first time, Macomb Community College needed to develop a strategy to attract and maintain students.[18]

In order to deal with the decline in enrollment and satisfy policymakers' interests, Al Lorenzo considered having the college offer an applied baccalaureate degree. While this term was utilized by some four-year colleges with general technology curriculum specializations, such as Ferris State or the University of Wisconsin Stout, Al Lorenzo's proposal focused exclusively upon specific occupation fields relevant to the local economy. He advocated that Macomb should offer degrees that were based on specific advanced technical occupations in subject areas where the college already had a substantial capacity and a well-established record serving local employers. The belief was this would attract both individuals with some college who wanted the four-year degree to advance into higher level positions, as well as those with no degrees who wanted to start the process. While this was not implemented, the college did develop a three-year advanced program in auto body design. Students received a certificate, but there was no attempt to offer a degree.

In addition to this initiative, Macomb College continued to forge ahead with new forms of partnerships at the University Center. In 2007, Macomb secured the Detroit campus for MSU Osteopathic Medical School at the University Center, making Macomb the first community college in the nation to house a medical school. This was a sign of the increasing importance of health-care occupations to the careers of community college students. The college also initiated discussions with both Wayne State University and Oakland University to expand their offerings in Macomb County. With Oakland University, the college developed a joint admission program where students were admitted to both schools simultaneously with a joint transcript keeping track of their progress in both institutions. When Michigan Governor Granholm convened the Cherry Commission in 2004 to investigate ways to increase the number of adults with postsecondary credentials, these Macomb initiatives were cited as models for what needed to be done by Michigan community colleges.[19]

One of the reasons Al enjoyed a long tenure as president was his ability to control the board to support his efforts. However, from the staff's point of view, the board was often perceived as out of touch with the institution's needs. As enrollment declined, especially among the faculty and administrators, there was a concern for the future of the college, and it led to the unions working to elect new candidates for trustee positions that would be more independent from Al's control. They began to ask questions about college priorities and the perception that staff salaries were lagging behind other community colleges in Michigan.

In the winter of 2007, Macomb received its reaccreditation status for ten years by the Higher Learning Commission. In the spring of 2007, Al Lorenzo announced he would retire from the presidency in June 2008 after serving twenty-nine years as the leader of the college. His long tenure was extremely unusual for community college presidents. During that period, he built the institution into a multi-campus complex organization with many new and creative programs. While he did not choose to play a major national role in community college activities, Macomb enjoyed the reputation of a well-run, mission-driven institution through his innovations. Within the Detroit metropolitan area, Macomb was considered a significant center for workforce development, focused on serving the workforce needs of the auto industry.

My Economic Forecast

I was absent from many of the Macomb activities discussed above. I was still an employee of the college, but my work at CCRC rarely led me to perform any duties on the campus. Much of this period was spent commuting from Detroit to CCRC in New York. Even though I was now a college administrator, I was not a member of the President's Council, the senior leadership team where major institutional decisions were made. In retrospect, my absence from the day-to-day activities of the college aided me when I applied to the presidency. I had not created any recent internal enemies or opponents within the college, which normally is the central obstacle confronting an internal presidential applicant.

However, I did follow the decline of the region and the issues affecting the auto industry through my Economic Forecast. My only significant local activity during this period was the preparation and delivery of the annual Economic Forecast for Macomb County. This was an extremely high visibility event that became an annual tradition in the developing civic culture of the county. This event started in the mid-1980s when I was still teaching economics at the college. I was asked by the local Chamber of Commerce to discuss local economy trends. Since no one had ever gathered empirical evidence on the local economic activity in the county, it became an annual event at the start of each year. With the support of the Chamber, the forecast became very popular, drawing 250–300 individuals from the Macomb business community and local elected officials. I intentionally grew this annual activity, adding PowerPoint slides and lots of empirical data on the county. Much of it was public and accessible to anyone who took the trouble to collect it, but because Macomb County rarely received any attention from the Detroit media, these facts were often considered news, including by the media. I became one of the few local "experts" on the economic, social, and political trends in the county. As the forecast grew in popularity, I obtained a great deal of very specific unpublished information on county economic trends from local public officials and private businesses. With both the public data and the private additions, I was able to weave together an informative presentation. The forecast was often held on campus, and it reinforced the widely held perception that Macomb was a vital community resource. Al Lorenzo was very supportive of the event in part because the college received very positive community feedback.[20]

This event not only elevated my personal standing in the community, but it permitted me to organize a well-documented narrative on the strengths and weaknesses of the county, which I shared with new data each year. This perspective was critical of the Macomb County leadership on many issues (such as racism, a lack of appreciation for new immigrants, and a refusal to play a more aggressive role in regional economic development), but at the same time, it was supportive of the county's emphasis on manufacturing and local economic growth and stability. I also raised the issues of the growing income polarization between the poor southern end of the county and the wealthier northern communities. Not all my remarks were well received by some of the conservative and right-wing business groups. Typically, after my talk, the local newspaper, the *Macomb Daily*, did receive some negative responses. One of my favorite comments was a letter to the newspaper that tersely stated: "Calling Jacobs an economist is like saying Jeffrey Dahmer was an operating surgeon."

Figure 5.1 Each year for thirty-four years of my career, I presented an Economic Forecast for Macomb County at Macomb Community College. Image courtesy of Macomb Community College.

These forecasts did promote me into a respectability among county political and business leadership. There were very few other people in the county who had an understanding of the social and economic challenges faced by Macomb County and who could articulate an approach for dealing with them. I was asked to serve on the board of a local community bank, which even though I was working in New York City, provided me with a means of keeping in touch with local conditions.

Peoples State Bank

My annual Economic Forecast was also instrumental in my being invited to join the Board of Directors of Peoples State Bank—a local community bank. Peoples State Bank was founded in Hamtramck after the First World War by a few successful Polish businessmen. The board was composed exclusively of white local businessmen, most with years of experience running small successful companies. I was the only non-private sector member invited to join because of my knowledge of Macomb County—a major developing market for the bank.

This was my first experience in leadership of a for-profit entity. While I contributed very little to the economic success of the bank, I did learn something important about private sector investment decision-making. I was somewhat stunned by how quickly the directors made decisions on loans for multi-million-dollar projects. There was little independent review of information, and what little information was presented before decisions were made typically came from the clients. Deliberations were often more focused on who was asking for the money, their history with the bank, and their personal ties with other companies. Little information was validated or confirmed through independent sources. Sometimes competitor activity motivated choices made, but rarely was data or historical context utilized at least by the directors when we met each month to consider investments. The operating culture of the board was based on speed and instinct, not deliberation and reflection. Previous track record with customers, particularly if there were any negative experiences, counted a great deal. Sometimes errors were made. One time the bank granted a significant loan to a grifter who claimed to be inheriting an overseas fortune. On the other hand, if an error was made in a bank decision, there was a swift process to adjust or rectify the mistake. Adjustments were made rapidly, and you "moved on." This decision-making process was almost the opposite of my experience in the educational sector, but it made me understand the culture of this private sector and how small and median size businesses make economic decisions. The bank played an important role in providing capital for investments of the newly emerging ethnic communities. Originally the bank was created to aid Poles, but by the time I joined the board, the main customers were from the Chaldean, Albanian and Bengali communities. These individuals, often new immigrant investors and entrepreneurs, could not meet the credit requirements of the larger banks and sought out relations with our bank.

However, despite filling a real community need and 100 years of successful operations, this did not save the bank from the realities of modern capitalism. Peoples State Bank became a victim of the Great Recession, which the board was unprepared to handle. Many of the directors suffered significant financial losses, and the community lost an institution that did make a difference in the financial lives of many new immigrants and their businesses.

Life at CCRC

My goal at CCRC was to aid in building the organization into an effective research unit whose work could be utilized by community colleges. While CCRC was housed within a major research institution that attracted many talented academics, I was primarily interested in how relevant this research could be to improve the functioning of community colleges. This would be a challenge. Not only did community college leaders believe academic research was often irrelevant to the practical day-to-day issues affecting the institutions, but there was a strong aversion and defensiveness within the community colleges to any empirical research. In large part, the insecurity of the colleges concerning their role within the postsecondary sector resulted in many leaders not trusting or utilizing research for fear it would disseminate "bad news" about them to the communities. Instead, they depended on anecdotes or specific individual stories of student success to confirm what they were doing right and dismissed many empirical data-driven analyses as done by people "who don't understand us and want to be critical."

The original idea for a research center devoted to community colleges came from an interaction between Tom Bailey, a faculty member at Teachers College, and Jesse Ausubel from the Alfred P. Sloan Foundation. At the time, most higher education research concentrated on Ivy League colleges and flagship public universities; there was little recognition or understanding of the significance of community colleges in American postsecondary education. Through his research, Tom developed an appreciation for the importance of community colleges. Although he had little experience with their internal operations or had any ties with the major practitioners in the workforce field, most importantly, he had an appreciation for the work of the colleges and an empathetic perspective on the problems they faced.

In this initial period, my contribution was to focus CCRC's academically sound research on topics that were real problems confronting the colleges. This research may lead to conclusions that identified the problems in their work, but it was always projected from a perspective that understood the challenges the colleges faced. In order to ensure that CCRC would receive critical feedback from the field, I helped Tom create an Advisory Board of community college leaders.

While part of my role at CCRC was to help form the organization and steer its priorities, I also was conducting research in workforce development. One of my first topics was to examine the growing utilization of certifications in the information technology sector and their impact on community college occupational programs. Many information technology firms, including Microsoft, Novell, and Cisco, created firm-specific certificates to validate the skills of their employees and new hires to work in their companies. These quickly developed into a set of standards separate from degrees or any traditional education credentials to be utilized by educational institutions. There was a concern that these certifications were creating what an educational researcher Clifford Adleman called "a parallel universe" that was competing with the credentials of the existing educational delivery system. Our research found that, rather than competing with community colleges or posing a threat, these certifications were being assimilated into community college programs and delivered by both college credit and non-credit divisions. Moreover, the beneficiaries of the "certs" were primarily employees already in the industry. The companies were using them less as a hiring device and more as a means of determining occupational advancement. In the information technology sector, firms rarely hire individuals with certifications but no experience.[21]

In this project, I worked with the late Norton Grubb, one of the most creative and thoughtful educational researchers I ever encountered. Not only was he a gifted thinker and a dazzlingly fast writer, but his broad knowledge and curiosity motivated him to conduct research on very relevant questions for the field. He helped me organize my thoughts on IT certification into an understandable paper. His untimely death in 2015 was an enormous blow to the field of community college research.

I also worked on research projects involving the National Science Foundation's Advanced Technology Program, specifically designed to aid community colleges in educating "technicians" in emerging technical fields.[22] Through these projects, I was able to utilize my knowledge of technology adoption and routinization learned at ITI with the emerging skill requirements of community college programs. Vanessa Morest, then a young researcher at CCRC and now Provost and Vice President of Academic Affairs at Westchester Community College, helped me understand how to conduct field research and a site visit to NSF centers. In 2002, CCRC added Davis Jenkins, a very talented researcher based in Chicago, who developed much of the guided pathways approach to curriculum and student services, which would become the most widely adopted organization change model.

I also initiated one of the most controversial research issues CCRC ever took up. As mentioned previously, the nursing programs of community colleges were being threatened by the development of four-year programs offering a BSN. The American Association of Community Colleges asked CCRC to examine these arguments made by the four-year nursing programs. Working with Kathy Hughes and Melinda Mechur Karp, I learned how researchers could approach this controversial topic and make a meaningful contribution to the field. We found there was little research basis for the four-year arguments. Melinda was the lead researcher in this project and often had to make presentations before two- and four-year nursing organizations, dealing with people who had had strongly held but often empirically unsupported views.[23]

Near the end of my time at CCRC, I worked on a crucial community college workforce issue: the relationship between credit and non-credit programs. This study was led by Michelle Van Noy, and she was one of the first researchers to systematically obtain state data on non-credit activities. We found enormous inconsistencies in state data gathering and little understanding, both within the colleges and in policy circles, of how non-credit and credit programs could be linked together. The specific policy suggestions that emerged from this study are now being implemented by community colleges. Later, when I became president of Macomb, I drew upon this research as part of my approach to combine credit and non-credit programs.[24] Even though it was completed over fifteen years ago, it still has relevance to the field.

By combining these research projects with my experience as a workforce practitioner, I was well positioned to participate in the policy work that CCRC undertook. As the major foundations began to invest in community colleges, they often turned to CCRC for assistance in ongoing evaluation and assessment of these activities. One of the first projects to involve CCRC was the Bridges to Opportunity grant of the Ford Foundation, which supported six community college state systems. As a participant in the grant, I obtained a firsthand perspective of how state community college systems functioned. Michigan was one of the few states with no postsecondary state authority, and through this project, I learned the advantages of state leadership to increase collaboration and innovation within the colleges.[25]

Achieving the Dream (ATD), originally funded by the Lumina and Kresge Foundations, also utilized CCRC in their initial research and program design efforts. ATD focused on institutional changes within community colleges to increase their low-income students' completion of degrees. This project focused on change in all major aspects of community college practice, from developmental education and counseling to encouraging institutional changes in curriculum and instruction. Much of CCRC's original research in developmental education reform and course selection sequencing was utilized by ATD staff in the creation of a career pathways approach to community college designs of curriculum and program data.[25]

My participation in the research projects and shaping the agenda for the foundations was helping CCRC grow and sink roots into the community colleges. Tom made me the associate director of CCRC, which gave me a leadership role within most major initiatives. As I participated in the CCRC research projects, I was also becoming familiar with the challenges facing many of the colleges. In addition, I was learning what the interests were of the foundations and government agencies in the potential of these institutions. One important conclusion I learned from these experiences was that community colleges were different from one another depending on the specific economic context they faced. A good community college understood its community and developed programs and activities to deal with the major issues affecting their districts.

My experiences at Macomb gave me a broad understanding of workforce trends, but I was quick to point out that the workforce specifics of dealing with the domestic auto industry were considerably different from what rural colleges in California, Montana, or New Jersey faced. But the essential process and the issues for each college to consider when they needed to understand their communities were common across the colleges. I was finding that my ideas for change were being taken seriously by a wider group of policy experts and researchers. People acted upon my suggestions, not despite my political views but often because of them. Initially, this came as a great shock to me—I had not understood how few people in the community college could combine three elements: practical work at an institution, relevant research knowledge, and a vision that could inspire new policies and programs to improve these institutions.

Second, and probably equally important, as I moved in these circles, I felt very much at home and equal to the tasks of administering and managing complex large projects. In my previous work, I did not believe I was acquiring administrative leadership skills. I had not read the organizational theory books or taken any management classes, nor did I embrace the educational jargon that was endemic among community college administrators. However, I found that this was not a significant drawback. Indeed, my political background as an organizer gave me the skills to convince people to participate in our research projects. In addition, my experiences at ITI, Peoples State Bank, and the college provided me with an understanding of employers and gave me a perspective on working with business leaders that was more knowledgeable than many educators, even those from the career and technical community. While I was at home dealing with the private sector, at the same time, I always took into account the mission and goals of a public community college. Businesspeople disagreed with me, but they appreciated my knowledge of their issues, and my willingness to understand their needs.

Third, my involvement with research projects outside of the workforce development area gave me a greater appreciation for the complexity of the institutions and for the need for a more holistic approach. The colleges had to understand the needs of their communities with a much broader perspective than just economic development of companies. The importance of student services, especially for first-generation students, was central to their success at community colleges. Good teaching mattered, as well as the commitment of the staff to work with students, but the organization of the institutions and its practices were crucial to its success. Taking these into consideration would result in discarding the belief that "the market" or "individual self-interest" would take care of college issues. There needed to be designed interventions to increase equity and opportunity for students from low-income backgrounds, and that required community colleges to be intentional about the interventions they pursued.

The business community was not going to respond without significant community college prodding and advocacy for our students and communities.

Finally, my participation in CCRC helped foster one of its most significant achievements of the organization—overcoming the community college fear concerning research on their activities. CCRC's thorough and very thoughtful approach to important questions facing the colleges won many community college leaders over to the belief that good research would improve the practice of community colleges. As a practitioner with years of community college experience, I played a backup role. Ultimately, Tom's openness and empathetic approach were the most important reasons for the success of CCRC with community colleges. Through his leadership, CCRC emerged as the most important research organization for community college practitioners in the United States.

CCRC's research agenda was attracting large grants from foundations and federal agencies to conduct its research. As a result, Tom was building a significant team of researchers. Much of the actual research was based on site visits to community colleges, interviewing administrators, faculty, and often students. On these site visits, I excelled because I always felt at home on a community college campus—I could grasp their issues and often could frame relevant research issues for them. I also added some dimensions from my political organizing days to help build the CCRC, framing community college issues within a broader perspective of their importance to working-class students and the communities they served.

No doubt, being at Teachers College gave me a national platform to initiate my ideas and concepts. It gave me great confidence in my abilities to know that my ideas were now being accepted by community college leadership. I also interacted with and learned from some of the great community college presidents, such as Gail Mellow, Bill Law, Diane Troyer, Eloy Oakley, Scott Rawls, Christine McPhail, Roy Church, Ken Ender and others on how they handled issues at their institutions. I had no specific career plans nor considered myself geographically mobile, but for the first time, I was thinking seriously about being a president.

National Council for Workforce Education

While at CCRC, I became president of an important community college workforce organization, the National Council for Workforce Education (NCWE). The organization was formed in the late 1970s by occupational deans and their workforce staff to influence national discussions of workforce education as well as professional development for the membership. The traditional education organization for career and technical educators, the American Vocational Association, was so dominated by K–12 educators that community college occupational administrators felt a need to create their own organization. NCWE was affiliated with the American Association of Community Colleges but responsible for its own financial and organizational status.

Given the increasing emphasis on workforce education, I was surprised how relatively small and isolated NCWE was from many of the recent national trends in workforce development. The organization was always on the brink of financial collapse. With such a national interest in workforce development, there should not be a financial crisis within an organization of workforce practitioners. I saw the opportunity for NCWE to grow and develop a sustained financial base by our membership collaborating on projects with research and policy groups. This would not only sustain the organization but elevate it into becoming a more critical force in the development of community college workforce policy. As president, I began seeking out foundation grants for our work. Working with Jobs for the Future, we secured a significant grant from the Mott Foundation to develop a project named "Breaking Through," which would link Adult Education Programs to community college workforce development programs. This brought revenue to the organization and, with these funds, we began developing a group of workforce administrators (not just occupational deans) committed to workforce education.

Through our efforts in a relatively short period, we doubled conference attendance and began earning money from participating in other grants, which enhanced workforce practice within the institutions. When I left my one-year term in office, the board created in my honor a James Jacobs Research Scholarship, which is given each year to support a graduate student in completing their doctorate on a workforce development theme.

Considering the Presidency

Through my work at CCRC and participation in the National Council for Workforce Education, I realized that I was as knowledgeable and capable as most of the current community college presidents. In addition, my politics (which I always considered to be a liability for any leadership position) actually was turning out to be an asset. My critique of present workforce activities and the need to understand how they were being shaped by inequality and racism was finding support in the mainstream dialogue about community college practice. By observing talented community college good presidents in action, I was aware that you could initiate changes that made both students and the community better. I began investigating potentially open presidencies in the New York area. There were some open positions, but the salaries did not seem sufficient to uproot Gabriella and me. In addition, I had no interest in taking the typical presidential pathway, which was to accept a position at a smaller, often rural community college and then attempt to win a job at a larger, more urban institution. Since Detroit was my home for many years, it seemed difficult for me to leave. So, I was resigned to stay at Macomb, continue my work with CCRC, and help Tom build the organization. Ironically, just as I concluded I should remain in Detroit, Al Lorenzo announced his retirement.

What I did not follow very closely were the significant changes in the Board of Trustees at the college. Two new board members were elected in 2006—one was a UAW staff representative, the other a former mayor of Eastpointe, a Macomb city. Their election was supported by the UAW local administrator's union that I helped organize a few years before. Some of these administrators had suggested that I consider returning as president, but I did not think there would be much support. Knowing Lorenzo's careful decision-making style, he probably had selected a preferred candidate before his announcement. The campus speculation pointed to a former provost who was now a president at another Michigan community college.

However, in the summer of 2007, after his retirement announcement, the UAW representative, now the chair of the Macomb Board, asked if I would be interested in applying for the presidency. While I was never told why she asked, I am sure some members of the administrative union (now a UAW local) had contacted her. While I responded that, yes, I was interested, I had no real strategy for making this happen. When the job was posted, there were several internal candidates and at least three external candidates who were already college presidents. It is highly unusual for the college to select someone from within the institution, especially when external candidates have presidential experience.

However, there were also some factors working in my favor. Since I had spent the last seven years at CCRC, while technically still employed at Macomb, I was not identified with any problematic issues within the institution or forced to take sides in any internal conflicts that typically would produce internal staff opposition to my candidacy. Second, the board chair put together a very unusual presidential search committee which included the leaders of each of the seven unions at the college. This gave me a significant edge because my past support for unions was well-known in the institution. Finally, I received some great advice from other community college presidents, one of whom advocated an approach that I adopted. He told me "Look, they know who you are. So don't tell them about your qualifications—tell them what you are going to do." Armed with this insight, I applied for the position with a six-page letter of application outlining my plans for the college if I was selected. These were to significantly increase our efforts at student success for low-income students, dealing with the growing diversity within the student body and in the county, and playing a more regional role in the economic and workforce developments of the Detroit region. I also needed to distance myself from some of Lorenzo's present policies, while at the same time not being directly critical of him. I confronted this issue by saying, "I am following a Legend, and here is what I would do to build upon his work." I knew some of my agenda were changes he had little interest in, including how much I valued the unions and the support of present staff at the institution.

The presidential selection process consisted of three rounds—an initial screening of the thirty-plus applications, then a narrowing down to eight candidates to appear before the search committee, and lastly selecting three finalists for a day visit at the college to meet with all staff groups and a night meeting with the board. Then the board would make the decision. I made it through the first round easily enough. In many institutional searches, all internal applicants are automatically passed on. The second round was in front of the entire selection committee, and during this round, I was asked what I considered a decisive question "What is the regional role that Macomb College should play?" I outlined how racism and isolation had hurt both the county and the college and said that, as president, I would advocate for Macomb to become a regional asset that was welcoming to students from Detroit. I knew this could be a deal breaker, but this was something I had to say because it was at the heart of my belief system. After my response, the interview was abruptly stopped, and I assumed this was my exit from the process. Later I learned it was stopped because most of the committee liked the answer!

From that point, I became a front-runner for the position. In the final round, I knew I would have support from many of the staff but was unsure how my candidacy would be considered by newer employees. I had been away seven years, so there were many new employees now working at the institution I did not know. As I entered the room, however, right in the front row, I saw some old familiar faces. They were the retired clerical workers from the college, who were leaders of the 1970 strike. They were there to support my candidacy for president. The presence of these retirees who came back to support my application for the presidency was very moving for me. They gave me confidence that day, and I did well at the meeting. The actions of these retirees reaffirmed my faith that context matters—my previous actions were contributing to my present support. By the end of the meeting, I knew the staff was supporting my candidacy.

My last interview that day was with the Board of Trustees. I knew the board chair was supporting me; I didn't know about any of the others, so I was unsure what to expect at my final meeting before they made their selection. A few attended my meetings with the staff but never said a word. It was a snowy March night, and I suspected the board would either cancel the meeting or delay the ultimate selection. Nevertheless, they went ahead with the meeting and asked a few perfunctory questions—and soon I was dismissed to drive home through the snow. I no sooner arrived home when a representative from the board called and said that by a 5–2 margin, they voted to offer me the job as president! Later, I discovered that the chair of the board had the votes already committed before the meeting. Given her background as a long-time UAW elected official, I should have realized Nancy Falcone knew how to assemble and accurately count the votes. With that decision, my life changed dramatically.

Notes

1 There are at least two theoretical explanations for the bipartisan support of community colleges. The first was developed by Grubb and Lazerson in their 2009 book titled *The Education Gospel*. They present a historical analysis of the emphasis on schooling to support vocations from 1900 until 2009, when their book was published. They argued that America has long held the belief that "education reform can lead to economic and social and individual salvation." W. Norton Grubb and Marvin Lazerson, 1. The second theoretical explanation is a more overtly political explanation tied to the functioning of capitalism, which both major political parties support. John Levin situates this bipartisan support within the ideology of corporate liberalism. This is an explicit development of capitalism that promotes opportunities for student development and growth but within "a business-like approach, pursuing revenues, working for increased productivity, and marketing itself as a salvation for local and even state and national economies through economic development." John S. Levin, *Nontraditional Students and Community Colleges: The Conflict of Justice and Neoliberalism* (Palgrave Macmillan, 2007), 57.

2 Allie Grasgreen, "Community colleges lifted via Obama," *Politico*, May 18, 2015, https://www.politico .com/story/2015/05/community-colleges-lifted-via-obama 118077.

3 A 2004 national survey funded by the Ford Foundation conducted by Douglas Gould and Company revealed "highly favorable attitudes toward these colleges [i.e., community colleges], many of those attitudes formed through first-hand experience." Belden Russonello & Stewart, *Expanding Opportunity: Communicating about the Role of Community Colleges* (Douglas Gould and Company, 2004).

4   For the best, up-to-date national data on community colleges, visit the Community College Research Center at https://ccrc.tc.columbia.edu/.

5   This critique is best articulated by the major work of the CCRC during this period: Thomas R. Bailey, Shanna Smith Jaggers, and Davis Jenkins, *Redesigning America's Community Colleges: A Clearer Path to Student Success* (Harvard University Press, 2015).

6   Joel Vargas, Sarah Hooker, Michael Collins, and Ana Bertha Gutierrez, "Eliminating the Gap between High School and College," in *13 Ideas That Are Transforming the Community College World,* ed. Terry U. O'Banion (Rowman & Littlefield, 2019), 191–212.

7   Community College Research Center, "Understanding Dual Enrollment," accessed October 9, 2024, https://ccrc.tc.columbia.edu/publications/understanding-dual-enrollment.html; Schwartz and McKittrick, 4–11.

8   Melinda Mechur Karp, Juan Carlos Calcagno, Katherine L. Hughes, Dong Wook Jeong, and Thomas Bailey, *The Postsecondary Achievement of Participants in Dual Enrollment: An Analysis of Student Outcomes in Two States* (Community College Research Center, 2007).

9   John Fink from CCRC has mapped dual enrollment programs in rural colleges. See John Fink, "Acceleration for All? Mapping Racial Equity in Access to AP and Dual Enrollment," *Community College Research Center*, https://ccrc.tc.columbia.edu/easyblog/mapping-racial-equity-ap-dual-enrollment.html.

10 Matthew Zeidenberg, Sung-Woo Cho, and Davis Jenkins, "Washington State's Integrated Basic Education and Skills Training Program (I-BEST): New Evidence of Effectiveness," CCRC Working Paper No. 20 (Community College Research Center, 2010). For further information about I-BEST, see Washington's Community and Technical Colleges, "Integrated Basic Education and Skills Training (I-BEST)," December 2022, https://www.sbctc.edu/resources/documents/about/facts-pubs/i-best.pdf.

11 Elizabeth Meza and Ivy Love, "When Community Colleges Offer a Bachelor's Degree: A Literature Review on Student Access and Outcomes," New America, March 28, 2023, https://www.newamerica.org/education-policy/reports/when-community-colleges-offer-a-bachelors-degree/.

12 Deborah L. Floyd and Michael L. Skolnik, "The Community College Baccalaureate," in O'Banion, *13 Ideas*, 103–27.

13 Melinda Mechur Karp, James Jacobs, and Katherine Hughes, *Credentials, Curriculum, and Access: The Debate Over Nursing Preparation* (Community College Press, 2002).

14 Center for Automotive Research, 15.

15 Ibid; James Jacobs, "Economic Forecast for Macomb County," presented January 2008.

16 Nathan Bomey and John Gallagher, "How Detroit Went Broke," *Detroit Free Press*, September 15, 2013; Nathan Bomey, *Detroit Resurrected: To Bankruptcy and Back* (W.W. Norton & Company, 2016), 1–18.

17 Bomey.

18 College enrollment declined from 1987 to 1997. In 1995, Macomb Community College hired the Office of Adult Learning Services of the College Board to conduct a study of adult enrollment: College Board, *Policy Recommendations for Educating Adults* (College Board, 1995).

19 Commission on Higher Education & Economic Growth, *Final Report of the Lt. Governor's Commission on Higher Education & Economic Growth* (State of Michigan, December 2004), 18.

20 In 2007, Macomb Community College's self-study for the Higher Learning Commission referred to my economic forecasts as "sharing regional economic forecasts with community leaders and elected officials, with particular attention to the status of manufacturing and manufacturing related employment." Macomb Community College, *Self Study Report* (February 2007).

21 James Jacobs and W. Norton Grubb, "The Limits of 'Training for Now': Lessons from Information Technology Certification," in *Defending the Community College Equity Agenda*, ed. T. Bailey and V.S. Morest (Johns Hopkins Press, 2006), 132–54.; Clifford Adelman, *A Parallel Postsecondary Universe: The Certification System in Information Technology* (Office of Educational Research and Improvement, Department of Education, 2000).

22 Thomas Bailey, Yukari Matsuzuka, James Jacobs, Vanessa Smith Morest, and Katherine L. Hughes, "Institutionalization and Sustainability of the National Science Foundation's Advanced Technological Education Program," Community College Research Center, Teachers College, Columbia University, October 2003.

23 Karp et al., *Credentials, Curriculum, and Access*.

24 Michelle Van Noy, James Jacobs, Suzanne Korey, Thomas Bailey, and Katherine L. Hughes, "The Landscape of Noncredit Workforce Education: State Policies and Community College Practices," Community College Research Center, Teachers College, Columbia University, April 2009.

25 "Bridges to Opportunity for Underprepared Adults: A State Policy Guide for Community College Leaders," Community College Research Center, Teachers College, Columbia University, 2008, https://ccrc.tc.columbia.edu/publications/underprepared-adults-state-policy-guide.html.

6 **Becoming a President**

I was hired by the board in March 2008 with a starting date of July 1. However, since I was already employed at Macomb, as soon as the decision was made, I started planning my transition to the presidency. Al Lorenzo included me in all leadership meetings, and even though I was working for the Community College Research Center (CCRC), I started to spend more time at Macomb, maintaining my little cubicle office. The only noticeable difference was the new deference being paid to me by some of the staff. When my family attended college events, my kids noticed how the maintenance workers and campus police were now calling me "boss," something they found very amusing.

College staff members who had known me for years and who had barely acknowledged my activities, let alone supported them, were now extremely solicitous to me. Some of them were senior administrators who I knew were uncomfortable with my ascendance to the presidency. A few of them announced their retirement shortly after my selection which, while presenting some immediate staffing issues, probably helped me overall by creating opportunities for others who were more supportive of me and my plans.

While I engaged in the presidential search process in the winter of 2008, it was apparent to me that the Great Recession had already begun in the Detroit area. The economic picture for Detroit was extremely grim in January 2008, eight months before the collapse of Lehman Brothers and three months before the failure of Bear Stearns, another major investment firm. Wall Street's financial crisis led to a national economic downturn. But Michigan already was in recession. Auto sales were down in 2007 as the first impact of the subprime mortgage crisis was being felt by consumers. Financial markets were in turmoil because no one could be sure of the real value of these subprime instruments. The damage to the United States economy was enormous. From 2007 to 2010, 4 million homes were foreclosed, median household wealth income declined by half, and between 27 and 40 million jobs were eliminated worldwide.[1]

Community Colleges and the Great Recession

The Great Recession increased attention on community colleges and highlighted an important trend in higher education. After the Second World War, the United States had the greatest number of citizens with postsecondary degrees of any advanced industrial nation. However, by 2012, a study by the Organization for Economic Development and Cooperation found that the United States ranked nineteenth among nations whose twenty-five to thirty-four-year-olds held college degrees. Many low-income students were enrolling in college but not completing a degree. All too often, students would enroll in postsecondary education through community colleges but not finish their programs. For policymakers in the Obama administration, there was great concern about how to increase the rate of students who completed college. As the economic trends in advanced industrial nations called for more "knowledge-based" skills, college completion became an important priority for success.

One approach sprang from a program initiated in Kalamazoo, Michigan, in 2006, to slow suburban flight and maintain the city's population. A group of local donors created the Kalamazoo Promise, which provided free in-state college tuition to every student who graduated from the Kalamazoo Public School District. There were no income or merit qualifications. The program was incredibly successful; the population of Kalamazoo increased as families moved into the city to take advantage of it. Moreover, the number of Kalamazoo public school students who enrolled in college rose sharply, especially students from low-income families who had not previously considered attending college.[2]

This local innovation suggested to federal policymakers that eliminating tuition costs would increase the number of students enrolled in colleges and universities. While few cities or states could afford to implement the Kalamazoo Promise for four-year colleges, the Obama administration announced that one of its goals was "free community college" for low-income students. If the cost of tuition was a major barrier to college enrollment and completion, then federal initiatives, coupled with state and local strategies, would provide a free community college for all. Community colleges were encouraged by the recognition they received and worked closely with the federal government in this effort. During the Great Recession, community college credit enrollments increased by 20 percent between 2008 and 2010. In the same period, enrollment in credit programs by adults aged twenty-five and older increased from 2.7 million to 3.1 million. In addition, thousands more adults took non-credit workforce programs at their local community college.

The Great Recession's Impact on the Detroit Region

The impact of the Great Recession on the auto industry and the Detroit region was profound. Many lost their homes as their financial situation worsened, and those who did not face foreclosure were "underwater," meaning the value of their home was now less than the amount they still owed on their home mortgage loan. In Macomb County, the average selling price of a home in 2009 fell 35 percent from the prior year. Auto sales slumped, and in January 2009, Chrysler Corporation, the single largest employer in the county, laid off more than 10,000 employees and shut down all of its assembly plants.

By January 2009, Macomb County's economic growth declined for the first time in more than sixty years. Manufacturing employment in the county declined by 35 percent from 2008. The labor force participation rate dropped by 6.3 percent. In 2008, residential housing starts (an indication of population growth and the backbone of the local economy) declined from 4,000 in the prior year to 508. More than 70,000 Macomb County residents sought help from the local federal employment agency, Macomb-St. Clair Michigan Works.[3] As I assumed the presidency of the college, there was a real concern about the institution's future as well as the future of Macomb County.

However, as difficult as conditions were in Macomb County, they were much worse in Detroit. From 2000 to 2010, the city lost 25 percent of its population. Detroit mayor David Bing was forced to cut 4,000 city workers, one-third of the city's workforce. As a result, city services became almost nonexistent. Half of the streetlights in the city were not operating, response time for police on high-priority calls was over thirty minutes, and there were almost 85,000 blighted structures, nearly one for every eight residents, which remained uneradicated.[4]

Despite the cuts, Detroit's finances continued to decline, forcing the city to borrow significantly. In 2008, the city owed its creditors almost $8 billion, and this excluded an additional $10 billion in pension costs and health-care benefits for existing retirees and interest on its debt. Detroit became the poster child of a failing industrial city during the Great Recession. When people in other parts of the country complained about their conditions, the response was often, "At least we are not Detroit!"

From the start, I knew I had to move quickly to help the college and the broader community. I would need to scrap the conventional wisdom for new presidents, which was to spend six months getting to know the institution and then proceed to reorganize, promoting some staff, bringing in others, and perhaps eliminating a few positions. The rationale for this was the notion that any new president needed "their own team." Not only was this approach time-consuming, but it could drain morale as staff jockeyed for recognition or key positions. I decided to skip both the six months' wait and reorganization process. I wanted to move more quickly and avoid needless confrontations and institutional drama during major reorganizations, so I chose to advance my agenda using the existing staff. I knew it would be easier to provide strategic direction for the existing staff than spend time and effort reorganizing the institution, changing their jobs, or replacing them. I was helped by the fact that I knew many of the senior staff. I knew who I could depend on and trust. I had already told the board what I was going to do. Now, I wanted to get started.

First Activities with the Board

Before I did anything, I needed to navigate an extremely critical initial ritual: the negotiation of my contract. Many presidents consider this to be the most essential aspect of assuming a community college presidency. Once an initial employment contract is negotiated, it is extremely hard to change it; typically, you can only make financial modifications at contract renewal times. There is a cottage industry of lawyers, consultants, and ex-presidents who advise new college presidents on how to negotiate contracts. Much of the advice is directed at strategies to increase the president's income and benefits with little or no transparency for the public. I decided to forgo this approach because I did not want a long-drawn-out process that might discourage board support for my programs. Instead, I asked my friend Dick Soble, our lawyer during the Red Squad case, who was now a successful arbitrator, to negotiate my contract. I instructed Dick not to press for a larger salary but to ensure that I would be able to continue consulting with organizations such as the CCRC. This arrangement was unusual, and I knew some on the board might feel uncomfortable with the request. While maintaining my consulting work did create another income stream for me, my main reason for the request was to continue to learn from the practices of other colleges. Trading a bigger paycheck and fringe benefits for the opportunity to learn from others seemed to me like a good trade-off. Dick successfully negotiated a workable contract that contained general guidelines for my involvement in non-Macomb College projects.

Residency is an issue that often arises in these contract negotiations. Many community colleges, particularly in Michigan, require the college president to live in the college district. While I had been working at Macomb for more than forty years and had previously lived in the county, I was no longer a resident and had no intention of moving. I wondered if some members of the board, particularly those who voted against hiring me, would demand residency as a condition of my employment. Fortunately, when the issue was raised within the board, the chair cut off the discussion by stating, "He has been here for forty years. What more will we gain if he moved into the county?"

An unanticipated issue emerged during my contract negotiations, giving me a preview of what I might face with the board. As part of the contract settlement, presidents are given a monthly allowance for expenses related to the performance of their job, such as membership dues for local organizations that are important for the college and financial support for community events. One of the board members who voted against me becoming president refused to support the allowance as a means of demonstrating his dissatisfaction with my selection. After a long executive session of the board, at the meeting where I was to officially sign my contract, a compromise was reached: the monthly expense allowance was withheld for the first six months, which gave the dissident board member a "win." It was a petty issue that had little impact on my behavior, but it showed how an unhappy board member could hamper my activities.

During the transition, I was thankful for the support and advice of my predecessor, Al Lorenzo. While we had quite different perspectives on the mission and leadership of the college, he very kindly put that aside and was extremely helpful in my transition to the presidency. One of my "blind spots" in assuming the presidency was failing to consider the varying needs of board members. With guidance from Al Lorenzo, I began to see how important it was to have positive relationships with the board and to view this as a critical duty, albeit a time-consuming one.

I was reluctant to adopt Al Lorenzo's approach to the board, which required lengthy discussions with individual members and obtaining majority support before bringing an item for a vote by the board. The result was an almost scripted process, with board meetings like a well-rehearsed play, and each member often reciting words scripted for them by the staff. Anyone attending one of these meetings for the first time would be hard-pressed to know what was happening.

While I was not interested in reliving the experience of chaotic Wayne County Board meetings, I was unwilling to invest the focus and time as Al Lorenzo did with board members to ensure smooth adoption of agenda items. I wanted to concentrate my effort on the staff, the students, and the community. In addition, long-standing personal differences between some board members contributed to a behind-the-scenes drama, and I did not want to get caught up in this conflict. I also knew the two board members who voted against me becoming president would continue to oppose my efforts. For these reasons, I decided to leave in place the prevailing board culture but omit the lengthy interactions with individual board members. I met regularly with the chair of the board, who was my supporter, and allowed her to organize the board's deliberations and votes. While this gave me time to focus on changing the college, I got used to not dealing with the board very much, which was an error I regretted the longer I remained president because boards can play an essential role in institutional change.

My political background was also a handicap for me in my relations with board members. I was used to collaborating with people on common political issues. Even in non-political organizations, such as the Peoples State Bank board, members were motivated from a common perspective: a desire to increase profits. In contrast, people choose to serve on publicly elected Boards of Trustees for various interests and reasons. I had to adjust to the fact that many serving on the board did so for individual, personal reasons, rather than a shared political agenda. As president, I needed to unite board members and their diverse personal and political motives behind a strategic vision for the institution. This took time and effort, which at the time I was not prepared to give.

Empowering the Staff

While I greatly respected Al Lorenzo and viewed him as an extremely talented administrator, I knew my approach would be a departure from his "old school" leadership style with traditional lines of control that centralized power and authority in the office of the president. Al had hired many talented senior administrators, but their ideas and skills were underutilized. They rarely participated in national community college organizations, and even within the institution, they were given little freedom to solve issues creatively. I outlined a different approach to the board in my statement of candidacy for the presidency:

> I would draw on my skills to create an organizational team from the talented members of the college staff who share my vision and commitment to the college. My goal is to manage the institution through setting goals with measurable outcomes that hold team members accountable for their programs. I would encourage professional growth to catapult our senior college leadership into the forefront of national programs that teach and that contribute to the development of the college as a leader in institutional innovation. I believe in shared institutional leadership success and have demonstrated that I can put that belief into action.

There was a very pragmatic reason for taking this approach. Since I assumed the presidency relatively late in my career, I knew I had a short amount of time to implement my agenda. It was important that I not spend much time or effort on "building my team" through a lengthy administrative reorganization. I was determined to work with the present administrators and develop a more collective approach to the college's issues. I wanted to focus on substantive issues and make changes through the existing systems. Far too many institutional "reformers" stumble when their first steps disrupt institutional processes or personnel. This approach often results in wasteful procedural wrangling and internal conflict, delaying the implementation of major change within the institution.

However, I knew there was a risk to this strategy. Some senior administrators, particularly those in nonacademic areas, did not share my opinion of the college unions and did not want them to be involved in major institutional decisions. My approach was put to the test at the start of my administration, as one of the first issues I confronted was negotiating with the faculty union over renewing its contract. I did not want these negotiations to create distrust that could impede other activities. Fortunately, I was aided by the retirement of the Employee Relations Vice President, who had a long, contentious history with the faculty union. In the interim, I had his role filled by the provost, who had a background in faculty labor-management negotiations. The provost's views about the need for union participation were similar to mine, and he was extremely helpful in securing renewal of the faculty contract in my first year, with minimal conflict or hostility.

Maintaining a close relationship with existing staff and seeking collaborative relationships did not apply to my initial treatment of the institution's senior administration. I have always believed in starting major institutional changes at the top, with the most senior and highest-paid employees. This would serve as a model for others to follow and reinforce the idea that change was going to impact everyone, regardless of standing within the institution. I focused on the President's Council (PC), which was composed of the institution's senior leaders and was the major internal decision-making body for the college. Taking advantage of the retirements of two senior leaders, I reduced the size of the council from twelve members to seven, making it a more effective decision-making body and pushing many of its responsibilities downward, mainly to middle-level management. In my experience at the college and from my knowledge of organizational theory, significant institutional change requires support and buy-in from the administrators closest to the front lines, which in the case of the college meant the associate deans and directors of non-instructional units. I initiated regular weekly reports to the President's Council on the unit activities to encourage cross-collaboration and eliminate the organizational barriers between the units. I also recommended articles and books for President Council members on practices at other community colleges so that we could adopt the best ideas, even if they originated elsewhere. I assumed that the issues we faced at the college were not unique and we could learn from the experience of others. I also encouraged all the senior leadership to play national roles in their professional community college organizations as part of their personal staff development plans, which they submitted to me on an annual basis. My assumption was that the more active we were in community college professional organizations, the better our leadership would be.

Changes to the President's Council were only the first step toward establishing a new organizational reality at the college; the unions also needed to play a role in the new collaborative approach. Macomb employed a bit more than 2,000 individuals and only twenty-five were "at-will employees" unrepresented by a union. There were seven separate unions, some of which were independent bargaining units and others which were affiliated with national unions, such as the United Auto Workers (UAW), the American Federation of Teachers

(AFT), and the American Federation of State, County, and Municipal Employees (AFSCME). All had separate contracts that often contained different definitions of important workplace issues such as overtime, the selection process for new hires, and layoff procedures. It was a significant task simply to administer seven separate agreements. I needed to simplify these contractual agreements as well as develop new forms of collaboration so that the unions could play a greater role within the institution. I knew major changes could not be achieved without their support. Moreover, I thought this would be an important way to demonstrate my commitment to change at Macomb and win support for my ideas from an important constituency at the college. I already had a solid reputation and institutional "capital" in this area because I had been a leader in the faculty and administrative unions and was fired in 1971 for my support of the clerical workers' strike.

To start the process, within a few months of assuming the presidency, I held monthly meetings of all the union presidents and the new Vice President for Human Relations. The meetings were not to raise collective-bargaining matters, contracts, or employee discipline, but to provide advice and input on collegewide issues. The meetings would help me learn more about issues the staff thought were important and provide an opportunity for the union leaders to raise general matters of institutional importance directly with me. I hoped that even if the unions disagreed with my decisions and actions, they would understand the process and the reasoning behind them.

Originally, I intended to have these meetings to be private ones between the union presidents and myself, with no minutes or official recordkeeping. Our Employee Relations Vice President, previously a private-sector HR manager whose workforce was represented by multiple unions, was extremely uneasy with that idea. He insisted on being present and I agreed to have him attend the meetings and witness what was said. However, I ran the meetings and in consultation with some of the union presidents, set the agenda. Most of the presidents of these unions had never discussed collegewide issues jointly, so it was a learning experience for them.

My emphasis on collaborating with all the unions was intentional and designed to alter institutional perceptions of who was important within the institution. Many staff, especially the faculty, believed the full-time faculty union was the most important facet of the college workforce, but I knew that the clerical and technical staff were vital to student success. The college could not run without the work of the technicians in our computer and science labs, or the student activities coordinators, or the campus police. Unlike the faculty, the non-teaching staff were at the college daily, interacting with the students and the community. In addition, the non-teaching staff tended to live within the county and often sent their children to Macomb schools, including the college, so they were strategically positioned to tell me how they and their neighbors perceived the institution. They could be a critical asset in any millage and board elections by campaigning as local residents in support of the college. Moreover, as union members they could help us gain support from other local unions in Macomb County, which have significant influence on electoral activity. My goal in these efforts was to make clear that all the employees at the college contribute to the success of the institution.

I also needed the staff to educate me about areas of the college where I had little familiarity and about the impact of the non-teaching staff on the college environment, which affects student learning. Maintenance people are responsible for clearing the parking lots and sidewalks during snowstorms so that students can attend classes. Clerical workers are essential to the functioning of important units such as Counseling and the Office of Financial Aid. Yet their input was rarely considered in strategic planning or goal setting for the institution.

I took the advice of Gail Mellow, former President of LaGuardia Community College, part of the City University of New York (CUNY), to learn how non-instructional areas of the institution function. I asked the maintenance staff to give me a tour of the heating and cooling systems at our South Campus, which still relied on equipment installed when the campus was constructed in 1964. Climbing over pipes and entering the complex tunnel arrangement below some of the buildings gave me an appreciation of how fragile these systems were. Moreover, the knowledge of how to maintain, adjust, and repair this aging equipment was stored in the heads of a few veteran employees who were close to retirement. We needed to make sure this knowledge was transmitted to younger staff members who were expected to fill these roles in the future. I discovered that far too often, important information on essential workplace functions is informally held and I knew that as the college grew, we needed a more formal and transparent approach.

Using Staff Input in Decision-Making

As an example of my goals, in my first year as president, I used the expertise of the maintenance people to redesign one of the most important decisions many colleges make in winter: the determination of the snow day. The decision to close a community college for a snow day is always contentious. It was the only time I got nasty phone calls or emails from staff, and sometimes students or parents. Typical were ones from parents who asserted I was trying to kill their child when we kept school open after a major snowstorm.

When a snowstorm was predicted, our maintenance staff arrived at work at 4:00 a.m. to clear the parking lots and often worked sixteen to eighteen hours a day in the days that followed. During the first of these "snow days" of my presidency, even if the college was closed, I came to work and had pizza delivered to the maintenance workers to show my appreciation for their efforts. More importantly, I used their input to change the decision-making on snow days.

Under the process in place, the decision to close the college due to weather rested with a maintenance staffer who made the call at 4:00 a.m. based on whether he believed the parking lots could be cleared of snow by the start of classes. At 7:00 a.m., when the rest of the staff arrived, we informed local radio and TV stations if the college was open and posted the information on the college website. While we thought this approach worked well enough, the decisions were not communicated in time for our students to alter their commute to campus if needed. Nor were these decisions made in coordination with other schools, particularly the four-year institutions based at the University Center. Most importantly, the process was not transparent: no one really knew who was responsible for the decision or the criteria that were used. In the face of this uncertainty, students and parents bombarded the school with phone calls the night before an approaching storm. With the advent of social media, the telephone calls were replaced by endless speculation online, which increased tension and uncertainty for faculty, staff, students, and their families.

As we considered changes to the decision-making process, I started with a premise that I knew would be unpopular, namely, that if McDonald's is open in a snowstorm, the college should be open. As an institution of higher education, our role in the community was at least as important as McDonald's, so why would we be closed when it stayed open? With this, I made it clear that my preference was to remain open in the face of bad weather. I called for Macomb Community College to establish and publicize criteria that would be used to make the decision on closing. We developed a new approach and under it, if bad weather hit, we first consulted with the Macomb County Road Commission on the state of the roads leading to our campuses. If there was difficulty clearing these roads, we would not hold classes. Second, we would monitor decisions by other higher-education institutions in our area, including Wayne State, Henry Ford College, and Oakland University. If they were closing, we should follow their lead. Third, we would get feedback from our maintenance staff and campus police on whether they could clear the parking lots for the start of classes at 7:00 a.m. Based on this information, I and our "snow queen," the Vice President of Business, Libby Argiri, would confer at 4:00 a.m. to make the decision. This information was immediately transmitted to students through an emergency text message system that we established and posted immediately on the college's website.

We shared the new criteria and the decision-making process with the staff and students. This seemingly minor change took time and effort to execute, but it demonstrated to our workforce that important campus issues could be changed for the better. We provided a system with clear guidelines in place of the uncertainty that previously existed. I still received nasty communications about the snow-day decisions, but they were at least more informed ones!

Another change I made was to amend the college calendar. For years, the college remained open on the weekdays between Christmas and New Year's Day, even though the fall semester was over, and the new one had not yet begun. This was very unpopular with non-teaching staff, as they were required to take vacation days if they wanted to be with their family during this period, while the faculty were not affected. After discussions to determine which college operations had to remain open, such as campus police and some registration functions, I announced that in the future, we would close the college during this period and would give most of the staff time off to enjoy the holidays.

A second calendar change, making MLK Day a college holiday, was important as a political statement. Even though Dr. Martin Luther King's birthday was a national holiday, the college had never officially celebrated it. We announced that we would cancel all classes on MLK Day and give the staff the day off, but we encouraged staff and students to use their free time for volunteering on or off campus with community-based organizations in honor of the late civil rights leader.

Both of these changes were ones I made unilaterally, and I am sure some of the legal and HR senior leadership were not happy about that. The conventional wisdom in a collective-bargaining setting is to never give anything up without winning some concessions in return. However, I was more interested in having the unions support other institutional reforms, and I implemented these changes quickly as a sign of others still to come.

In part, I was able to make changes immediately without internal conflict because I inherited an extremely well-functioning institution with no crisis to manage. There were no outstanding financial issues and no major personnel questions. The board was happy with the college, and its reputation in the community was extremely positive. Many new college presidents do not have this luxury; instead, they must contend with extreme dysfunction and spend valuable time and energy cleaning up past mistakes before they can implement their own plans. I was extremely fortunate in that regard, but because the college was functioning well, its staff was reluctant to embrace change. The attitude of many on staff was, "If it's not broken, why fix it?" I soon learned that when I was making changes, it was best to justify them as building upon past success, not upending or replacing it. When making changes, it is never useful to blame others, particularly your predecessors, and to instead be on the side of "progress" and serving the community.

One area I could not easily change was the increasing cultural difference between the two main campuses. The South Campus was the original campus constructed in the early 1960s, and the Center Campus was completed twenty-five years later. (Plans for a "North" campus were abandoned as the county's population growth stalled.) While the two campuses were only 8 miles apart, they reflected demographic differences in the communities and the students served. The South Campus, home to our industrial technology programs, was closer to Detroit, in the most diverse part of Macomb County, whose residents generally had lower incomes than those attending the Center Campus. The Center Campus was the site of the University Center, the Macomb Center for the Performing Arts, the Lorenzo Cultural Center, and all of our health-care programs. The Center Campus was nearer to the most affluent suburban communities of Macomb County. There was a general perception, especially among the white students and staff, that the Center Campus was a more desirable place to take classes than the South Campus. Indeed, even before I became president, the enrollment at the Center Campus exceeded that of the South Campus. While never explicitly stated, there was a clear racial undercurrent in the perception of the campuses that I knew needed to change. Even though there were facilities available for me to move to Center Campus, I maintained my office at the South Campus and tried as much as possible to ensure that all college functions were evenly distributed among both campuses. In our annual construction plans, I prioritized renovations of the older South Campus and looked for ways to bring new programs and activities to those facilities. This was often difficult to accomplish as our Performing Arts Center and Cultural Center were located only at the Center Campus, but I was able to renovate a smaller facility at the South Campus and utilize our library and student union for cultural activities. Nevertheless, the real and perceived differences between the campuses remained for my entire presidency. They reflected the economic and social differences within the county, which were extremely difficult to combat, even with my intentional efforts.

Teaching at Macomb

Even though I had been a community college instructor for more than forty years, I wanted to learn more about recent teaching practices at the institution. In my first year, I tried to attend a credit class at least once a week, particularly in the areas where I had no direct knowledge of the curriculum or substantive background in the discipline. I also wanted to understand how some of the new learning technologies were being utilized by our instructors. Under our faculty union agreement, administrators could only attend class if invited, so I had to get permission to attend from the faculty. In my initial meeting with the faculty at the start of the semester, I requested invitations to observe their classes. Most of the faculty were extremely supportive; many said that no administrator had ever observed their teaching. I also knew that many faculty inviting me into their classes had reputations as being some of the best instructors, so I was getting to see some excellent teaching practices. For my purposes, this was fine, as I was interested in seeing "the best" Macomb had to offer students, which could aid me in determining what changes were needed. I was impressed by how much technology played a role in the day-to-day classroom. Many of the textbooks came with computer-generated exercises and tests, and I wondered the extent to which that might curtail classroom discussion on relevant issues. Thankfully, the instructors were supplementing these texts with discussions often broader than the textbook. In addition, it was comforting that the career and technical classes remained "hands-on." Students learned welding or how to move robotic arms by doing it under the guidance of instructors. In a physical therapy class that I attended, all the students and I practiced physical therapy exercises on each other. Learning by doing was an important pedagogy to emphasize, especially to prepare students for the workplace.

Much to my regret, the one area I did not emphasize in my classroom investigations was our growing online learning classes. This was a major error on my part. Online instruction continued to grow; the classes offered were extremely popular and filled up quickly. By 2008, about 15 percent of all Macomb Community College classes were delivered online. However, our online classes were also ones with the largest number of students withdrawing or receiving a grade of "incomplete." Instructors that I spoke to thought that these classes attracted students whose lives were already full of work and family responsibilities. Taking classes online eliminated the time to commute to campus, but students did not realize that it can be harder to succeed in online classes than in a traditional classroom setting. In a sense, their busy lives made them select classes which they were more likely to struggle with and fail. There were also students who took courses online because they believed they were "easy classes." Of course, the opposite was often the case, and many students could not keep up with the work and dropped out rather than get a poor grade.

After discussions with the instructors, I was uncertain how to intervene in this area. For instance, should we insist on certain prerequisites for students before allowing them to enroll in online classes, or develop interventions to help them with their learning issues? Or conversely, should we require assessing all students' abilities to be successful? And if so, how would we do that? For many low-income students, their problems may have been due more to their computer equipment and wireless connectivity than to themselves and their own ability. After I retired from Macomb, I was involved in an online course designed by Google for unemployed students seeking work in the information technology sector. One of the barriers we found was that the students did not have adequate computer technology at home and could not download the assignments. While our knowledge of how to deliver online classes has advanced since 2008, the issues involved with successful student completions remain. Moreover, since the Covid-19 pandemic, enrollment in online classes has increased. In 2024, more than one-third of Macomb credit students took all of their classes online.[5]

One non-instructional function of Macomb I knew well was institutional research. Through both my experience at CCRC and my work at Macomb's Center for Community Studies, I was familiar with the operations of institutional research and the ways research units might help transform the college. Research was an important activity for establishing an internal culture that would be unafraid of introducing changes, as long as there was research supporting it.

In many community colleges, institutional research was exclusively focused on responding to compliance demands from federal, state, and local agencies. However, this was not true at Macomb. Research was valued by Al Lorenzo, and he created a sizable well-functioning unit who took on many unique activities. Since Macomb was the only local postsecondary institution in the county, the college took on some research functions for the community typically performed by four-year institutions. For over fifteen years, the college conducted a semi-annual random telephone survey of Macomb citizens to determine their views on major county issues. Focus groups were also used regularly to test opinions of students and the community about issues affecting the college and the community. This information was regularly utilized for college planning, but also widely distributed to county leadership through the Center for Community Studies.

My goals were to build upon this very solid foundation in three dimensions. First, I wanted to end the isolation of the unit from other parts of the college, the most significant areas being instruction and grant making. One researcher who has significant interest and understanding of neural networks was assigned to the Provost's Office to help provide information for student success initiatives. Our grant writing unit regularly called upon the research area asking for specific information to be incorporated within our proposals.

The second dimension was to extend the institutional research capabilities beyond the institution. As a large college with significant innovations and a rich well-kept data set, I knew Macomb would be an attractive research target for the growing number of academic researchers who were focusing on community colleges. If their research interests could help solve our practical issues, I welcomed their participation with our staff. I especially concentrated on building ties with CCRC and the University of Michigan's School of Education researchers who had track records of producing well-designed relevant research. In many of these projects, we jointly raised foundation money to conduct research. We were able to engage these researchers in helping us determine how to create a better enrollment and counseling system, what success our students were having at four-year institutions, and what the economic outcomes were for career and technical occupations. I maintained a close relationship with Tom Bailey, so CCRC staff regularly interacted with our staff and often the two groups made joint presentations at conferences. These interactions encouraged our staff to see research as not an imposition, draining time away from their job, but part of the process that any good community performs.

This goal of creating positive research relationships with other organizations sometimes did not work out. We were asked to participate in a long-term random assignment study of some of our programs by a major research and consulting group. They wanted to utilize the "gold standard" of having some students receiving a specific treatment, with a similar group that did not—something that is difficult to implement in a public setting. In addition, they also demanded we not change any of the proposed programs of study during the tenure of the research—a seven-year project. Their refusal to allow program changes seemed inconsistent with our goals of program improvement, so we did not participate.

The third dimension was to use our institutional research for quick secondary analysis of our data that could aid us in making short-term adjustments with our initiatives. This strategic or tactical research could help us make immediate decisions. For example, in discussing our nursing program, we examined the student course-taking patterns to determine how many of the students accepted into this high-demand competitive program started in developmental education courses. I was surprised to learn that 18 percent of the students accepted into our nursing program started in developmental education. Were there any commonalities among these students in the courses they took or other enrollment patterns that could account for their success? Another issue we considered was whether students who enrolled in class after the semester began were less successful than those who were able to start the semester on the first day. I utilized some of this tactical research at public events. Before every graduation, our research unit surveyed students scheduled to receive their degrees, gathering information on their age, background, interests, and occupational plans—and I would incorporate these findings into my remarks at the graduation to give the students and the audience a sense of who we were. This also maintained our "brand" of being an institution of opportunity for first-generation students.

Learning About the Institution

While teaching was an area that I knew, there were other parts of the institution that affected the learning environment, of which I had little understanding. Again, I educated myself as much as possible through direct observation. This meant observing food service personnel as they planned menus, watching campus police as they performed nighttime inspections, and visiting the financial aid office to observe how student applications were received. There was a great deal to learn from these segments of the college, including how they affected student success and what, if anything, could be done to improve them. I believed it was important that I was not chained to my desk in meetings with the same senior staff, only learning about campus issues through reports from others. I also believed that getting out of my office and seeing so many areas of the college would help me win support for policies to change the institution.

My Four Initial Goals

In my first year, the economic crisis in the community demanded a response from the institution. Since I was not "new" to Macomb or the community, nor was I attempting to reorganize the institution or recruit a new leadership team, I was able to concentrate on my initial goals. I wanted them to be understood by the staff and considered important for the institution. Also, they had to be relevant, meaning they would specifically address the issues the college faced with the students and the community. They could not be abstract educational rhetoric; after thirty years of working with one president, the college staff expected change, but it had to be understandable and build upon the existing reality. Most working at the institution didn't believe it was broken or in need of fixing, so attempts to change all aspects of it were not going to fly. The initial approach would need to be seen as building upon the good work of the past, not departing from it. I also wanted my goals to be measurable, as I assumed they would be initiated in the first year but followed for years to come.

I consistently asked three questions of any college program: what is the importance of the activity, who are the customers of the activity, and how do you measure success? For example, a look at our enrollment process revealed that many students who applied and were accepted to the college never registered for classes. Some who also were applying to four-year colleges had submitted their application to Macomb as a "safety option" in case their application to the four-year program was not accepted. Others failed to attend a voluntary orientation program or meet with a counselor and simply did not register. We formalized the enrollment process with mandatory steps for students, which included an orientation session, meeting with a counselor, and other activities aimed at increasing student registrations. This process began in my first year and was refined and implemented over a number of years, thanks to a grant that allowed us to work with CCRC on this effort.

Priority #1: Workforce Development

Developing initial goals was not difficult. Since I came to the presidency at the beginning of the Great Recession, the immediate priority was the workforce and economic development of the community. The auto industry was suffering its worst downturn since the Great Depression of the 1930s, and many in the community were unemployed. Even for those who still had jobs, it took years before they were recalled to the workplace.

Macomb had many different workforce programs. The issue was not to initiate more but to organize them so the community and students could understand and effectively utilize them. To begin, we combined credit and non-credit workforce programs into one unit under the same internal administration. The internal conflict between the credit and non-credit units was known at the college, and I was well aware that combining them was only the start of our overhaul; the cultural changes needed to make it effective would take years.

For far too long, workforce programs had been housed in separate organizational silos reporting to different vice presidents. These units had frequent disputes, particularly about utilizing campus facilities, and competed over relationships with local companies. In some cases, the same company received a separate visit from the credit and non-credit units, urging it to work with their program. At best, this was confusing, and worse, it may have caused companies to question the college's abilities and decide to distance themselves from collaborating with it.

I knew from experience, as well as the research at CCRC, that the college's careful delineation between credit and non-credit programs was irrelevant to most adults. Those who lost their jobs in the Great Recession wanted to get back to work and, to do that, they needed to acquire new skills quickly. Responding to this demand gave us an opportunity—and a justification— to unify credit and non-credit programs under one vice president.

Both areas needed a stronger focus on the overall goal of student success. The proliferation of non-credit education programs attracted large numbers of adults to community colleges. Many of these students may want to obtain a degree and perhaps transfer to a four-year institution. However, since non-credit programs were isolated from the credit part of the institution and often not considered a part of the "core of the institution," students in non-credit programs were unaware of the options they had.

For their part, the non-credit staff considered themselves to be more effective, creative, and customer-driven than the rest of the institution. Their isolation contributed to their belief that they operated outside the college's overall mission and values. The non-credit units needed to understand how their efforts fit within the institution's goal of student success. Putting the credit and non-credit programs under a single administrator was a necessary first step. We also need a new team to bring all the elements together and to do some major institutional rethinking on curriculum development. The conventional wisdom was that the college had to offer many different programs so students could choose an option that fits their interests. The cafeteria-style approach assumed that students came to occupational courses with well-conceived knowledge of their occupational goals and the current job market. In truth, the economic upheaval meant that students, especially younger ones with little work experience, needed far more guidance and structure to help them identify realistic employment goals and chart their path toward achieving them.

Moreover, the speed of technological advances and the impact on employment made it difficult for colleges to keep their curricula current. Preparing students for increasingly specialized occupational skills requires community colleges to stay in close contact with employers and devote significant resources to equipment and faculty development. The resource demands required shrinking the array of career and technical programs offered and concentrating on what looks like the safest investments for the future of workforce programs and the workforce. The "comprehensive" community college could no longer offer fifty or seventy-five high-quality occupational programs and might realistically focus on six to eight that are targeted to the interests of employers and the community.

Although I was never able to substantially reduce program offerings at Macomb Community College,[6] I was able to focus on our credit and non-credit programs to meet the needs of the dominant sector in our community: the auto industry. Through grants from the National Science Foundation and the US Department of Labor, the college intensified its work with the auto sector. One benefit to us from the Great Recession was that it allowed us to hire many individuals with extensive industry experience who retired early or were laid off due to the downturn. Some became excellent administrators for these grants, and others became instructors in our auto programs. To maintain our knowledge base within the auto industry and increase our abilities to be proactive, I joined the Board of Directors of the Center for Automotive Research (CAR), an organization based in Ann Arbor, Michigan, which specializes in auto-industry developments.

Priority #2: Educational Partnerships

Another important issue for me was how the education sector responded to new needs in our communities arising from the economic upheaval. If there was one common theme in Macomb County, it was the need for more postsecondary education, so that younger people and adults could move from unskilled or semi-skilled work to higher-skilled and technical work, including outside of the auto industry. This demanded collaboration by all sectors: elementary, middle and high schools, community colleges, and four-year institutions. Yet in Michigan, a state with no centralized educational approach, this collaboration did not exist. I wanted Macomb Community College to take the lead in promoting collaboration and mutual understanding, at least within the Detroit region. Since community colleges are sandwiched between the K–12 public school districts and the four-year colleges and universities, I sought to strengthen our relationships with these larger and more powerful educational sectors. The college had worked with both of these areas for years; now the task was to focus our collaboration on preparing students for academic success in postsecondary education.

About 35 percent of Macomb high school students attended Macomb Community College after they graduated. A small number want occupational programs that might prepare them for an entry-level job. But very few viewed an associate's degree as their end goal; many of the students and their parents saw community college as a vehicle for obtaining a four-year degree. Although some low-income and first-generation students might be unsure about whether college is a good option for them, they enrolled because it was relatively easy to do, close to their home, and inexpensive.

We also had a small number of high school students attending Macomb Community College while still in high school. Before I became president, the college had initiated a dual enrollment program that made it easier for these students to attend classes at the college. There were even discussions about constructing a building on the South Campus where high school students could attend classes. The college faculty were ambivalent about the idea, and it seemed to me that setting the high school students apart from the rest of the campus was not consistent with providing them with an authentic college experience.

The dual enrollment program came at a time when the K–12 public school districts in Macomb County faced declining enrollments as the school-age population in the county continued to decrease. Given this decline, it would have made sense to consolidate the school districts and reduce overhead. However, no governor or legislator wanted to close a school district because that would generate significant opposition from parents and local school authorities. Rather, in the late 1990s, the Michigan legislature created a system based on "open districts," allowing schools to enroll students who did not reside in their district. Not only did this fail to resolve the issue of declining student enrollment, but it encouraged fierce competition between the districts for students. As a marketing tool, all wanted to boast of a close relationship with the college.

Dealing with the school districts was an area I knew well because of my past connection with School to Work activities. Creating individual programs for twenty-two school districts would have been challenging, but fortunately the Superintendent of the Intermediate School District (ISD) took the lead on an innovative program where the ISD would serve as an aggregator for the school districts in their relationship with Macomb. When I became president, we abandoned the idea of building a separate facility for high school students in favor of integrating them into our normal for-credit classes. An excellent program was developed under the leadership of Ed Stanton, who had collaborated with me on School to Work and was well acquainted with the high school and ISD staff.

We named our program Early College. The administration for the project remained in the hands of the ISD, which was responsible for the financial matters and coordination with the twenty-two districts. The high school students had to apply for the Early College program through their school district. We urged the school districts not to restrict the program to honors students but to open it broadly, including to students who may be undecided about attending college at all. We wanted a diverse group of high school students, particularly those students who had not previously considered college. However, we restricted their number to no more than eight in a class so that high school students would not dominate the class and would have an authentic college experience.

Along with college courses, the Early College program included a seminar organized by ISD counselors to help students think about their occupational choices as they attended their high school and college programs. Early College students also took part in a summer work program organized by the ISD in coordination with nearby employers offering job shadowing, co-ops, apprenticeships, or other work-based learning experiences.

Perhaps the most attractive thing for the families was that there was little cost to the students. The ISD paid for the students' tuition and gave each a computer; the students paid only for their books and transportation costs. The Early College program was funded by participants agreeing to remain in high school for five years, which allowed the school district to receive state aid and reimburse the ISD for the costs of the program. Upon completion of the fifth year, the dual enrollment students were able to earn a high school diploma and an associate degree. They received their high school diplomas in the afternoon, and then in the evening, they received their associate degrees with the rest of Macomb's graduates.[7]

At first, the Macomb faculty were concerned that the high school students would not be prepared for college-level work. When it became clear that the dual enrollment students' grades and classroom performance were often better than many of the regular credit students, those concerns faded away. We started the program in 2010 with sixty students, and, by 2015, we had expanded it to more than 700 students.

The Early College program became an important new enrollment source and, as it grew, so did faculty support and interest. Before I left the presidency, Ed had expanded the program by developing relationships with Oakland County school districts and played a major role in the Detroit Promise program with the Detroit Public Schools. This program, funded by the Detroit Chamber of Commerce, provided free tuition for any Detroit Public School graduate at any participating community college. We learned a good deal from participating in this program, which is discussed in more depth in Chapter 8.

To recruit dual enrollment students, we had graduates of the Early College program visit their former high schools and speak to the students about it. We held separate orientation sessions for students and their parents to prepare them for their experience at Macomb. At these orientations, the most frequent question from parents was whether college credits earned at Macomb would transfer to a four-year college or university.

Parents were right to ask, because when our students transferred to four-year institutions, they often did not receive credit for having completed Macomb programs and courses. In many cases, the four-year colleges only transferred community college courses as electives, meaning students still needed to retake any required introductory courses. This encouraged Macomb students to spend as little time as possible at the college, sometimes no more than a year, and select only courses whose credits would transfer to a four-year college or university.

In my first year as president, I knew we needed to address the transfer function in general and our relationship with our University Center partners in particular. As discussed in Chapter 4, the development of the University Center twenty years earlier was one of the most important national innovations to link community college and four-year institutions. These activities, however innovative and creative in 1988, needed refreshing twenty years later. For starters, as online education expanded, the attractiveness of the University Center's labs, classrooms, free parking, and campus security had to compete with the attractiveness of distance learning. We needed a relationship with four-year institutions that went beyond where classes were to be offered, or what new programs could be covered by articulation agreements. We needed more compelling reasons for four-year institutions to maintain their interest in the University Center and our students.

As I tackled this, I realized that we had little interaction with our four-year partner colleges beyond dealing with the courses and programs at the University Center. We needed more information, such as how our students were performing at their institutions. Did our curriculum provide a suitable beginning for them and ensure they were appropriately prepared for a four-year course or university? Did they change their field of study after they transferred? What orientation was needed to ensure the transfer process was successful?

Although a few private college University Center partners provided Macomb with information on the progress of our students, most of the Michigan public colleges typically gave us enrollment and grade point data. There was typically a ceremonial "presidential" meeting between the two institutions when an articulation agreement was signed. However, despite these efforts, there was little staff attention paid to how these documents could encourage student success both at Macomb and four-year institutions. It was assumed their existence would make things "better" for the students without intentionally connecting the agreements with student success initiatives at the institutions. This needed to change. I assumed that the primary reason four-year institutions maintained ties with us was to understand how our preparations helped transfer students succeed at their institution. It was not the facilities that brought us together but our mutual interest in student success. Based on this understanding, we initiated regular meetings between our staff and the administrators at our four-year partners to discuss our relationships and how we could collaborate better to support our students in earning a four-year degree.

These initial discussions revealed how little we knew about the success of our transfer students, including what four-year programs they selected when they transferred, how well they performed in these programs, and how many actually graduated with a four-year degree. I obtained a grant from the Kresge Foundation to engage the CCRC in a study of our graduates who enrolled in four-year institutions. Sharing data between institutions was not an easy matter. Each of the colleges and universities maintained their own records systems which were often not compatible. The project expanded to become an information technology exercise, so data could flow between institutions. The study showed that many of our students who transferred maintained their academic focus and did not change majors. We also discovered a phenomenon of what we called "swirlers," students who moved back and forth between two- and four year colleges, a group we had never before recognized in any of our planning. As a result of this research and our monthly discussions, several of the four-year colleges established orientation programs specifically for community-college transfer students. In these discussions, I felt that we were respected by the four-year institutions as real partners—all trying to improve the experience of our students.[8]

While these general discussions were extremely useful, we also needed a more targeted and strategic approach to the transfer process for our students. For many years, Macomb cast a broad net and sought to obtain transfer agreements with as many four-year colleges as possible, believing that doing so offered more options to students who wanted to transfer. However, when we looked at our transfer data, we found that almost 75 percent of Macomb students transferred to just four institutions in the region. Thus, we concentrated on strengthening our relationships with those institutions as they were clearly the most important for our students.

Our relationships with four-year institutions required particular attention to the needs of our workforce students. As skill requirements in many occupational areas were increasing, our occupational students wanted the opportunity to transfer to a four-year institution after completing their apprenticeship. How did these students fit into the transfer process?

There were significant issues for transfer students in our health-care programs, especially the nursing programs. The four-year nursing programs traditionally offered "hands-on" nursing courses in the third and fourth years, while community colleges provided them in the first two years. The four-year colleges were reluctant to give credit for community college nursing programs, forcing our students to repeat these introductory courses. This was particularly inappropriate for students who were already nurses, those who had their associate's degree and experience working as a nurse, who had applied to a four-year nursing program to obtain a Bachelor of Science in Nursing (BSN) degree. Fortunately, we were able to negotiate a nursing articulation agreement with Michigan State University. Under it, our students attended MSU courses while they completed their nursing program at Macomb, and when they transferred, they were 80 percent of the way toward completing the requirements of their BSN program.

Priority #3: New Sources of Revenue

Amid the Great Recession, we could not expect an increase in revenue or resources from traditional sources of support. The time was ripe for a comprehensive approach to revenue generation. We had to develop new ways to secure grants from public institutions and private sources while also generating income from our alumni, nearby companies, and others in the community.

I knew from my work at CCRC that there were many federal government agencies with programs that could grant us funds for needed projects. In addition, foundations and other private-sector organizations were keen to support community college student success and workforce development. Macomb had applied for and received grants in the past, but only sporadically. I wanted to make the pursuit of grants and foundation investment a routine college activity, which led to the development of a new grantmaking unit with a small staff based in my office. In a break from past practice, I commissioned our business unit to determine what overhead rates we should use in grant applications, so that our proposals were consistent and our costs would be covered. Our goal was to avoid being stuck with "a grant that keeps on taking." Moreover, I encouraged our college administrators to use this unit to seek grants for new projects and embed grants in their annual financial plans.

Another part of our strategy was to repurpose the Macomb Foundation, which mainly had been used to fund scholarships for students, not to raise external resources. The foundation board was comprised of senior college officials and aside from dispensing scholarships, its other main function was to channel surplus college revenues to student support activities. I wanted to expand the Macomb Foundation into a major external fundraising arm with outreach to the community and to retired Macomb Community College staff and alumni. I changed the composition of the board by appointing noted local community leaders and successful Macomb alumni. The math was not complicated: more than 150,000 Macomb alumni live in the Detroit region, and even if a small percentage of them regularly contributed to the college, it would bring in significant revenue. If we were able to convince 1 percent of the alumni to donate an average of $100 annually, it would amount to $1.5 million of new revenue for college programs.

Our work with local employers was based on the same calculation, that is, we focused on financial support for the college from employers in the community who were hiring our students. To do so, we needed better data on our student employment and how closely it tracked with the occupational programs chosen by students. This data would enable us to articulate the "value" of the college to local employers and seek contributions from company foundations and executives to support an institution that was increasing the profitability of their company. This required staff resources and research capabilities, which we did not have and, given other priorities, we were unable to develop.

We were more successful in obtaining contributions from retired Macomb staff. Under the leadership of now retired Jim Varty, we started a retiree association. While the association mainly held events to help retirees maintain personal ties with their former coworkers, we also used it to raise money for the college. Since some of the retirees had moved south, my good friends, now retired, Art Ritas and Sue Calkins helped us organize a winter outreach program for retired staff and alumni living in Florida. In at least one instance, we were able to obtain a six-figure donation from a former instructor. Based on my experience, I believe community colleges can generate significant funds from their alumni, retired staff, and area employers, but it is likely to flow in a way that is quite different from contributions to four-year colleges. Financial support from these groups will not necessarily yield major one-time donations but can bring in steady revenue each year from people who value the impact a community college has had on themselves and their communities.

A final fundraising strategy was to work more closely with many Michigan foundations, exploiting a strategic advantage Michigan possessed. Due to the wealth created by the auto industry, Michigan is home to several major foundations, including the Ford Foundation, the Kresge Foundation, and the Mott Foundation. Each of these foundations had specific interests in Michigan, and often the Detroit region. We began by meeting with foundation officers to learn about their priorities for the region, and then sought funding for programs at the college which we believed could mutually benefit the goals of both organizations. This did not mean altering our agenda but rather aligning it with the interests of the foundation. The main missions of the college, namely education, enrichment, and economic development were broad enough to fit into the priorities of almost any Michigan foundation.

I also added another aspect to our definition of student success—the issue of place. In our attempts to make students successful, I believed that a critical issue should be whether they remain in the community after graduation. Some of this was motivated by enlightened self-interest: why wouldn't a community college, whose financial future depends on a strong local economy, want to maintain its graduates within the community? It also would benefit the broader community by ensuring that those with a higher education remained in Macomb County, rather than moving elsewhere. I focused on the Kresge Foundation, whose CEO Rip Rapson, and staff understood the vast potential of community colleges. Many of the Kresge staff resided in Macomb County, and over the years, we became close friends and confidants. Our goal was to use the foundation grants to fund activities that we could try out and, if successful, would seek to integrate into the college's general operating budget. For example, our relationship with the National Science Foundation (NSF) on automotive technology led to the creation of new technology programs in electric vehicles for first responders. These programs were offered both at Macomb and then with the assistance of NSF to other community colleges. It was example of a grant leading to an innovation that was incorporated into our regular programs.

Priority #4: Emphasize a Regional Focus

My fourth goal, which was possibly the most important, was to bring a regional focus to all Macomb College activities, a departure from past tradition. Many of the county's elected leaders and local businesses viewed the county's separation from Detroit as a strength, not a liability. Political leaders often won their elections by being "anti-Detroit." This approach was parroted by businesses and community-based organizations despite the county's dependence on the auto industry. Census data reveal the interrelationships between the county and region, and I knew a regional approach was needed for our workforce educational activities to be useful.[9]

The commitment to a regional approach extended beyond workforce labor markets. As discussed in earlier chapters, racism was a major reason for Macomb County's isolation. Almost all of Macomb County's growth from 1945 to 1980 came from white families leaving Detroit as the city's population became more African American. Those moving into the county wanted little contact with the city, a stance often articulated in racist views. Even though these were working-class voters, their fear of Detroit and Black people moved them away from the Democratic Party and they increasingly supported Republican candidates. Political pundits coined a phrase for their political transformation, referring to them as "Reagan Democrats."[10]

Fortunately, by the time I became president, significant changes in demographics and new county leadership meant that my regional vision faced a less hostile environment. For the first time, there were a significant number of African Americans working and living in Macomb County. In 1992, there were about 21,000 Black residents in the county, comprising less than 2 percent of the population. By 2008, the number of Black residents had increased almost fivefold, with 108,000 residents, or 13 percent of the county's population. In some school districts in the south end of the county, Black students accounted for 25 percent of the student population. Black student enrollment at Macomb Community College grew from just over 4 percent in 2000 to 13.8 percent by 2014. Many were new residents of Macomb County; others lived in Detroit but had taken advantage of open district high school enrollment policies to enroll in Macomb school districts and, upon graduation, go on to Macomb Community College.

Unlike white residents who wanted nothing to do with the city, the new Black residents maintained family and cultural ties to Detroit, erasing the notion that Eight Mile Road was a border not to be crossed. In my first year as president, I was approached by a pastor from a large Detroit Black church to place one of their associates at our student center. Many of their parishioners had moved to Macomb County but still attended church in Detroit.

Regional decision-makers could not ignore the trend. Organizations such as the Detroit Institute of Arts recognized they had to include Macomb County in plans for programming. Moreover, as the auto industry considered the future of electric and autonomous vehicles, it recognized that the skills and knowledge underpinning these technologies often were found in Macomb County.

A change in the governing structure of the county also contributed to a friendlier view of regionalization. In 2008, Macomb County voters adopted a County Executive model of local government, which already existed within Oakland County and Wayne County. Macomb's first elected County Executive was Mark Hackel, the former County Sheriff, Macomb Community College graduate, and adjunct faculty member. Mark was now a recognizable face to represent the county in the region and saw his role as a cheerleader for the county and its community college. Mark Hackel became the Macomb County Executive at almost the same time I became the Macomb Community College president. My support for his regional activities meant that I was asked to join the boards of a number of regional organizations. My service on these boards is discussed in Chapter 9.

What I Learned

I learned to leave some free time on my calendar because there is a delicate balance between sticking to a schedule and addressing unexpected issues or community events. I also had to balance requests from staff to settle long-standing grievances, which I had been warned would no doubt arise. In my case, it began as soon as I was selected by the board. I was already at the college, and my open work style made staff members feel at ease requesting favors. Many of these appeared harmless, such as changing a job title. However, at colleges, job titles affect contractually determined levels of compensation and cannot be modified easily. Other requests and complaints took time to consider. I needed to reject some outright and sidestep others, sending them back to the "chains of command."

Sometimes, requests came from outside the institution and were initiated directly with our board, raising more significant issues for me. These were particularly troublesome when they came from elected officials asking that their friends be considered for open positions at the college. My consistent answer was that while I had final authority in the hiring process, I would not interfere with the selection process. Managing these issues was a key part of my early learning curve because my past experiences had not taught me how to carefully reject requests without harming critical external relationships.

Another balancing act came from my intention to push decision-making downward and allow the individuals who do the work to decide how it should be done. On my first day as president, that intention was put to the test. I was asked to approve plans for a driveway on campus, because the president had to approve all new construction, no matter how small. I met with the construction supervisor, who arrived armed with blueprints for the driveway. I asked the supervisor how many driveways he had built or rebuilt for the college during his many years on the job, and he said it was more than ten. I told him I had never designed or built a driveway, and that if he thought this was a good plan and there was a need for it, he should just do it. He left dumbfounded at my response and concerned that I had misunderstood my role in this process.

While I initially congratulated myself for being true to my values and letting people who do the work make the decisions, a few hours later, I began to have second thoughts. What if the driveway project was bid out to relatives of the supervisor? What if the materials were purchased from vendors who were kicking back funds to the supervisor? Corruption or abuse was a possibility, but I decided to take the risk and trust the staff at the college to make the right decisions. In retrospect, I wonder if that was always the best way to proceed. I had the advantage of knowing these individuals and I believed I could trust them. For presidents entering a new situation without knowledge of the workforce, it may not be such a good idea.

Finally, I learned that staff willingness to support change does not happen without a consistent repetition of goals and an almost obsessive recitation of the reasons for initiating a change. You could not just mandate things to happen. This is particularly important in educational institutions where "new ideas" and innovations are introduced so often that staff do not have the time to understand them, much less assimilate or implement them. Not surprisingly, people who work in schools and colleges become numb to and often cynical about the next "exciting new idea" proposed by their administration. Implementation never happens, or the idea gets no more than lip service, because staff know that it will soon be replaced with an even newer initiative. I knew it was vital to keep my focus on a few straightforward changes and continue to repeat them so that the staff knew I was serious about implementing my goals.

One quality of leadership, often underappreciated by many academics and consultants, is the need for leaders to stay on course—to be consistent when seeking long-term change. You will win more support through consistency than with a brilliant argument or binders of data. Once people see that you are determined to realize your goals, even those who disagree will respect their significance and not obstruct their implementation. I put this into practice at Macomb, where the four goals I initiated during my first year stayed consistent for my entire time as president.

There were some things I considered but rejected, including a campus "climate study" to survey staff on their priorities for the institution and use the results to create a strategic plan. In part, I relied on my deep knowledge of the institution, feeling confident that I understood it and the community in which it operated. In retrospect, this was a mistake. I was not as knowledgeable as I thought, and having been away from the college for almost a decade, I no doubt could have used a refresher course. In addition, such a study would have given me staff input and helped me align my objectives to their needs. Even though I thought of myself as open to new ideas, I came to the presidency with specific goals and objectives, which perhaps were viewed by others as unresponsive to the needs of the institution or even arrogant.

Macomb and the Great Recession

Many of my first-year initiatives were tied up with two critical national developments. First was the Great Recession, which intensified the economic challenges facing our community. Macomb County was extremely hard hit: there were massive layoffs, and two major automakers, General Motors and Chrysler, were forced to declare bankruptcy. By the summer of 2009, the official tally showed unemployment in Macomb County was close to 15 percent of the workforce, and unofficial observations suggested it was more than 20 percent. The staff at the college could see the impact of the Great Recession on their friends, neighbors, and their own families, and as president, I could not ignore it.

Macomb Community College was one of the few institutions in the community to benefit from the downturn. Enrollment at the college rose substantially with the recession. Thousands of unemployed autoworkers came to the college looking for programs to get them back to work. Our credit enrollment increased from 20,000 students in 2005 to more than 24,000 students in 2008. In addition, there were more than 18,000 students attending non-credit workforce programs, almost half of them adults.

I was able to win support for the changes I wanted to make with the justification that these were necessary responses to these new conditions. The lesson was simple. You do not need to manufacture a crisis, but you should respond to it in ways that align with your goals for the institution. The economic crisis of the Great Recession and its massive disruption of the status quo in Macomb County made it easier for me to win support from the staff for my agenda. They accepted the idea that in the face of this crisis, we had to make changes.

Another boost came from the election of President Barack Obama in 2008. This brought to the White House a president who viewed community colleges as important institutions to spur economic recovery, particularly in the auto industry. Macomb was uniquely positioned to play that role. My formal investiture as president in March 2009 occurred one day after GM and Chrysler declared bankruptcy and were placed under federal receivership. One of the speakers at the ceremony, US Congressman Sander Levin, highlighted the need for the college and its new president to help save the auto industry.

Fortunately, from my work at CCRC, I was acquainted with some of the staff serving in the US Department of Education and the US Department of Labor in the Obama administration. Being viewed as an ally of the administration's programs had an enormous institutional payoff for the college and my agenda. In July 2009, President Obama came to Macomb Community College to announce his administration's strategic plan for community colleges. It was his first major speech on community colleges, which became an essential part of his presidency.[11]

The visit by President Obama was a fitting capstone to my first year as president. It reinforced my efforts because the staff could see that my ideas had support from the highest level of government. It increased the reputation of the college and validated a point I always tried to convey to the staff, namely, that what we do matters because the most pressing problems in American society—and their solutions—are found within the college itself.

Notes

1 Gary Gerstle, *The Rise and Fall of the Neoliberal Order* (Oxford University Press, 2022), 220–1.

2 Read more about the Kalamazoo Promise www.kalamazoopromise.com/.

3 James Jacobs, *Economic Forecast for Macomb County*, February 3, 2019, PowerPoint presentation.

4   Bomey, 45–6.

5   Di Xu and Shanna Smith Jaggars, "Examining the Effectiveness of Online Learning Within a Community College System: An Instrumental Variable Approach," Community College Research Center, Teachers College, Columbia University, https://ccrc.tc.columbia.edu/publications/examining-effectiveness-of-online-learning.html; Macomb data is from IPEDS data, Fall 2022.

6   In 2007, Macomb offered associate degrees in seventy-eight different subjects, both academic and technical, and seventy-six certificates for one-year programs. Before I retired, through mergers in some areas, we reduced the number of subjects to sixty-five and the number of certificates to sixty-two. For example, three separate electronics degrees were reduced to one by 2016. A new program in Automated Systems Technology replaced Welding, Metallurgy, and other technical areas. We were more successful in decreasing the number of degree programs by increasing what we called "specialized skill certificates." These were shorter credit and non-credit programs whose skill-specific courses would provide entry-level work. In 2007, there were thirteen skill-specific programs; by 2014, the number had increased to twenty-five. These changes were slow and very time-consuming and often resisted by faculty members who worried about their impact on faculty employment. No full-time faculty were eliminated during the process.

7   For a review of the Early College Program, see Macomb Intermediate School District, "Early College at Macomb," https://ecmacomb.org/pdf/2023-2024/ECofM_brochure_2024_web_version_Accessible.pdf.

8   Community College Research Center, "Building Transfer Student Success at Macomb Community College: A Report on Transfer and Degree Completion," Teachers College, Columbia University, https://ccrc.tc.columbia.edu/publications/building-transfer-student-success-macomb-community-college-report-transfer-degree-completion.html.

9   The Census Data on transportation patterns revealed the interrelationship between the counties: In 2008, 57.7 percent of the Macomb County residents traveled outside the county to work. During the same period, 48.7 percent of the people employed in Macomb County resided outside the county.

10   For a discussion of the Reagan Democrats, see Peter Brown, Minority Party: Why Democrats Face Defeat in 1982 and Beyond (Regnery Gateway, 1991).

11   The White House, Office of the Press Secretary, "Remarks by the President on the American Graduation Initiative in Warren, MI," July 14, 2009, https://obamawhitehouse.archives.gov/the-press-office/remarks-president-american-graduation-initiative-warren-mi.

7 Getting Our Students Back to Work

The visit by President Obama in July 2009 affirmed Macomb Community College's reputation as a national leader in workforce development. His visit also helped to validate my work with the staff at the college—I must be doing something right to obtain such national attention. I also used the Obama visit to promote the college with many national and local foundations. As soon as the visit was confirmed, we quickly invited many foundations and national foundations to attend his speech. Their hearing President Obama praising our efforts ensured Macomb's proposals would be taken seriously. In addition, since Obama's speech also unveiled his community college agenda, many community college leaders around the country came to Macomb to attend the event. It was a great public relations boost for the college.

Federal Initiatives Under President Obama

President Obama's remarks established a federal agenda for community colleges with specific milestones for them to attain. The Obama administration proposed a ten-year $12 billion initiative to increase the number of community college graduates. Most of these funds would come from already existing federal programs of direct student aid, such as Pell grants; only about 2 billion would be distributed directly to the colleges. Considering the total budgets of all public community colleges in the nation were about $42 billion, this was a 2 percent annual funding increase—not very much to sustain current activity, let alone expand the capacity of these institutions. Moreover, since most non-tuition funding for community colleges came from states, there was a strong likelihood that the increased federal funds would be used as a pretext to reduce state support for these institutions, further decreasing the resources needed for change. The Obama community college initiative was a start. It was necessary, but it was not sufficient to transform the colleges. Tom Bailey and I wrote a brief article that recognized the positive initiative of Obama but called for direct funding of the colleges to increase their capacity to promote student success.[1]

No Worker Left Behind

The Great Recession inflicted significant economic hardship on metropolitan Detroit. It also challenged our ability to provide an economic recovery for our students and the community. Despite the attention and accolades we earned from the president's speech, the college was still confronted with how to effectively respond to our dire economic situation in Macomb County. Enrollments at most college occupational programs increased as more laid-off and unemployed adults enrolled at the college hoping the programs they chose would prepare them for employment. They were also encouraged to return to school by a new state program, "No Worker Left Behind," initiated by Governor Granholm. This program granted every jobless Michigander two years of free community college tuition provided they selected an occupational program in high demand. It was led by Andy Levin, who later succeeded his father as our Congressional representative. As a former union organizer, he was a major supporter of community colleges. I quickly found common ground with him, and Macomb had the largest number of program participants among the Michigan community colleges.

Successful implementation of the "No Worker Left Behind" program also required a positive working relationship with the federally funded local workforce board. Fortunately, over the years, I developed a good relationship with John Bierbusse, the Macomb County local Workforce Board executive director. He encouraged the college's involvement in workforce board issues and was willing to strategize with us on what needed to be done. John co-located his counselors within our counseling area so we could jointly assist unemployed workers in their choice of college training programs.[2]

Yet, even with these available resources and the commitment of some talented program administrators, it was difficult to match laid-off workers with immediate employment. The labor market realities facing laid-off auto workers were often challenging. There were some service jobs available, but they paid significantly less and often did not possess any fringe benefits that individuals who worked in the auto sector possessed. The "good jobs" that had higher wages and fringe benefits often required degrees or certificates that would take significant time for students to complete. For most laid-off workers, especially those with families who could not sustain a long period of unemployment, they did not have the time that would be required for completing a degree. In addition, many have been outside of formal educational institutions for several years, so their foundational skills in communications and mathematics may need some forms of developmental education. During this period, the mass media sometimes focused on a small minority of laid-off auto workers reinventing themselves to become health-care workers, but this transition was far less common than the newspapers suggested. The length of time for an auto worker to complete programs in health care stretched into years, making it unlikely that this transition was feasible for anyone who was a primary breadwinner for a family.

Most laid-off adults desired to get back to work as quickly as possible. What was more likely was for workers in specific industries to acquire new skills to enable them to continue working in their field or seek employment in jobs that could utilize their existing skills. Occupations such as truck driving, welding, or nursing assistant became fields of choice for auto workers wanting a job quickly. There were often low-paying jobs that didn't offer the benefits auto workers enjoyed, however. Ironically, many of these occupational areas were also significantly disrupted by Covid a decade later.

Even getting back into the auto industry was going to be very difficult for some of the laid-off workers. Employment in the auto industry was undergoing a long-term transformation in skill needs, and that transformation was going to make it difficult for short-term training programs to sufficiently prepare people for employment. Auto companies were looking for skills in new technologies, such as artificial intelligence, computer-aided design, electrical engineering, and big data management, requiring skills associated with four-year degree programs. The design, production, technical, and administrative hub of the industry was still concentrated in the Detroit region, but the local composition of work was moving away from hands-on production toward employment in research and development occupations.

A study of the Detroit automotive workforce conducted by an MIT project called the *Work of the Future* found that between 60,000 and 75,000 auto industry jobs could be changed as a result of a movement toward electric cars. The report noted:

> *New technology is changing the skills demanded of workers, but as one head of operations at a Tier 1 supplier suggested, the work is "different, not more difficult." New technology does not demand a wholesale change in the workforce but a shift in skills, mindset and incentives. The flood of information potentially unleashed through new data-driven manufacturing techniques makes the organizational and domain knowledge of all workers more valuable, not less. Worker domain and systems knowledge proved valuable time and time again as firms looked to workers to identify pain points and facilitate technology adoption. With multiple generations of workers on the shop floor and large divides in technical and domain expertise, knowledge transfer between groups is critical, particularly in integrating new technologies and talent with the knowledge to navigate current systems.[3]*

While this research indicated there would be some difficulty for high school graduates in Macomb County to seek jobs in the automotive sector, the implications of the report for the Detroit Public Schools (DPS) were considerably more ominous. At the time, the Detroit Public Schools had less than half of their students who started high school earning a degree in four years. In addition, the Michigan student assessment scores were indicating that Detroit students were scoring significantly lower in mathematics and English than public school districts in the rest of the state. There was a critical need to increase college attendance and completion among DPS students. In 2011, Michigan Governor Rick Snyder initiated a plan to fund community college education for every DPS graduate. By 2013, a coalition of education and business groups led by the Detroit Regional Chamber of Commerce initiated the Detroit Promise. This plan called for free tuition for any DPS high school graduate at one of the regional community colleges. It was modeled after the Kalamazoo Promise.[4]

We knew the changes in auto production processes and products were going to affect many of our manufacturing programs, although the speed of this implementation was hard to gauge from the outside. For example, the utilization of more composite and plastic parts was going to diminish the need for metallurgy and welding skills and increase the working knowledge of adhesive, plastics, and injection molding technologies. Yet, how fast this transformation was going to occur and what the impact would be on our current programs in welding and chemistry was hard to determine. Unfortunately, as a result of the Great Recession, our regular contacts in the auto industry who kept us up to speed on the state of the industry were either terminated or reassigned to other work in their companies.[5]

In this period, one organization that we should have sought out for more collaborative activity was the UAW. The union was much better positioned than us to understand what their members would need to continue employment in the industry. In addition, the union had won through collective-bargaining negotiations a union-management education and training organization to prepare workers for some of the anticipated new jobs. While most of the money in the joint programs had been used for members' personal educational activities, or to pay for courses at postsecondary educational institutions, there was a possibility for funding technical preparation for workers to adapt to these changes.

Though UAW president Bob King was a progressive union leader willing to support new programs, the union was confronting significant OEM efforts to slash costs through plant closings, eliminating thousands of jobs. The union was on the defensive, fighting to keep certain facilities open and as many of its members employed. In retrospect, I should have been more responsive to the issues faced by the UAW and determined how we could have worked together to deal with some of the education issues, both within the auto industry and outside of it.

Despite the reputation of the college in the workforce and the commitment of our workforce board partners, we were challenged by the conditions we faced in both the needs and the interests of the students coming to the college. The complexities of handling the new reality were important issues for me as president to consider. They called for a reassessment of our workforce strategies, and in at least one area, we started to implement that approach.

Do We Have the Right Programs?

In this period when jobs were scarce, my concern about the appropriateness of our programs became even more important. I had always believed that not only did we have too many career and technical programs to be successful, but I questioned whether some of them fit the job markets our students faced. How were the changes in the local job market reflected in the changes in the curriculum? This was not just the substantive content of the curriculum, but also the length of our programs. The anecdotal feedback from employers was that many of our students may be *overprepared*; that is, they possessed too many specialized skills that many employers either did not need or believed they should be taught within their workplace. In addition, while we prided ourselves in knowing what was the "cutting edge" in terms of new technology or innovations in the field, we were less adept at understanding the speed and depth of how the innovations were implemented within a sector. For example, auto companies were committed to "lightweighting": that is, the use of plastics and composites to replace steel in their construction of vehicles. This suggested we should be teaching chemistry to many of our technical students. As metal use in auto manufacturing diminishes, we would expect that skills, such as welding, would be in less demand. These changes were not yet felt in employer demand. Welding jobs remained plentiful, and demand for students with chemical skills remained very low. The issues of supply and demand in occupational programs always focused on numerical job openings, when the issues around meeting the needs of employers were far more complex and nuanced. They required consistent review and adaptation, and

I was unsure how well our faculty was prepared to make these adjustments. We needed far more research capacity than we had the ability to support.

Even though we lacked more detailed knowledge of the timing of the changes, during this period, the mismatches between our occupational programs and the new skills needed on the job were becoming more apparent. More equipment utilized in the manufacturing process required electronic and computer controls that some of our faculty were not as familiar with as they should be. The implementation of information technologies was also challenging our business programs, rapidly making some of the curriculum obsolete. Programs such as accounting and office management were faced with occupational changes that placed far more emphasis on computer skills and the ability to utilize computer applications in the areas of analysis and data collection. In health care, an entirely new field of medical records technologies emerged, which became significant with the new national health-care system. Our criminal justice and law enforcement programs needed new curricula dealing with cybercrime. While not directly affected by technical change, even our flagship nursing program was being threatened as hospitals sought more BSN nurses from the four-year programs. The good jobs required more skill and different skills, and we were faced with resource challenges to invest in upgrading our present programs.

At the same time these changes were raising the bar for increased skills, we also faced growing employer demand on the other end of the employment spectrum: entry-level work skills, particularly in non-union manufacturing. Employers were coming to us complaining about labor shortages. The wages employers were paying were often too low to attract young applicants. Many smaller manufacturing firms, traditionally a major employer of our students, were offering starting wages barely exceeding the fast-food sector. While these smaller manufacturers gave workers stable work schedules, opportunities for overtime, fringe benefits, and substantial advancement into higher-paying work, their initial low wages did not attract young students into manufacturing. The enrollment of young people right out of high school and into manufacturing programs at the college continued to diminish. However, young students were enrolling in occupational programs such as Veterinarian Technology or Culinary Science. These were oversubscribed by students even though their initial entry wages were often lower than fast-food restaurants—and the prospect of any advancement slim.

This reality raised a troubling issue for me. I was always opposed to tracking or any command process by which young people were told what to study. On the other hand, I also wanted to develop some form of local occupational information system which would provide them with relevant information on long-term prospects for employment in certain jobs. Wages or plant visits were insufficient. To recruit students, I organized a meeting between an owner of a machining company that produced parts for satellites and a group of high school students. He came to the meeting with his pay stubs from his workers to show the wages his workers were earning; however, the students were unimpressed and barely paid any attention. Every year we organized an event for high school students and many of our local manufacturers. The firms brought simulations and sometimes real machines to show the students what they did. This was held in the daytime at our athletic facility and the school district sent busloads of students. Over 4,000 students attended. At night, the students were able to come back with their parents to talk with the firms about potential jobs. There were few students interested; however, many of the parents made contact with these firms for employment.[6]

For young students, besides the lack of social status that manufacturing brought, it was unattractive because it was primarily an authoritarian culture, where they were forced to stay in one place, and they had little access to their cell phones or any privacy at the workplace. Despite numerous national, state, and local programs that aim to attract young people into manufacturing, there were few young students enrolled in hands-on manufacturing work, such as welding, machining, or robotics. If students considered manufacturing careers, they were usually in the design areas, auto repair technicians, or pre-engineering manufacturing technology programs. The only exception was those students who were admitted to our apprenticeship programs, but given the substantial decline in any new hires by the companies, there were few students enrolled in these programs.

Finally, given these complexities, we also needed to determine which of the student constituencies should be the target of our efforts. While there was a great deal of effort made to bring career choices to younger students, given the impact of the Great Recession, I believed we needed to concentrate upon young adults with families in the community who lacked sustainable-wage employment. The main group enrolling in hands-on direct manufacturing programs are typically between twenty and thirty years old, often with families or other dependents who needed jobs with benefits. Many have been exposed to low-wage service work and, in some cases, started at a postsecondary institution but never completed. Some had criminal records that prevented them from being employed in other sectors, such as health care. For these individuals, manufacturing work was a second chance at earning sustainable wages. When young people and their parents are provided with information about manufacturing employment opportunities, the unfortunate stigma of these jobs often trumps other concerns. They perceived college as providing them with an opportunity to get a "better job" in the white-collar or service sector. Increasing the interest of younger students in manufacturing programs remained a challenge we never resolved.

However, there was another important constituency of students who were very interested in taking occupational courses. These were often called "skill builders," young adults already working within a sector who were taking very specific courses to increase their skills and opportunities for occupational advancement.[7] For example, engineers from a small manufacturing company would take a programming language course to gain skills to operate a new computer application on their machinery. This group of adults was uninterested in degrees or any formal institutional certifications, nor did they need counseling or student support services. They knew exactly what courses or programs to take and often disappeared from the college after taking a few classes. It was hard to judge the size of this group, but they played a significant role in some of our manufacturing and business programs.

To add to the confusion of trying to synchronize student demand with occupational markets, college associate degree policies were often opaque and not well aligned with the reality of the labor markets. Like many community colleges, Macomb awarded more than one associate degree. In fact, students at Macomb were offered five different associate degrees and two kinds of certifications, often leaving students without much guidance as to the implications of these credentials for future employment or college transfer. This was not a failure of the staff, but a greater institutional dilemma. We simply did not know the value of these different degrees in the occupational marketplace or at four-year colleges.

There were degrees offered in liberal arts (which was considered transfer degree) and three occupational areas (health care, business, and manufacturing). However, the most popular selected by students was the general studies degree. Originally conceived as a means by which students could choose a variety of courses to meet the degree requirements, it became a default path for students to avoid taking what they perceived as difficult math and science courses. At graduation, there were typically four or five times as many graduates in general studies as in any of the other degrees. While some students used the general studies option to take precisely the courses they needed to transfer to their selected four-year college, they were the minority of students. Most importantly, the selection of the general studies degree did little to prepare students for any specific occupational area or an academic subject to pursue in a transfer to a four-year institution, and it also didn't effectively prepare students with a set of skills to enter the workforce.[8]

Especially for students coming to college right from high school, the pursuit of this degree had little economic value. Employers did not demand it and most rarely understood what it meant. Often, parents assumed postsecondary institutions were the appropriate place for a student to "learn what they wanted." Just going to a four-year college became a goal, and it was there that your career interest would be determined. While college should be, in part, an institution to explore your interests, the general studies associate's degree did not prepare students well for the selection of programs that would aid them in being successful in the new workplace.

The New Suburban Student: The Working Poor

At the same time, our occupational programs needed revision, we were faced with a growing number of students whose background brought new challenges to our efforts. The Great Recession exposed the myth that the suburbs were comprised of individuals living the middle-class American Dream. The disappearance of auto unionized jobs and the proliferation of low-wage service sector employment, along with the growth of single heads of households, was creating significant economic inequalities among the working-class residents in Macomb County. Through the research work of the United Way, a new concept of the "working poor" was developed. It has a strange acronym: ALICE (which stands for Asset Limited Income Constrained, Employed). In Macomb County, as a result of the Great Recession, almost 40 percent of the population met the ALICE data definition. These were primarily people working full-time at low-wage jobs (some with more than one job) with little benefits and limited, if any, possibility for advancement. For this group, postsecondary education was one of the few options to break out of their economic condition. However, their ability to complete a college education was often faced with considerable barriers outside of the institution. An illness, a work accident, a sickness of a close family relative, a car breaking down, a housing foreclosure, or many other unanticipated occurrences in the daily life of the working poor easily disrupted their education, and they too often dropped out of classes.[9]

These individuals defied the conservative stereotype of poor people being lazy and unwilling to work. However, serving the needs of the working poor requires some rethinking of what a community college could do to retain this population within the college. This was particularly true for the communities we served in Macomb County. When the county expanded in the 1960s and 1970s, there was little attention paid to public social services. The assumption was most of the population was "middle class," working in stable jobs, owning their homes, and requiring little support from local government. The Great Recession and the decline of the domestic auto industry shattered these assumptions, and most of the suburban communities in Macomb County were unprepared to provide necessary support for this new group of working poor.

Nor did the creators of Macomb Community College design college programs to appeal to this new constituency. It was assumed that college was an opportunity for students from families with a stable economic background who desired to better themselves with a college education. The major policies and practices at the college to handle the needs of low-income individuals were to reduce college costs through Pell grants and foundation scholarships. Neither of these was adequate to meet the economic issues that working poor students experienced in their struggle to remain at a community college.

The Crisis of Student Financial Aid

The federal Pell Grant program provides low-income students direct financial assistance for their participation in postsecondary education. It was originally designed to provide low-income students funds for tuition and other college-related expenses to complete their college degree and rise out of poverty. While Pell grants are cash outlays to individual students, they can only be accessed through their enrollment and completion of programs at a postsecondary institution. The amount of money distributed to students is determined through a complex formula, which includes not only the income of the students but also the total costs of the college and the number of courses students take at the college. As a result, individuals attending institutions with higher tuition costs receive greater Pell grant funds than low-cost community colleges. This formula also encourages students to get the most amount of Pell grants by taking many classes which, when added to working full-time and/or raising a family, can become a significant barrier for them to achieve student success. But most importantly, the Pell grants are distributed in lump payments and assume students would be successful in planning their financial lives to utilize these monies carefully throughout the semester.[10]

Pell grants greatly influence college practices. Pell grants and student loans are accessible to all students who qualify, regardless of their abilities to be financially literate. In addition, if students drop out, the colleges are obligated to recover any funds given to them when they ceased to attend. The college is an agent of the federal government and is required to meet all federal rules and regulations and be held accountable for all funds incorrectly distributed.

College financial aid offices are expected to operate like a financial institution distributing the funds, making sure the students are completing their courses each semester, monitoring their progress, adjusting their grants when their financial situation changes, and recovering money if they cease attending. In 2008, almost 25 percent of the Macomb student body received Pell grants, resulting in $10 million distributed annually by the college. By 2015, that number jumped to 40 percent of the students receiving Pell grants, and the college distributed over $30 million to students. Federal student loans also increased from $2.25 million in 2008 to over $10 million by 2015. Even for a well-run college, the distribution of Pell grants is always a risk, and clerical errors made by college staff can be extremely costly.[11]

There is an even greater danger to a college with the federal student loan system, which all institutions that grant Pell grants are required to offer. While the federal student loan system makes the college operate like a bank, there is one critical difference. Student loans are guaranteed for every student who qualifies, regardless of their financial knowledge or previous financial history. In the private sector, individuals who apply for loans can be denied for their financial inability to pay back the funds. But that is not the case with federal student loans. In fact, federal rules do not permit a college to deny anyone a loan. Individuals can be cautioned that going into debt at a community college is unwise because the costs of attending a four-year college would exceed any community college costs. And students can be advised it would be more prudent to save any borrowing until they reach a four-year institution. But colleges cannot deny students who wish to borrow money. While the policy assumption (particularly during the Obama administration) was that student loans were "rights" of students as part of the federal commitment to opportunity, reports suggested that the for-profit sector of higher education encouraged poor students to borrow as much federal money as possible. As public institutions, we were concerned about our students going into debt, but for-profit private institutions had no compulsion about urging the students to borrow as much as they were entitled, forcing students into significant debt before completing their education. When students were unsuccessful at the for-profit schools, they often came to Macomb already carrying significant student debt. The "freedom" to obtain funds to complete a postsecondary education quickly turned into a major constraint on their lives for years after. However, student aid was such an important part of most community college students' lives, the colleges were reluctant to suggest ways of changing the system for fear that the amount of money given to students might be decreased.

Three months into my presidency, I was faced with a federal investigation and audit of our Pell grant activities. Without any explanation, the college received a letter from the United States Department of Education indicating that a team of auditors from Washington were coming to the college, and we were required to have our president and legal counsel available to respond to their inquiries. By their rules, we were being investigated for our financial practices with Pell. Since the letter did not indicate the specific nature of their concerns, we could not prepare very much for their visit. This was very unsettling for our financial aid office and the business office. I also wondered whether I might want to rethink my career plans. At our first meeting with their team of investigators, we discovered a computer software error in our system was incorrectly coding the marital statuses of our Pell students. This computer error triggered Macomb Community College as having the largest percentage of single heads of households receiving Pell grants in the nation! Fortunately, the error was easily rectified, and most importantly, we had not incorrectly distributed any funds. However, while the federal auditors went through our records, they found some other smaller issues which cost us significant time and some funds to fix.

In 2008, our financial aid office operated as a silo, independent of any other student services. They were most concerned with carefully complying with the complex federal regulations for Pell grants, often resulting in forcing students to submit many supporting documents. This focus on compliance kept them from appreciating how their operations fit within any student success strategy. The result was often long delays in notifying students of their aid allotment and long lines in front of the financial aid office as students waited to be served. Many Macomb administrators considered Pell grants like welfare distribution and believed they should be difficult for students to attain. In addition, students were discouraged from taking on federal student loans at Macomb and encouraged to only use them when they transferred to a four-year college. The office policies were motivated more by our fear of making a mistake leading to a significant financial penalty rather than implementing a policy that would encourage student success and help students escape poverty through their completion of a college education. Pell was not welfare, but a means out of welfare.

Outside of Pell grants, the college did maintain several private scholarships established through donations to our Foundation. Typically, these were established by families of deceased staff members to honor their loved ones. While motivated by the best of intentions, these scholarships were often significantly restricted in terms of who could obtain them. For example, contributions to the college in honor of a deceased art teacher resulted in a scholarship for students taking art classes, generally not very attractive to the interests or needs of low-income students. Some scholarships maintained by community civic organizations were also directed at very specific groups. For example, the Italian American Society had scholarships designed for students taking Italian language classes.

Not only were these scholarships often very specific, but they were also difficult for students to learn about or understand how to apply for them. Their existence was maintained in lists by our Foundation Office located in a remote college administration building near our Center Campus but inaccessible to any low-income students from South Campus who lacked automobile transportation.

When our financial director retired, I hired Doug Levy, an experienced financial aid administrator from the University of Michigan who transformed our system. In his view, financial aid was a critical part of student success, so it should be responsive to students by quickly determining their awards and coordinating it with other forms of financial assistance. He worked with our information technology staff to develop a system of online submissions of forms, scanned all student paperwork into a database, and established an online system by which students were able to access information about private scholarships. Most importantly, his office became a participant in our student success initiatives. Through that process, not only were we able to comply with the federal rules, but our student default rate was less than 10 percent, far lower than the average Michigan community college default rate of 18 percent.

The Need for a New System

What is needed is a new approach to student financial aid. The entire system is based on a private sector assumption that students are "consumers" who are purchasing postsecondary education. Giving the "rights" to the students for these funds, without a clear understanding of their responsibilities, provides private sector higher educational institutions a significant cash incentive to exploit. A shift is necessary that ties student financial aid to both school performance and career selection. It may start with student access to public tuition support and loans, controlled by a non-education entity, but as a student makes a career choice, the process could shift into the private sector. Just as medical students find banks and other financial institutions willing to fund their medical school education, because once they complete medical school, their employment opportunities and corresponding salary would permit them to repay the loans, there should be financial support for students who want to complete a program in automotive repair, nursing, computer repair, design, and other high-wage, high-demand occupations. This would establish a relationship between the bank, the student, and specific community needs, which would benefit all groups. It would also remove the college from the financial aid process, an area where we don't have the skills or the institutional capacity to regulate well.

This approach would also force college occupational programs to focus their efforts on providing only programs that would result in sustainable-wage jobs. I floated this idea to a few local financial institutions, but there was no one who was willing to pilot a program that linked financial aid to the high-wage occupations. The Aspen Institute's College Excellence Program has begun to explore ways colleges should reform and scaffold programs so they lead to high-demand, high-wage careers.[12] They advocate that measures of student success should include workforce program awards by post-completion value (the higher, the better) and average student debt upon completion (the lower, the better). Indeed, for community colleges, the goal needs to be much more than access to higher education, and program completion is also not fully sufficient either. Overall, colleges should prioritize helping students achieve post-graduation success.[13]

While Pell and private scholarships were fundamental to provide support for student tuition, we needed a financial option to respond to the financial needs of the working poor while they were enrolled in classes. Twenty years earlier, many of the activities we initiated by the college during the Great Recession would have been considered as aid for "unemployed poor people." Instead, these initiatives were directed at this new group of working poor students. The college-initiated food pantries at each campus were often stocked with goods contributed to the college by our staff and students. The food pantries operated within the Macomb County cultural norms, which meant they provided aid as anonymously as possible. There were no records kept of who was using the pantry; food was placed in student book bags so that people who used the pantries on a regular basis could not be easily identified by other students.

Within our student services unit we also initiated a new emergency fund named "Dream Keepers" that gave students immediate access to small grant awards to assist them with short-term life disruptions, such as utility shut-offs, car repairs, or rent payments. A student could apply for the funds and immediately receive them, eliminating the typical wait time required of the federal student aid process. These grants were funded through our Foundation Office, and while the typical grant was less than $500, its impact on student behavior was significant. Of all our intervention programs to aid student retention, this program maintained the highest percentage of students who completed their semester and registered for the next semester. Over 80 percent of the students continued their education into the next semester and 41 percent graduated.

We centralized the food pantries and emergency funds into a new office which provided direct student assistance for food stamps, housing vouchers, and other forms of governmental aid not under control of the college. The new program was called Student Options for Success ("S.O.S."), and it was open to all students who needed assistance during the semester. In four years of operation, the program served 1,300 students—48 percent of them with families, 37 percent working part-time, and 50 percent coming from households earning less than $10,000 annually. The college was responding to the new needs of the working poor in the community.[14] Many community colleges and some four-year institutions such, as Georgia State University, developed similar programs which recognized the need to support student financial emergencies during the semester.

Achieving the Dream

Dealing with the economic needs of the working poor while they attended college was one important step, but we had to ensure that curriculum and programs were leading to successful transfer or student employment. Like most community colleges, Macomb had broadly measured its success by the number of students we enrolled in each semester. This neglected to consider how many students completed their course of study and what happened to them because of this completion. If we considered student completion and post-graduation success as indicators of the success of the college, the initial data we collected suggested we had work to do.

In 2008, 14 percent of students entering Macomb Community College for their first postsecondary experience earned zero credit hours in their first semester. For entering Black students, 37 percent completed their first semester without any credits earned. Of those students who completed their first year with some credit, only 50 percent continued into their second year at the college. After six years, only about 16.2 percent received an associate degree and 36 percent who transferred with no associate degree completed their four-year degree.[15]

Even though Macomb's outcomes were comparable to other community colleges located in working-class suburban communities, these results were unacceptable. We had to improve student outcomes, and this would require changes in our instructional processes. To emphasize the importance of changing our systems, as well as to continue the concept of learning from others, it seemed useful to join the national program that promoted student success called Achieving the Dream. Through the Kresge Foundation, we secured an initial grant to pay for our membership in Achieving the Dream (ATD).

Our involvement in ATD produced some mixed results. Many already-dedicated teachers enthusiastically joined the ATD task forces and played a role in encouraging change at the institution. However, these faculty members were the same instructors who always stepped forward to support educational innovation efforts. There was little outright resistance to ATD activities, except from a few liberal arts instructors who believed these efforts undermined their efforts at developing quality programs. Of greatest concern for me was most of the faculty who played little or no role in the project. These were faculty who were dedicated to their students but believed the college seemed to be operating well. They did not view the low completion or retention rates as significant concerns. They were unconvinced that their role was to get all students to succeed. They responded well to their academically inclined students and encouraged their success. They were less likely to spend time with poorly prepared students, preferring to have these students seek remedial programs and personal tutoring to be successful. They considered themselves to be good teachers, fulfilling the requirements spelled out in the collective-bargaining agreements; they were doing their job.

Many of these faculty who were uncertain about the student success initiatives proposed by ATD stated that ATD "did not understand their students." These words were typically followed by statements of how disappointed the faculty were with the quality of the students who enrolled from the high schools. In a few instances, they also interpreted our poor results as reflecting on the growing numbers of low-income students who were enrolling, and their examples often, unfortunately, referenced incidents with our Black and immigrant students.

My response was always "You teach the students you have, not the students who you would like them to be." I borrowed this phrase from ATD, and it was shared by many of us within the organization. Our students' previous educational experiences may not have prepared them very well. But that is a challenge we often face at community colleges—how to help ill-prepared students be successful. In the higher education landscape, American community colleges should be the institutions that possess the knowledge and the programs to make all students, regardless of background or previous education experiences, successful.

For a small number of the faculty, their own status insecurities made them take an elitist approach. Students who were deemed as "not college material" were not given adequate encouragement or support and, as a result, often did not successfully pass their courses. These faculty believed I was not appreciating the need for academic quality and rigor. They wanted us to operate as the University of Michigan or an Ivy League school. Of course, the irony of this view was that if this argument were applied to them, few of these faculty possessed the credentials or specialized expertise to teach at the University of Michigan or any elite university.

Most of these faculty were often ones with high seniority who were close to retirement. Many of the newer faculty wanted to be at a community college precisely because they were interested in teaching community college students.

Unfortunately, while sympathetic to activities that would promote student success, the faculty union also was hesitant to advocate for the goals of ATD. Efforts to reform teaching and learning were never opposed by the union as long as they were not contractually binding. The union did not want to negotiate contract revisions to issues related to quality teachers and student success, arguing these were very subjective and could be used to harm faculty whom the administration did not like. In addition, the full-time faculty union did not want part-time members involved in student success activities, fearing their large numbers would dominate the discussions and overwhelm their interests.

While I understood their concerns, I was disappointed that they did not embrace the project. As a strong supporter of union involvement, I thought I would be able to obtain their participation, but that was not the case. In retrospect, I underestimated the need to have more faculty understand that community colleges have a mission that is different from being a "junior" college. Community colleges should not operate like four-year institutions. We have a different role within higher education that focuses on a specific and important higher education problem—how to welcome and enroll underprepared or under-resourced students and help them to be successful. In many cases, underprepared students result from income inequities, family disruptions, or other issues, but the goal of community colleges must be to help students obtain higher education while also helping them overcome the challenges they face in life. When I discussed this concept with faculty, their response often was "I am not a social worker. I should not be expected to deal with these student issues." At best, I could get them to at least know how to spot student issues and refer students to other units of the college where these issues could be handled. As a field, we need to develop a more convincing argument and be clear about what our mission entails. Until more community college faculty members embrace a more holistic approach to supporting students, our attempts at increasing student success will remain positive but marginal within the entire institution.

The ATD project also provided me with a "coach," a former community college president who could advise me on how to encourage faculty participation. My coach was Christine McPhail, a former president from California who became the director of the community college leadership program at Morgan State University. She was particularly helpful in getting me to understand the needs of our Black students to be successful in a majority white environment such as Macomb.

Our efforts in ATD did achieve important changes in specific curriculum areas. The mathematics faculty changed their curriculum and developed an entirely new course emphasizing practical approaches to mathematics. Our data indicated that students who took these courses had a much greater success rate than in the traditional math class. Led by several younger mathematics faculty, these individuals became the core faculty who championed our efforts to transform teaching and learning at the college.

In addition, we consolidated all our counseling and student services and established a new Vice President for Student Services in 2013. Under the leadership of our Vice President for Student Services, Jill Little, with assistance from the Community College Research Center, she was able to develop a new enrollment and student orientation system. She also implemented a new student success class for students who were defined as "at-risk"; that is, they scored below our assessment test cut-off scores. This course started in 2011 with 43 students; three years later, there were 325 students. Those who completed the course had a 10 percent greater persistence rate than students who did not.

Changing Occupational Courses

In our ATD work, I was troubled by the lack of participation by many of the career and technical faculty. I had always been impressed by their teaching styles, which resembled coaching more than the formal academic model. I thought the liberal arts faculty would benefit from interactions with them. Yet, especially in the manufacturing and health-care programs, there appeared to be little interest. To understand the reluctance of the technical faculty to participate, we started to examine some fundamental issues regarding the occupational programs and courses within the career areas. Even glancing through our catalog of courses I recognized, we were stretched far too thin to confront the reform of community college workforce curriculum. The sheer number of the occupational programs we offered made it impossible to expect excellence in all of them. In 2008, the college had over 235 credit workforce programs and 51 non-credit programs. In many cases, the differences across our programs were difficult for our students or employers to appreciate. For example, we were teaching electrical technology, electronics, and electrical controls as distinct programs. There was a machine tool design program, a computer numerical control program, a machine tool program, and a tool and die apprentice program. While there were distinctions in each of these areas, the differences were subtle, more nuanced, especially at the introductory level. From the perspective of employers, many of these specializations' differences were best taught at the workplace. Not only was this vast number of occupational programs far too difficult to manage, let alone ensure they were of high quality, but it was expensive to maintain up-to-date equipment, find instructors to teach these new skills, and market them to employers for securing employment for our students.

In addition, to meet the challenges of maintaining appropriate student enrollment in these many programs, the technical faculty instituted a paradoxical practice of increasing the number of required classes to complete each program. While this provided them with teaching loads, as students continued to register for the many required classes, it created a situation where students were needlessly kept at the institution and away from the workplace, attempting to complete a program. As provost, Jim Sawyer performed a long overdue empirical review of each of our occupational programs and found that in some cases, the mandatory program completion was between 61 and 92 hours of courses, well above the traditional 60 hours for an associate degree. All these additional courses were technical courses. Even if they enrolled full-time, students would need to take more than two years of coursework just to complete the program.

This length of time required to complete a program raised an important issue of what was essential for mastery, a question often posed but rarely agreed upon by either employers or faculty. I knew from research and practical experience that most companies did not believe advanced technical specializations were necessary for most entry-level hires. If recruits possessed good foundational skills, they could learn on the job effectively and become advanced. Once these students were working, employers were very willing to pay tuition for their continued education and obtaining a degree. Our lengthy programs precluded students who needed to obtain immediate employment and discouraged employers who were often wary of hiring individuals with what they considered overspecialized skills that did not fit their needs. Most importantly, many technical programs did not adequately prepare the students for on-the-job learning experiences, which employers believed were fundamental to their success and advancement at the workplace. Given this data, we needed to reduce the number of courses students were required to take to fulfill either an associate's degree or a certificate. Obtaining more technical faculty participation in ATD would give us an institutional context to move ahead with some needed changes.

We also initiated some changes in our mechatronics occupational curriculum program, which combined electronic, computer, and mechanical skills. We benefited from a combination of having faculty interested in offering general skills in these areas alongside having real employer demand for individuals who were cross-trained in these skills. Our new mechatronics program enjoyed a significant positive reaction from local manufacturers. Many of the students who enrolled found jobs or were promoted within their present workplace before completing the program. The success of this program encouraged me to consider the growing appeal of short-term training programs for employers. Many programs in our career-technical areas were traditional two-year degree programs or one-year certificate programs. Short-term training programs could not give students comprehensive skills packages, but their advantage was that they produced a fast track into the workplace. At the workplace, continuing work-based learning would give the students the necessary skills to succeed. I began to consider our task as training employers to undertake work-based learning activities successfully.

A New Approach: Project Redesign

During this initial period, we initiated a new approach to workforce programs which emerged from our efforts adapting the auto design occupational program to the challenges of the Great Recession. As discussed earlier, the auto body design sector was an important part of the local Macomb County economy. The Great Recession resulted in the auto manufacturers and suppliers laying off designers in their efforts to cut costs. To respond to both employer needs and the needs of the community, we initiated a very specific retraining program—Project Redesign.

In February 2009, Macomb Community College held an unusual student "graduation" in a suburban office building. There were twenty-five "graduates"—all former Macomb Community College design students, many of whom had ten to fifteen years of experience as auto body designers working for original equipment manufacturers (OEMs) and their suppliers in the Detroit metropolitan area. They were also unemployed because of the Great Recession as the domestic auto industry downsized. Our task was to initiate a unique "skill builders" program that would find work for these individuals within another industrial design sector. With support from the local workforce board, these individuals completed a college program to transition their auto design talents into designing nuclear power plants, petroleum refineries, and new subway systems being built overseas. These auto design students were mastering the lexicon and techniques of design, all built upon a collaboration with Macomb College and a local employment service firm, Talascend. After students "graduated," the employment service firm would market them to companies in the southwest states or international construction firms that were in need of design talent. The immediate goal of the program was to find work for unemployed individuals, but there was also an economic development strategy embedded within Project Redesign. The employment service firm was trying to obtain employment for these workers with the goal of bringing design work back to the Detroit area, creating new markets for the current auto design firms and new employment opportunities for designers in our region. Part of the retraining effort was to encourage new economic development in the county and decrease the dependence of the design sector on auto-related work.[16]

In addition, for those laid-off design workers who could not commit themselves to work as designers in other sectors, the college initiated a free "updating and retraining program" which would allow unemployed designers access to our laboratories, so they could keep their skills current. The program (called Project Retrain) was also funded by the local workforce board and existed alongside Project Redesign. With this retraining, they would be able to return to work easily when the auto industry restarted itself immediately. Both programs were extremely popular among our former design students and hundreds attended the program which lasted until 2014. I sat in some of these sessions and typically tried to speak at the end of the program to the graduates.

These classes were extremely well attended, and the focus of the students was exceptional. They were present to learn skills that would keep them employed when the industry rebounded. The results of Project Retrain were impressive. Over 500 unemployed auto body designers went through the program between 2008 and 2014. Many maintained their skills and were prepared for work when rehiring began by 2012.

While these efforts focused on only one sector, they suggest some important criteria that could be applied to the future design of community college workforce development efforts. Macomb could not assume that the role of the college ended when students who took our technical courses found themselves hired for their first job. The college's responsibility was to maintain ties with them during their work careers and continue to refresh their technical skills as they advanced in their careers. Adopting this perspective makes the college a lifelong partner with these individual students.

In addition, adopting this approach to student technical education implied more emphasis on developing shorter training cycles, which would get an individual within the workplace quickly and then provide abilities to return to longer programs for credentials and degrees. To implement this on a broad scale, community colleges need to maintain better mechanisms to facilitate the pathway of the students between school and work. At Macomb, we had to maintain the capability to remain in contact with former students and interact with them to ensure their skills did not become obsolete. In the case of Project Redesign, we were dependent upon the workforce board for these connections.

Second, while the college could be responsible for the development of initial skills for students to find employment, their upgrading and specific skills acquisition continued within the workplace. The college may assist firms in the development of workplace learning activities, but much of the process could require assistance from private sector organizations that have more regular and systematic interactions with the private sector than we could maintain. Connections with private companies became an important aspect of community college workforce efforts. In some cases, the college may become a training resource for employers' on-the-job learning efforts. Establishing these relationships was central to the success of any of our career and technical programs.

Third, many of the skills needed by the firms were best learned and mastered at the workplace, not the classroom. This meant that both company and college had to collaborate and develop a detailed understanding of where the "hand off" between the educational instruction and the private sector implementation happens. Not only would the college need to prepare students for work-based learning, but there would be a new activity for the college in helping employers understand how to effectively deliver and evaluate on-the-job learning—particularly for students who may not have any previous knowledge of their chosen sector. The community college can become a knowledge hub for the education and training of adults and employers and should be able to draw upon these resources to construct their programs.[17]

Fourth, bringing new work back into the community underscores how a community college can synthesize workforce and economic development efforts for the students and the community. The design industry was an important part of Macomb County's local economy. The college had a responsibility to maintain these firms, not just for obtaining work for our students, but because of their significance to the overall economy of the region. The college can become an anchoring learning institution for the community. While it primarily meant strengthening the present economic institutions in the community, it also would include college participation in efforts to attract new sectors and grow the local economic base.

Finally, to develop this new approach, the college had to collaborate with many other public and community partners. Public collaborations mattered not just with the workforce board, but with economic development agencies, school systems, and community organizations. One institution could not initiate all the programs necessary to encourage community growth. The typical transactional relationship where the colleges just listen to the present demands of the employers needed to be replaced with a broader understanding that partnerships also must happen across the students, the community, and the employers. The exchange of information and the ability to see this relationship as independent from the typical business cycle or just the immediate demands of firms would be an important perspective for community college leadership to develop, on all levels of public policy.

This new approach to workforce development discussed above would mean significant internal institutional changes. The careful distinctions the college had made in the past between credit and non-credit courses were irrelevant to many students taking workforce courses. Many students wanted immediate skills to obtain work. Colleges have sought to separate themselves often into two types of workforce curricula: credit and non-credit. In theory, the curriculum for credit is created and taught by full-time faculty, who are subject matter experts. These individuals are selected through a process that validates their knowledge of the discipline, either through degrees or previous work experience. The term "credit" comes from a college's accreditation, a process that is performed every few years by a nongovernmental accreditation agency. It is very important for the colleges to have accreditation. Students cannot obtain federal grants or loans unless the institution is accredited.

Non-credit instruction does not have this process. Programs can be taught by part-time adjuncts who may lack degrees or skills the faculty may consider appropriate. In addition, the curriculum may be developed by a third party, an employer, or other training provider. This form of learning sits outside the credit decision-making process, as well as the regular college rules on faculty credentials, length of instructional period, and cost of instruction. As we mentioned in early chapters, non-credit education was an essential part of the workforce activities at Macomb.

To engage in economic development work, the college had to collaborate in new partnerships with both public and private organizations. It utilized the skills of the companies (i.e., the employment service firms) to serve the needs of the students but also attempted to provide a potentially new form of economic development for a community. By providing the former Macomb students with new skills, we created opportunities for them and tried to seed a new industry for the community. The program was aiding the designers but also creating an economic development opportunity for the community. Unfortunately, while some designers got hired in these new sectors, we were unsuccessful in bringing design work back to Macomb County. Before we could build long-term relationships with companies in other parts of the country, the auto industry began to recover and rehired our designers.

But the lessons learned in Project Redesign will become important in future workforce activities, not only for Macomb but also for other community colleges. However, there was one important downside, which was a major barrier to development in other workforce areas. Despite external funding, there were significant college resources tied up in this project. This suggests a reconsideration of the number of key career and technical programs. Even a large and well-financed community college such as Macomb could not undertake this sort of effort in more than four to six programs. In our present financial condition, we were unable to attempt this program in other areas.[18]

Economic Development Focus

Despite our successes with auto body design students, and even with a recovery underway, we knew the automotive sector would not regain all the jobs lost in the Great Recession. There would be a need to support the development and expansion of the private sector. One of the three missions of the college expressed in our college logo was economic development. Macomb from its initial days was always committed to entrepreneurial education. For years we taught a class in our business area devoted to students initiating their own business startups. With the impact of the Great Recession, I knew activities in this area would need to be increased significantly. In 2010, in partnership with Wayne State University, we joined the Goldman Sachs Small Business Program to create 10,000 small businesses through a program developed by the investment company but taught by our instructors. The owners of small companies, selected through a rigorous applications process, participated in an eight-month program to learn how to successfully operate and expand their business. The college not only supplied the faculty members for the program but also participated in the selection process of the firms. One of the first success stories emerging from this program in 2011 was a cookie maker, Ethel's Baking Company from St. Clair Shores. The owner utilized the program to increase her sales and was able to get her products in national retail stores.[19]

Our involvement in the Goldman Sachs program also taught us that many smaller employers in our county knew little about the capabilities of the college. Most of our local Macomb employers who had completed the program had never utilized the college as a source for employees when they needed to expand. We assumed that these companies would know about the abilities of the college to provide them with talent, but that was not the case.

We faced a similar experience while providing economic development activities for one of the significant "hidden sectors" of Macomb County—the defense industry. The headquarters of the fourth largest domestic vehicle producer—the United States Army's Tank Automotive and Armaments Command Operations and Materials (TACOM)—is in Warren, Michigan. Attached to this administrative hub was the Tank Army Research Development and Engineering Center (TARDEC)—the research and development arm of TACOM. TACOM and TARDEC control the research, design, development, and production of all Army vehicles. TACOM's presence in Macomb County encouraged many defense producers to establish significant research and development centers in the county along with small production facilities. They also utilized the metalworking capacity of local tool and die and machine tool builders to source parts for military equipment. I remember visiting a small, unionized manufacturer located in Warren who was the only source for some highly specialized parts that were found in the most advanced Air Force fighter jets. One employer who played a major role in the Machinist Training Center made parts for NASA satellites. Each piece had to be made with very precise machining standards. Because there was a demand for military part-making, the college operated a Procurement Technical Assistance Center (PTAC) for the state of Michigan. The purpose of PTAC was to assist firms in obtaining manufacturing defense contracts. The organization ran seminars and trained local businesses on how to compete for defense contracts. In 2011–12, over $69 million in local contracts were awarded to 755 PTAC clients. Yet few of these clients utilized the college as a source of hiring.[20] There was a gap we had to close between the employers using the college for assistance in obtaining defense contracts and hiring our students to work on these new contracts.

We also needed to provide more opportunities for our students to initiate their own businesses. We started by establishing a Center for Entrepreneurship to aid students in developing their ideas for business. As part of this center, we received a grant from a local community bank to create a competition with a $1,000 prize for the best student concept of a business. The competition was modeled after the television program *Shark Tank*. I did not realize the interest the competition would generate within our student body. We held the finals of this competition as a public event where each student would present their idea for a business to a panel of local businesspeople. Over 200 people turned out on a Friday spring evening, and the winner (whose entire family was present) was a young Bengali student whose plan was to create a high-fashion clothing store for young Muslim women. It was a wonderful concept and demonstration to me of the talents of our students. Unfortunately, our funds ran out before we were able to continue this event, but this initial competition gave me a sense of the potential that students could contribute to the economic development activities of the community. In our Center for Entrepreneurship, we were able to maintain economic development consultants to help students with forming new businesses.

This experience also increased my interest in having the college play a direct role in business initiation that could lead to student employment. Through our relationship with the Community College Workforce Consortium, discussed later in this chapter, we learned about Lorain Community College's creation of an Entrepreneurial Innovation Fund. Utilizing funds from the state of Ohio, Lorain developed a unique system of providing financial support to entrepreneurs and emerging businesses to turn good product ideas into viable businesses. In a relatively short time, their fund produced over 130 new internships, 100 new community jobs, an average salary of $48,000, and a total economic impact of more than $65 million.[21] Their fund was established with collaboration among other four-year institutions in their area. I was very impressed with the project's creativity and was determined to implement it at Macomb.

However, we needed a funding source because an Innovation Fund was not something we could afford to start with our internal resources. I tried to remain consistent with my internal rule that all new activities would be initiated with external funding. In this way, I believed there would be less resistance to major changes because no one at the college would be forced "to give up something" to initiate change. We did every year, however, set aside some of our annual budget in our Strategic Initiative Fund to invest in innovations of the existing programs the college believed important.

Ironically, our search for funding for an Innovation Fund became successful because of the fiscal crisis in Detroit. The Detroit bankruptcy attracted attention from several major philanthropic and financial institutions. One of them was JP Morgan Chase, which made a number of significant commitments to the city of Detroit. As a result of our regional perspective, we were able to position our Innovation Fund as another means of helping Detroit's economic revitalization. JP Morgan Chase gave us $1 million to initiate the fund, as long as we matched their investment with contributions from our college Innovation Fund. By adding some other funds from our Foundation, we launched the Macomb Innovation Fund with $3.7 million in 2015. The fund would be administered by a committee of local business leaders who would analyze applications for the fund. In their proposals to the fund, each start-up company had to indicate how they intended to employ Macomb students in the business they were developing.

We became the first community college in the region to offer a funding program for new companies with awards as high as $100,000, provided the companies offered workplace opportunities for our students. In our first year of operations, we were able to award $800,000 to thirteen companies. Our initial belief that we had students with the skills these companies needed, however, proved incorrect. The technical skills needed by the companies were more than what associate degrees could offer. However, we were able to place students who were interested in their own entrepreneurial activities as interns within these firms. One of our first intern students was the woman who won the $1,000 college competition for her plan to start a clothing store for Muslim women. The experience of being involved in a start-up operation was attracting students, and their desire to work in new entrepreneurial activities was enough for companies to hire them.[22]

As we anticipated, some of the companies did fail and the Innovation Fund sometimes lost money. Many of the local companies are still operating, and at least one has emerged to become a successful national food company. However, my personal favorite was a company formed by two students who had studied in our non-credit sign reading program. To be certified as a sign reader, which would allow them to participate in court proceedings and other highly paid employment as sign readers, the students needed to complete a specific number of hours working in the field. The analogy was in the training of airline pilots—hours must be spent flying to achieve a level of competence. However, it was difficult for students to find hearing-impaired individuals to practice their skills. On the other hand, hearing-impaired individuals were excluded from many occupations and finding any work for them was a struggle. These students developed a business to connect students in the sign reading program with hearing-impaired individuals. They designed a website portal which had a video link between the students and the hearing-impaired. For a fee, a student could obtain access to a hearing-impaired person who would be compensated by the company to "talk" with the student. These practice hours counted toward their certification. The hourly fee given to the hearing-impaired person provided a needed source of income. The company the students formed was named "Sign-On C. R. P." and their business plan was to market the portal concept to other signing programs at educational institutions. I thought this was a remarkably creative idea that gave income to hearing-impaired individuals, supported students in completing their signing program, produced more trained sign language professionals, and benefited the community. It contained all the ingredients of a successful public-initiated economic development activity.

In retrospect, I believe our approach of funding companies that were willing to provide employment opportunities for our students was worth finding more financial support. This could be the creation of a new form of partnership between community-based institutions, such as local credit unions or community banks, and a college to formulate a local economic development strategy that would provide investment capital for companies willing to locate their enterprise in the community and hire students from the community college. Our efforts were only the beginning of what was possible for community colleges. I would encourage others to focus on this space through participation in organizations such as the National Association for Community College Entrepreneurship (NACCE).[23]

Recovery in the Auto Industry Begins

By 2011, there were beginning signs of recovery in the auto industry. Nevertheless, it was clear that the jobs that had existed previously, particularly in the semi-skilled and unskilled areas, were barely increasing at all. What was increasing was technical and information technology employment in both the development of electric cars and autonomous vehicles.

To understand these trends, we hired individuals fresh out of the industry, and through a grant from the National Science Foundation, we were able to develop a national center on advanced vehicle technologies to serve other community colleges in the development of their programs. Through this work we learned that the new electric cars were changing not just auto workers but the occupations of sectors that interacted with vehicles, such as first responders. We created the first course for first responders (such as EMS, police, and firefighters) in dealing with accidents involving electrically powered vehicles.

To search for answers on how to streamline and make curriculum more effective, I decided to seek out contacts with other community colleges, particularly those in communities served by the auto industry and that were facing similar issues. Perhaps we could learn from each other and work together to grapple with the new needs of these students and the community. These colleges included Harper College in Illinois, Lorain Community College in Ohio, Grand Rapids Community College and Mott Community College in Michigan, and the Ivy Tech system in Indiana. As presidents of the institutions, we convened to form a new organization named Community College Workforce Consortium (CCWC). While this organization was new and committed to perform more than customized training for companies, its roots were based upon the work done by the Mid-American Training Group almost thirty years earlier.

The CCWC was designed as a peer learning organization led by the presidents of the colleges, all of whom were committed to workforce development as a fundamental part of the institution. We held regular meetings encouraging joint work on projects and banding together to seek funding from the Department of Labor Trade Adjustment Assistance (TAA) grant. It was a place for me to learn from other presidents how to focus an institution on the workforce mission. The organization also broke significant ground for community colleges, which typically only relate to each other through state organizations. The CCWC was formed explicitly around the everyday needs of institutions as they dealt with the auto manufacturing sector.[24]

Many of these community college presidents were much more experienced than I in leading their institutions. While we all learned a great deal from our efforts, active participation by the presidents was very difficult to achieve. For all of us, collaboration between institutions was

Figure 7.1 Addressing the audience at the inaugural Innovation Fund Awards event at Macomb Community College in 2015. Image courtesy of Macomb Community College.

rarely a priority with our trustees. None of us were evaluated on how well we collaborated with other community colleges. Thus, CCWC work was placed on top of everything else expected of us, so maintaining the regular structure and meeting became a difficult task. I searched for some intermediary to maintain the organization, and by the time I retired from Macomb, CCWC had selected Jobs for the Future to become the administrative center for the organization. It continues to this day with more than twenty major community colleges involved.

What I Learned

Through these initial efforts, I began to understand that the education and training relationships between employers and community colleges were more complex than I assumed. Before becoming president, I accepted the traditional transactional model as the operating system for our work with companies. This "transactional" model assumes the companies knew the skills they needed, and the purpose of the college is to respond with a curriculum that meets these needs. The intended result is that students who take these programs would then obtain work. In some cases, these are spelled out in contractual arrangements if the firm is hiring the college to train incumbent workers. However, in practice, employers do not always know or can't always articulate the specific skills they need and, therefore, despite a college's determination, their programs may not always meet workforce needs. While there is some interaction between business and education, mostly these relationships are one-directional: the immediate market needs of the company are the driver of the community college programs.

As president, I interacted with senior company representatives, often with the CEOs of their firms. I was struck by how little they could articulate their specific needs and relied upon us focusing on some general "job ready" skills, which they could then supplement with any specific training. Nor would many companies be willing to answer our questions about their specific needs. They often treated us as another vendor who was offering their services, not a planning partner for the good of their firm and the community. During the Great Recession, as companies fought for their survival, they were unwilling to discuss their future education and training needs. However, with the beginning of recovery, the companies were focused on their return to growth, and they still were unwilling to project their future education and training needs.

With experiments such as Project Redesign and the Innovation Fund, I learned community colleges needed to develop an alternative approach to the transactional approach of workforce development. Employers, even large and well-financed ones, do not pay much attention to the training and educational needs of their employees or the individuals they wish to hire. Community colleges can become an important resource for them by providing employees. In addition, the college can assist companies with how to express their skill needs more comprehensively and determine the appropriate strategies for work-based learning. In this regard, we have much to offer firms, but we have often been too timid to assert our views with the management. We need to represent the interests of the community and the interests of our students more intentionally in our interactions with firms. In many European countries, educators play a role as "social partners" which companies accept as an important reference group in determining their skill needs. In addition, I found as president that it was important to engage company leaders in some of these discussions as equals, not simply pandering to them to obtain a contract. A good community college should be recognized by the private sector as adding value to their training and education needs.

The refusal of the private sector employers to discuss their future needs was not a phenomenon of the Great Recession. The companies continued to make short-term fixes for their workforce needs, not knowing and sometimes not trusting us to provide the skills they needed. Their preference was to hire people with experience, preferring to steal workers from each other or maintain their present workers past retirement to keep skills fresh. We needed a different approach that made the college not just respond to the needs of the companies but to help our students and the community pursue a more proactive outreach to the companies built upon our institutional strengths. We also needed a strategy to convince the companies we could contribute to their success with a strategy that encouraged long-term cooperation and collaboration.

As public institutions, community colleges are responsible for meeting the workforce needs of the communities they serve. Instead of looking at workforce development as a bilateral relationship between colleges and companies, we need a framework based around a more complex and developed understanding of the relationship between the college and students as well as the companies and the community. What appeared missing in these equations were two essential factors. The first was the context: that is, the community served by the institution. All communities have a specific set of local economic actors and a culture that needs to be understood by their community colleges. This context should shape the college's investments in programs, the alliances formed with businesses, and the emphasis placed on priorities and objectives. More than any other postsecondary institution, community matters for community colleges. This willingness to consider the needs of the community and the students also distinguishes the community college from private sector competitors. While some companies may automatically reject this perspective, from my experience, there is a growing understanding in the private sector that they have responsibilities to communities and community colleges can become significant allies in forging and maintaining these alliances.

Notes

1 Thomas Bailey and Jim Jacobs, "Can Community Colleges Rise to the Occasion?" *The American Prospect*, November 2009, 18–20.

2 Karin Fischer, "As the Auto Industry Shrinks, a Community College Retools," *The Chronicle of Higher Education*, May 8, 2009, https://www.chronicle.com/article/as-the-auto-industry-shrinks-a-community-college-retools/.

3 MIT Task Force on the Work of the Future, *Mobility and the Work of the Future* (Massachusetts Institute of Technology, March 2021), 3.

4 Detroit Promise, "About Us," https://detroitpromise.com/about/. For an analysis of the Detroit Promise, see Alyssa Ratledge and Stanley Dai, "The Detroit Promise Path Evaluation: Outcomes After Four Years," *MDRC*, October 2022.

5 Center for Automotive Research, 47–51.

6 Phelps et al., 28–30.

7 Peter R. Bahr, Yiren Chen, and Rooney Columbus, "Community College Skills Builders: Prevalence, Characteristics, Behavior, and Outcomes of Successful Non-completing Students across Four States," *Journal of Higher Education* 94, no. 1 (2023): 96–131, https://doi.org/10.1080/00221546.2022.2082782.

8 A CCRC analysis of credentials indicates students with general studies degrees are less likely to transfer to four-year colleges. Davis Jenkins, John Fink, and Tatiana Velasco, "Which Community College Awards Are Likely to Prepare Students for Post-Completion Success?" Community College Research Center, Teachers College, Columbia University, https://ccrc.tc.columbia.edu/publications/community-college-awards-for-post-completion-success.html.

9 United For ALICE, "The State of ALICE in Michigan: 2023," https://www.UnitedForALICE.org/Michigan.

10 College Board Advocacy & Policy Center, *Rethinking Pell Grants* (The College Board, 2013), https://secure-media.collegeboard.org/digitalServices/pdf/advocacy/policycenter/advocacy-rethinking-pell-grants-report.pdf.

11 Jill Little, "Student Options for Success: Non-Academic Financial Support for Students in Need," Macomb Community College, Internal Report, 2013.

12 Josh Wyner and Davis Jenkins, "Eight Strategies to Strengthen the Value of Community College Credentials," The Aspen Institute College Excellence Program, November 19, 2024, https://highered.aspeninstitute.org/blog-posts/eight-strategies-strengthen-value-community-college-credentials.

13 Aspen Institute College Excellence Program, "Focus Areas," https://highered.aspeninstitute.org/measures-student-successs/high-value-program-enrollment.

14 Macomb Community College, "Report on Diversity and Inclusion at Macomb Community College," Internal Report to President Jacobs, 2016.

15 Ibid., 22–3.

16 James Jacobs, "Build Upon the Strengths of America's Community College," Brookings Institution, Metropolitan Policy Program, https://www.brookings.edu/wp-content/uploads/2016/07/0927_great_lakes_community_college.pdf.

17 A study indicates how different firms' knowledge of community colleges is compared to the perceptions of community college leaders. See Joseph B. Fuller and Manjari Raman, *The Partnership Imperative: Community Colleges, Employers, and America's Chronic Skills Gap* (Harvard Business School, December 2022).

18 For further elaboration of these views, see James Jacobs, "Student Centered Vision for Workforce Development," Community College Research Center (Teachers College, Columbia University), 2023, https://ccrc.tc.columbia.edu/easyblog/student-centered-vision-workplace-development.html.

19 For a discussion of the national program, see Goldman Sachs, "Program Details: 10,000 Small Businesses," retrieved October 12, 2024, https://10ksbapply.com/program-details/.

20 Macomb Community College, *Macomb Community College Data Book*, 2016.

21 For more information about the Lorain Innovation Fund, visit www.innovationfundamerica.org/.

22 Macomb Community College, *Year One Report: Innovation Fund. Innovation Fund Report*, 2016.

23 For more information, visit the National Association for Community College Entrepreneurship website at www.nacce.com.

24 Jim Jacobs, Ellen Ullman, and Tabitha Whissemore, "You've Got a Friend . . . in Industry," *Community College Journal* 82, no. 1 (2011): 22–7; Community College Workforce Consortium, "White Paper: Aligning Demand Skills and Training with Sector Needs," 2013.

8 Running the College

In the first decade of the twenty-first century, over fifty years after community colleges emerged as important postsecondary organizations, these organizations were still operating with mostly a local focus. They had little interest in developing a broader, more national perspective on how they should serve their students and communities, and there was no real incentive to change that mindset. Until then, while there were similarities between the colleges, their goals and priorities were primarily based around local origins and/or state policies. Traditionally, the colleges dismissed attempts to develop a unified strategy, usually claiming that the local context of each institution was so different that "one size did not fit all." In addition, they argued that missions and processes were best evaluated by the accreditation agencies. However, as community colleges became more recognized as important parts of postsecondary American education, a growing and urgent need emerged for the development of a common approach to one of the most pressing problems faced by these institutions—the lack of students completing programs and earning degrees.

Several researchers, often funded by foundations interested in increasing postsecondary education outcomes, began studying the reasons for the low graduation rates at community colleges and identifying ways to mitigate the issue and increase community college student success. Through the work of national organizations, such as Achieving the Dream and Complete College America, the process of collecting and disseminating community college success initiatives became an important function. In 2015, these efforts and others were synthesized by Tom Bailey, Shanna Smith Jaggars, and Davis Jenkins from the Community College Research Center. Their book, *Redesigning America's Community Colleges*, became the most influential and comprehensive analysis of what community colleges should be doing to support student success.[1]

Based on over a decade of research, the authors argued that community colleges should move away from the then-typical "self-service cafeteria-style college" model, one that prioritized student choice and flexibility but provided students little assistance in navigating their choices of courses and programs.[2] For most students, this model leads them to taking much longer than necessary to complete a program, or worse, but also quite frequently, not completing at all. Instead, the authors argued that colleges should scrap the cafeteria model, redesign the college experience, and build intentional program pathways for students to follow. In these program pathways, students would take a pre-determined set of courses and would be closely monitored to make sure they stay on track, all with the goal that students can more efficiently and successfully complete degrees and other credentials. The crux of the book is that an overwhelming majority of community college students want to obtain a college degree, and therefore, the purpose of a community college should be to make sure this desire is met.

The steps outlined in the book were widely supported by major foundations and have been implemented in one form or another in over 400 community colleges. At least sixteen states have formally developed programs with community colleges utilizing the pathways approach. In essence, the four "practice areas" (or pillars) outlined originally by CCRC include the following: (1) mapping pathways to student end goals by developing a structured curriculum designed to meet student objectives, (2) helping students choose and enter a program pathway, both through counseling and intentional design of first-term courses, (3) keeping students on the path through instructive counseling and rigorous interventions, and (4) ensuring that students are learning through constant refinement of curriculum and development of metacognitive approaches. This pathway model is important for first-generation college students (i.e., students whose parents did not go to college) because it creates structure, provides proactive support, and minimizes how chaotic and overwhelming the college experience can be, even for students whose parents did go to college.

The practical work of implementing pathways has placed particular emphasis on the critical first semester and how incoming students can be nudged into early program adoption through a series of structured experiences within the institution. One feature of this approach requires them to take at least one class on a topic that interests them in their first semester at the institution to anchor their interest in completion. A required program completion plan by the end of the first term would follow this initial year.

While there are variations within the colleges implementing these designs, the data collected so far indicate that the pathways approach has helped students tremendously. In some cases, colleges have reported significant gains for non-white students and some initial indications that they are "closing the gap" between their academic performance and their white counterparts. While few colleges have taken all the steps advocated by CCRC, those that have followed these steps have reported very positive numbers of students being retained from term to term and an increase in student graduation rates as well. If colleges put in the effort, the pathways approach leads to permanent changes in their structure in terms of how they serve their students and in how their students and the communities perceive them—not just as open-access colleges but as open-access colleges that also care about student success.[3]

Redesigning Macomb Programs

I wanted to implement the pathways approach at Macomb Community College. However, you don't win support within your college with flowery speeches about how the institution must take a new institutional approach. When I became president of Macomb Community College, I knew that if I was going to make an impact on the institution, I had to demonstrate to the staff, students, and the community that my perspective would produce a better Macomb Community College that could fulfill its mission. I was working at CCRC when the early aspects of *Redesigning America's Community Colleges* were developed. While I was familiar with the structure and I utilized it to guide my activities, I was only able to make marginal advances in Macomb's course selection processes to mirror the pathways approach. There was faculty resistance to pathways, not because of major disagreement with the substance but rather an unwillingness to advocate one approach to teaching and course development. The faculty believed, as professionals, they should determine the curricula and teaching and learning processes. We did, however, begin the pathways approach and it still provides the "North Star" for the college today.

Implementing the pathways approach was also challenged by the lingering impact of the Great Recession on the community. By 2010, some of the federal initiatives of the Obama administration were taking hold in the United States economy, and these were being felt in Macomb County. For the first time in three years, the official unemployment rate decreased from 15.9 percent in 2009 to 12.3 percent in 2010. Auto sales increased, recalling some workers to Macomb auto manufacturing facilities. The passage of the Affordable Care Act encouraged the local expansion of health-care institutions, and the projected growth in health-care occupations was 25 percent. Finally, the new County Executive governmental system was established, which allowed county officials to coordinate aid efforts in a far more effective and efficient way.

Still, recovery was a long way off. The Macomb Food Bank served 151,150 residents in 2010, about 17 percent of the county population. Thirty-seven percent of the homes sold in the county were by financial institutions, indicating the homes had been foreclosed because owners couldn't pay mortgages. (While this was still a high foreclosure rate, this was an improvement from 2009, when it was 52 percent.) These conditions continued to suggest that our major efforts in the county should be to increase the number of residents employed in sustainable-wage jobs. It was within this still grave economic context that we tried to implement the pathways approach at the college.[4]

Macomb Student Needs

Any redesign of college activities must start with the students and a close examination of their needs. Unlike high schools or traditional four-year institutions where students are grouped by age and year of attendance (freshmen, sophomores, etc.), community college students are a large, undifferentiated, diverse group of individuals that are difficult to sort out. Every year I send out a survey to all the credit students who achieved a degree or certificate, and I read the results at graduation. In 2016, our graduation class had an age range of fifty-two years—the youngest was seventeen, and the oldest was sixty-nine. Over 50 percent of the graduates were over twenty-five years of age. Over 40 percent had children, and 60 percent were women. About 20 percent of the graduates spoke more than one language at home—with Arabic, Chaldean, and Albanian being the most common languages spoken. Most Macomb students had attended part-time while also working, which often meant years of classroom work to reach graduation. At each graduation ceremony, I would weave these survey results into my speech for the students and the community to understand how this diverse student body drives many of our activities.

Given this diversity, it was very difficult to develop a common perspective on how to deal with student goals, let alone craft programs to handle them. I tried to concentrate on the two main groups. First were the young students graduating from high school and entering postsecondary education for the first time. This was a relatively homogeneous group. It was possible to develop a structured set of experiences alongside significant interventions of counseling and other student services to reveal their learning interests and their desires to transfer or seek employment opportunities. Especially for these students and their families, success for many of them meant efficiently getting a degree and transferring to a four-year institution without taking on a significant amount of student debt. Based on our work with Achieving the Dream, we were able to streamline our student services, enrollment management, and counseling to fit these needs. These are the students most likely to follow pre-determined pathways.

For many of our older students (above twenty-four years old), occupational preparation became far more critical than academic success. For some, especially women reentering the workforce, their learning needs were often similar to the younger students. They needed a structure to plan their programs and achieve success. For the "skill builder" students discussed earlier, however, they needed little student or academic advising. They were utilizing the college to advance in their workplace and knew exactly what courses they needed. We estimated perhaps 10 to 15 percent of our adult students fell into this skill-building category. For our adult students, we were always focusing on their occupational goals and how to help students achieve them.

Student Participation

I was aware that many of our new activities at the college were changing learning at the institution, but they were often implemented without much student input. Even though the pathways approach focused on a structured set of courses and programs, most research on community college student success indicates that the more students participate in student activities at a community college, the greater their likelihood of success.[5] However, boosting student participation in extracurricular activities at a community college is very challenging. The typical community college student body is very heterogeneous, and students have a relatively short-term and more tenuous relationship with the institution than students at four-year colleges. For many community college students, school is usually the last consideration among their "big three" life priorities—family, work, and school. Typically, this means they have little to no time to devote to extracurricular activities. Most students attend part-time, and their on-campus time is usually measured by a few hours a week, not by semesters or years. It was a challenge to incentivize more student involvement within the institution.

The traditional student organizations tended to be dominated by younger (i.e., directly out of high school) full-time students, who actually represented only a fraction of the student body at Macomb. In dealing with these younger students, I was fortunate to have the support of a talented group of employees known as student coordinators, many of whom started their postsecondary education at Macomb. This group of dedicated staff had a strong community focus for the students. In my first year, while we recognized Martin Luther King Day as an institutional holiday, we organized MLK Day Service Day, which brought students and staff to work in food pantries and community-based organizations across our service area. The college faculty also helped to mobilize student involvement by embedding these activities within their course structure. As part of our MLK Day celebration, one of our heating and cooling technology instructors had his class install a new furnace for a low-income senior. This offered both a great hands-on learning experience for the students as well as a material contribution of the college to the community's well-being.

I tried to relate to the younger students through direct activities. As a regular jogger, I encouraged our student activities staff to organize a Macomb delegation of students to participate with me in some of the local county distance races. The running group also attracted some of the Macomb staff. This was attractive local publicity for the college when about forty students and staff showed up in matching Macomb shirts in the annual County Spring Run. We even held our own awards ceremony, giving awards to the best running costumes, worst color socks, best times, and so on. Mark Hackel, the Macomb County executive, was also a runner. He would appear before the race for a photograph and an informal discussion with the students. I felt this was an organic way to relate to some of the students, cutting across the student/staff divides.

Increasing the participation of adult students in student activities was more challenging. They were relatively uninterested in the traditional student activities on the campus, but they did take their education seriously. Recognition for good grades and completion of programs were significant signs of success for these students. I found they were able to relate to the community college honor society, Phi Theta Kappa, so our college chapter was often composed of adult students. They participated in many of the Phi Theta Kappa activities, which included speaking to younger students about their work or family experiences. They were also attracted to some of the occupational student groups organized by our occupational faculty as a means to promote career growth and development.

For all students, we encouraged them to register to vote and participate in the political process. Given their local mission, community colleges should play a role in encouraging civic participation and civic engagement. We partnered with a non-profit and non-partisan organization called TurboVote to encourage students to register to vote and stay informed. For example, TurboVote would email reminders to students when elections were occurring in their communities. Our efforts paid off, as we were in the top ten postsecondary institutions in the nation recording new participants in TurboVote registrants.

New Americans

Another important student constituency I wanted to engage at the college was the growing population of new immigrants to Macomb County. My years of doing the Economic Forecast for the county made me acutely aware that suburban areas such as Macomb County were rapidly replacing cities as the primary destination point for these new Americans. Many came to Macomb County from the Middle East and the Balkans. For example, Macomb had one of the highest per capita populations of Albanians of any county in the United States. Another immigrant group concentrated in Macomb County was the Chaldeans (Iraqi Christian Arabs).

Given the continuing conflicts in Iraq, the Chaldeans were political refugees leaving their homeland with little possibility of returning. With this group, I built a close working relationship with the Chaldean Community Foundation for both English language training and occupational education. Over 2,000 refugees were coming each month from Iraq, and we provided some critical services to them with specific ESL classes taught by their instructors. I tried to speak to each of these classes to welcome them to the college and the community. There was also a growing Yemeni community in Hamtramck, a city located in neighboring Wayne County, but historically whose school system sent many students to us. I did initiate ties to the largest and most influential Arab community-based organization in the area, ACCESS (Arab Community Center for Economic and Social Services). Through ACCESS, we established ties with local Yemeni and Arab businesses to help with small business assistance activities. In our machining program, we had an Arab-speaking instructor, and I explored the possibility of teaching one of our machining classes in Arabic, but we were unsure about the demand for this program. We did hire a student navigator in our student services area who was fluent in Arabic to aid students in their program choices and provide them with access to benefits, such as food stamps.

Working with new immigrants provided the possibility of new community college learning experiences. One of our outreach attempts to the Arab community involved inviting high school students to come to the college and learn about our occupational programs. Most of the students brought their parents who also became interested in some of the programs. From then on, we always invited immigrant families to attend our events, not just prospective students. In the future, someone at a community college should explore whether co-generational learning is a possible strategy in dealing with the needs of new immigrant families.

Many immigrants enrolled in our English as a Second Language (ESL) program, which had expanded to four levels of classes. In one of the levels, we included information for students about obtaining a driver's license, opening a bank account, and other important basic activities of American life that may be difficult for any new resident. As an individual whose wife came from Greece, I was very aware that these seemingly mundane issues are most challenging to anyone migrating to the United States.

We also tried to quietly deal with undocumented student issues by making a small but significant change. Without any publicity, I was able to convince our board to waive any citizenship requirements for attending college programs. The only information we collected that mattered was the residency of the students. My argument was if you lived in the county and paid taxes, going to Macomb Community College was your right, regardless of your specific background. The board supported it unanimously. We never framed this as policy in favor of any group for fear of a community reaction against our board, but I am sure some of our non-citizen students benefited from this board decision.

Women at the College

Since the majority of students at Macomb were women, as well as most of the staff, I also tried to directly address the issues women faced. Signs suggested we had work to do. Some discrimination claims at the college were filed by women on staff, and there were also sexual harassment complaints made by students. Federal mandates existed on how postsecondary institutions should handle student sexual harassment claims, which required us to develop a new college process. I decided to take on the issue both for the staff and for the students. For the first time, all college staff went through the required sexual harassment training as well as diversity training through computer-based packaged programs. In addition, we developed with board approval a very detailed process for dealing with any sexual harassment or discrimination complaint. These diversity programs were national programs and well designed, but they lacked any specific applications to the situations we faced as a community college. I was never sure how effective they were, but they did underscore our seriousness about taking on this issue. We monitored the implementation process and tried to get all full-time and part-time staff to participate. We also established a specific system independent from the college for any specific complaints of sexual harassment. As the result of these actions, sexual harassment complaints both by students and also by staff were reported more frequently.

While these actions helped focus our staff on these overt examples of discrimination, there were instructional issues of a critical subgroup of community college women students—single heads of households. I became aware of the issues these women face through the resolution of a student complaint in one of our most selective programs—nursing. Similar to most other community colleges, Macomb's nursing program was a high-demand program where acceptance was determined through both grades and an examination. Once selected, the instructors established some stringent internal rules for the students in the program. One of them was a rigorous attendance policy that stipulated that more than two unexcused absences from a nursing course would result in termination from the program. All students were required to sign a statement that they understood this policy.

However, a single mother completing her final semester in the program could not find childcare and missed more than two days in one of her classes. The faculty wanted to expel her from the program. She appealed this decision to me, and the best I could achieve was for her to remain in the program, but only if she repeated the course. This incident caused me to wonder how many of these incidents had happened previously in other classes which had never been reported. It also raised an issue of whether we were doing anything about childcare for these women students.

Macomb did not have a childcare center. When I became president, I was sure this was an important area for our students and staff. My involvement in a community childcare center years before made me somewhat familiar with the financial and logistical issues of maintaining a center. We examined some childcare centers at other Michigan community colleges and found they were operating with very mixed results. Few students used them; many remained viable only if they permitted their staff to enroll their children. Moreover, unless they were heavily subsidized through state and federal funds, they were extremely costly to maintain. Macomb had a childcare occupational program, and I thought the development of a center primarily staffed by our students would be a natural fit.

However, when we conducted a survey of our students who had children on whether they would be interested in a childcare center, we learned there was little interest in a college childcare center. Most parents wanted their children taken care of by relatives or friends they knew and trusted. We dropped the idea of a center and shifted to offering a training and certification program for Michigan home childcare providers. We also established a student discount with certified local childcare providers for our students to utilize. These small steps hardly resolved childcare issues, but they indicated to me that, at least in Macomb County, students were not willing to trust us to provide adequate childcare for their children.

Black Students

One of the major issues confronting the college was how to ensure that the growing Black student population was becoming successful at the institution. We would need to be very intentional with our programming. We also needed to start by dealing with the racist history of the county. Many students and their families had experienced racial issues while shopping or attending events in the county. Some confronted racism issues while attending Macomb K–12 school districts. These were students, often living in Detroit, but recruited by Macomb school districts through the open enrollment policies discussed earlier. Many of these students followed the traditional path taken by their white Macomb student peers and came to Macomb right after high school graduation. However, because their residence was outside the county, they were forced to pay the higher out-of-county tuition rates, even though they graduated from the same Macomb high schools as their white counterparts. They often came to the college via the anemic Detroit regional bus transportation system, typically forcing them to take two or three buses, resulting in taking more than an hour to reach the campus.

Despite these difficulties, there was a consistent rise in Black student enrollment at the college. In 2004, Black students made up only 4 percent of the credit students at the college. By 2017, Black student enrollment was over 15 percent. To help these students become successful, they needed mentors, people like themselves who completed our programs and were employed. We were able to get a few students paired with some non-white alumni who went through some of our technical programs. They were able to communicate what issues they would face inside some of these highly paid technical and gray collar jobs, where they would be one of the only non-white employees in their work unit.

I tried to meet regularly with Black students who were participating in our athletic programs. Encouraged by one of our coaches, we hosted informal pizza sessions. These meetings also taught me that many of our Black students had difficulty with the culture of our institution. The overwhelmingly white environment of Macomb County confounded them and often marginalized them. These issues were more critical to the students than what was happening inside the classrooms. Persistence in this educational setting was going to be based, in part, on how comfortable students felt at the institution. Most of these insights came from interactions with younger students; I wondered if these same experiences were true for adult Black students.

To help me understand the day-to-day issues faced by these students, I assembled a group of non-white staff members, including administrators, teachers, and clerical employees, to discuss what should be done to encourage more success of non-white students. They urged some specific changes, such as hiring more Black counselors and student advisors for our Black students. Some of the staff were willing to be advisors to a Black student organization that might be formed. They also suggested that the campus police should hire a non-white campus officer. To this last suggestion, I was successful in hiring a former Black Detroit police officer, but the seniority provisions of our police contract put him on the midnight shift! He was totally invisible to our students.

I also learned that many of our non-white staff possessed skills useful to the college that were far beyond their present positions. A woman who was in a clerical position at the college worked as a flight attendant on a German airline earlier in her life and was fluent in German. She could help us work with many of the German auto suppliers that were developing facilities in the Detroit area. Another individual who taught photography as a part-timer had skills in counseling. From these meetings, I realized that many of our staff, both Black and white, possessed skills beyond their formal position. I tried to work with our human resources department to come up with a process for collecting information on these skills and determine how we could utilize them to benefit the institution.

These meetings with our non-white students and our staff were important in preparing me for our participation in the Detroit Promise. The Detroit Promise was a program modeled after the Kalamazoo Promise, which provided free community college tuition to any graduate of the Detroit Public School system. While I was excited to participate in this program, few Detroit students chose to initiate their postsecondary education at Macomb. The one barrier already cited was the lack of direct public transportation connecting Detroit with Macomb campuses. In addition, Macomb County and the college were perceived as hostile, unknown territory for many students and their families. The previous racist culture of the county was well-known to Detroit Black families, so they were hesitant to select Macomb, unsure what sort of welcome they would receive.[6]

I needed to change this impression. We started small, and I welcomed the students personally, holding meetings with them and their parents, and alerting our counselors to respond to their needs as best as possible. We put together a special summer orientation program for these students before they began their semester. We were fortunate in the second year of the program to have the project assigned an on-site "counselor" dedicated to these Detroit students. She was an African American who had previously worked as a counselor at Detroit Pershing High School and was extremely perceptive as to the needs of the Detroit students. We gave her an office, and while she was not on our staff, I considered her input essential in shaping our efforts to make these students welcome and successful at Macomb.

Through her insights, we learned more about how racism shaped the issues that Detroit students experienced at the college. In their K–12 experience, few Detroit students encountered white students in their classes, and there was relatively minimal contact with white teachers and administrators. Their experiences made them unprepared to be inserted into the primarily white institution such as Macomb, let alone dealing with the specific racist practices that many of our staff often unconsciously exhibited. Since most of these students found the South Campus closer to Detroit, there was a greater concentration of Detroit Promise students at South Campus. This development was immediately stereotyped inside the college, referring to South Campus as "the ghetto campus." I was able to convene a task force led by some of our best faculty and administrators who took on these perceptions just as I was retiring from the institution. Their report produced some important empirical information on the condition of our diversity efforts and concluded: "Diversity and inclusion programs exist relatively independent of each other, as one respondent described 'with limited institutional oversight and direction by the college.'" This issue will continue to constrain student success efforts at the college and will not disappear without the intentional efforts of the leadership and staff at the institution.[7]

Many faculty recognized the growing diversity of the college and, on their own, formed the Macomb Multicultural Initiative (MMI) to promote diversity and inclusion projects. I strongly supported their activities and gave them time at faculty and staff meetings to discuss their projects. Out of this work, the college also developed a new organization, "Safe Macomb," for LGBTQ students. These were important recognitions of the diversity of the student body, and I was heartened to learn many of the newer faculty were taking the lead in these developments.

A New Program: Community Leadership

Finally, in a curriculum area I considered very important for the future of community college activities, we created a new community leadership certificate embedded within our sociology curriculum. Community leadership is an area I believe will be an emerging feature that distinguishes community colleges from other postsecondary institutions. Community colleges enjoy the unique advantage of having almost all of their graduates return to the same communities in which the colleges serve. This distinction has made them a key to community economic and workforce development strategies. Why shouldn't that be extended to civic participation and community leadership? Community college students could become a key resource for the creation of leaders for community organizations, semi-governmental bodies, and advisory boards. It might also be a pathway to a political career. We were fortunate to have an outstanding faculty member in the sociology area, Rochelle Zaranek, who over the years had developed relationships with community-based organizations within the Detroit area for class projects. She used these connections to help create a program where students were able to experience on-the-job learning experiences that would eventually lead to placement in these organizations. These students would receive a degree from Macomb and their credits transferred to social work programs at Wayne State University in Detroit.

I witnessed the power of this approach on student learning firsthand through one of Rochelle's activities. Every year, Rochelle took students on field trips during our Spring break as part of her courses. These were not vacations; the students went to low-income communities to perform necessary community work, maintaining food pantries or helping build houses. After Katerina, she took a group of students to help rebuild houses in the New Orleans' Ninth Ward as part of the recovery process. Since I was attending a community college conference in New Orleans the week she was there with her students, I asked her if I could visit the site where the students were working.

She provided me with the address of the house they were rebuilding. When I gave this address to the cab driver at my hotel, he shook his head, saying no one lived in this area; I must have the wrong address. When I insisted, he drove me to the address and was amazed to find this group of fifteen students working on reconstructing the house. It turned out that before Katrina, the cab driver lived a few blocks away from this house they were reconstructing. So, for the next 40 minutes, he stayed with the students, talked about growing up in the Ninth Ward, and what happened when Katrina struck. This was a learning experience in sociology, economics, and racism that no textbook or classroom experience could replicate. It reinforced my view that community leadership and civic participation programs are powerful new contributions that community colleges can make to their students and their communities.

Importance of the Faculty

While my original focus was with the areas I knew well—workforce development and economic development—the real test for me was going to be what changes I could induce in what used to be called the "center of the institution"—the credit instructional areas. While much of the guided pathways approach emphasizes the intake and counseling process for students, ultimately, the classroom experience is the most critical interaction of any community college student. If we were going to make any serious change at the institution, it would require faculty support and participation.

My experience over forty years ago in Basic Education taught me that systemic changes in credit instruction would be a difficult task. There were great teachers at Macomb and very few poor instructors. Most teaching was performed by very capable people who made their own decisions on how and what they taught. They were happy to consider new teaching pedagogies, course curriculum changes, or any other proposals the administration wanted to make, *as long as they were not mandated*. For most of the instructional staff, they believed the institution was not broken, so why try and make major changes. The only time serious discussions of curriculum and teaching values were held in the liberal arts classes was when faculty discussed textbook selection and attempts to introduce new courses or programs.

Any strategy to develop a more aggressive role with the faculty had to cross this line of how much was left to faculty professional choice and how much could be mandated by the administration. Unlike many other presidents who believed faculty should only concentrate on what goes on in the classroom and leave the rest of the college to others, I knew that any changes I would make at Macomb must have the support of the faculty. This was not a philosophical issue, but a practical reality. Both research on student perceptions of community colleges and my own practical experience indicated that community college students trust the faculty more than any other group on the campus to inform them about institutional policies. Since students spend so little time on the campus, the faculty is their main source of information. If we introduced non-classroom activities to help with student success, such as the food pantries, writing centers, or our strategic student aid fund, they would only be successful if faculty supported them and encouraged students to utilize them.

This meant faculty needed to be actively involved in promoting institutional student success priorities. But I wanted to add another dimension. While the primary role of community college faculty was instruction, I believed as part of this role they needed to become experts in the teaching and learning of community college students. This didn't mean engaging in academic research or authoring publications. But it did mean becoming knowledgeable in the pedagogical issues related to their field and also the use of various instructional modalities for the successful instruction of working-class and poor people. They needed to be professional experts on the hardest-to-serve students with the goal of making sure everyone in their classes finishes. Community colleges are not research institutions, but we should expect faculty to become practitioner experts on how to engage and teach students who may not have encountered a positive educational experience before. Our mission should be to ensure that all students can be successful. That should be the guiding principle of the faculty at a community college. While I was never able to meet my goal of redefining the role of faculty, we did take some initial steps.

Utilizing this perspective, we started by looking at the data we possessed on student behavior. While Macomb had many graduates—more than any other community college in Michigan—the rate of students who attended and dropped out without receiving any credential was over 60 percent. Perhaps more damaging, the college participated in a student survey done through the Community College Survey of Student Engagement (CCSSE) based in Austin, Texas, and the results indicated shallow levels of student learning activities. A minority of students reported they engaged in active class participation, paper writing, or team projects, suggesting the traditional style of teaching (known as "the sage on the stage") was still all too typical at the college. We took those survey results, coupled them with our empirical data on the limited success of our students, and identified them as institutional priorities that we discussed regularly in meetings with the faculty, hoping this would stimulate change.

We also tried to aid faculty by addressing some of the skill deficiencies of students by using interventions outside the classroom. In discussing the needs, the faculty identified writing as one of the most important learning skills that applied to all subjects in our curriculum. Along with mathematics, writing papers was an area most students struggled with and, if possible, tried to avoid. However, being able to write either research papers, fiction, or simple descriptive narratives was one of the central skills contributing to increasing their metacognition skills. If you know how to write, you will have the confidence to take many difficult curriculum courses. With this in mind, we initiated a writing center at both major campuses as part of our Achieving the Dream reforms. My colleagues in Basic Education had established a writing center years ago staffed by students who would help other students with their writing. It was only marginally funded and depended on a good deal of volunteer work. I was now in a position to make this concept a more permanent operation.

We hired a person who had worked at writing centers at the four-year level to help establish our efforts. She developed a writing center on each major campus and hired a group of writing coaches who would meet with students and help them with class writing and research assignments. We encouraged our faculty to encourage students they thought could use writing help to make an appointment at the centers. We opened the centers in 2015, and there was an immediate response—over 3,000 students met with our coaches during the first year of operation. The centers also served to confront the view, often held by students and some faculty, that "writing" was a skill only taught in English classes.[8]

In addition to the writing centers, I initiated a Faculty Innovation program that provided institutional funds for faculty to develop practical innovations in their classes. It was designed to encourage collaborations between faculty members, often from different disciplines. The first few years produced exciting collaborations. Physics and childcare instructors produced a "toolkit" for childcare centers that used physics principles to develop preschool activities. A group of biology instructors developed a new curriculum for wastewater treatment in Lake St. Clair. Marketing instructors developed a teaching kit for their students to start their own businesses. These were positive projects that promoted change in many of the existing programs. Unfortunately, they were primarily initiated and utilized by the same creative faculty that the college could depend on for introducing any new ideas and concepts to students. Even though we promoted the program and held an award event where other faculty could see and hear about them, we were still not very successful in getting a majority of faculty to participate.

While the Faculty Innovation awards were a partial success, they went to only full-time faculty. The faculty group that most needed a connection to the institution was the part-time instructors. Macomb, like most community colleges, was highly dependent upon part-time faculty. In 2008, when I began as president, about half the credit classes were taught by part-time faculty. They were in a separate union from the full-time faculty, and not only under-compensated but shut out of any decisions on books, curricular topics or issues, or the scheduling of classes. Those areas were exclusively the right of the full-time faculty. In addition, part-time faculty had no access to many of the college's staff development functions and were often hired right before classes began, so their ability to control their teaching schedules was always tentative until the last minute. The failure to integrate part-time faculty into the student success activities of the institution was a significant barrier to any effort to change teaching and learning at Macomb.

In liberal arts areas, such as English, psychology, and counseling, the part-time teaching staff outnumbered the full-time staff. This reliance on part-timers was especially true during the 2008–2010 period when enrollment increased substantially. While there has been a great deal written about part-time faculty, few researchers or policy individuals have recognized how very diverse a group they are. There were part-time faculty, many in the occupational areas, who enjoyed teaching a course each semester and were content to remain part-time. Many were paid far more in their private sector employment than their community college wages. There were others, however, who taught primarily in the liberal arts areas and whose goal was to become a full-time faculty member at a college. This would not only increase their wages but give them fringe benefits, something many strongly desired.[9]

As president, I knew their significance to our institution and wanted to substantially increase their role in the instructional process. During my time as president, they joined the American Federation of Teachers in a separate local. The full-time instructors did not want them in their local for fear of being outnumbered. As president, I bargained a contract with the part-time faculty that included for the first time funds for their professional development. They were also encouraged to attend faculty events and participate in the monthly union meetings. We also organized an annual evening event for part-time faculty, where awards were given for their service, which many occupational part-time faculty appreciated. Still, these gains were marginal. Part-time faculty remained as second-class citizens at the college without many of the benefits of full-time employment.

Good teaching was a skill that needed to be mastered. However, in the past there was little intervention by the administration to encourage good practices of teaching and curriculum development; these were always left to the faculty to make their own individual decisions. Years before, a Center for Teaching and Learning (which was established by some of my Basic Education colleagues) enjoyed token administrative support. The Center's activities to stimulate creative teaching and learning were considered by most of the staff as a boutique program. It was maintained and open to all, but it did not challenge or disrupt the traditional assumption that left these practices up to the individual faculty. The Center's existence gave the appearance of innovation and change, while not disrupting the traditional perspectives held by many of the teaching staff.

However, before I became president and through the collective-bargaining process, a fuller, mandatory version of a Center for Teaching and Learning was developed for all new faculty. Known as the Faculty Academy, all newly hired full-time faculty were required to attend. This was a one-year program of monthly meetings for new faculty to learn about the goals and mission of the institution, develop their teaching skills around this mission, and collaborate with other faculty across disciplinary lines. Originally, this was a one-year activity, but I extended this to a two-year experience. In the second year, each new faculty member was expected to develop a capstone or applied project designating a new approach to curriculum or teaching methods that was presented at the last meeting of the Academy. I made sure to attend this session to emphasize the significance of these activities to the future instruction at the college. For example, one new accounting instructor developed a software application where students could follow his topics using their cell phones. Another faculty member in health care developed a new system for gathering data on student performance at their "practicum" of hospital work experience. I regretted that the Faculty Academy was limited to only new full-time faculty—and excluded part-time faculty, who often provided the bulk of classroom instruction.

Finally, our counselors were in the same union as the full-time faculty, although their workload was a daily full-time schedule. The counselor role was to aid students in program selection and completion of degrees or certificates. There were far too few counselors, and as a result, they often saw students only for extremely limited amounts of time. Given the significant number of programs and courses, as well as the always-changing relationships between the community college and the four-year programs, there were significant gaps of knowledge within the counselor ranks. The result was conflicting messages to students depending on which counselor they saw and often inaccurate messages, particularly about transfer and nonacademic student services. Of all areas of the college, our internal student surveys rated the counseling services as the most in need of change. We brought in a University of Michigan School of Education research team who interviewed our students, and they found as follows: "Students generally expressed a desire for advising sessions that were more tailored to their needs and interests. Students were frustrated by meetings with advisors whom they felt did not have specific information about their programs or occupational interests."[10] These broad criticisms of Macomb's counseling and student services unit were common to most community colleges. Students always rated this area the lowest regarding being helpful to their efforts. This is an area where AI applications could be extremely useful for ensuring that accurate information is conveyed to both students and counselors before they meet to discuss a student's academic plan.

Cultural Activities at the College

To both stimulate student participation at the college, as well as help connect Macomb County to regional cultural activities, I tried to connect the college to the cultural life of the Detroit metropolitan area. Among the major regional cultural institutions, it was well-known that Macomb residents had low participation rates in organizations such as the Detroit Institute of Arts (DIA), the Detroit Symphony (DSO), or the Michigan Opera Theatre. Part of this can be attributed to the conscious isolation of Macomb County from Detroit during the expansion years of the county. Few leaders from Macomb County played any leadership roles in these organizations. When I was an instructor, I required my students to go to the DIA, but I was forced to make this a non-mandatory assignment when some students complained that their husbands refused to let them attend because they feared being sent to Detroit. However, part of the isolation was also caused by the substantial anti-working-class bias of these same cultural institutions that tended to stereotype the county as a cultural wasteland. They rarely marketed their activities in the county or promoted ties with any institutions in the county that might be supportive of their efforts.

I was determined to change both of these perspectives by developing sustained ties with regional cultural organizations and encouraging them to focus their outreach efforts at the college and Macomb County residents. At our Cultural Center, we were the first institution in the county to display artwork loaned from the Detroit Institute of Arts in Macomb County. The DIA had its own reasons for developing a better relationship with Macomb County, and we were able to leverage their interest and promote our own close ties. In a future chapter, I will discuss some of these relationships more thoroughly.

In 2011, after the Detroit Symphony Orchestra (DSO) settled a six-month strike, we invited the orchestra to perform at our Macomb Center for the Performing Arts to welcome them back into our community. We held a reception for the musicians and their conductor, and I think they were somewhat surprised by the positive audience response they received. Some of the Macomb staff brought their children who were learning to play musical instruments in their public school programs to meet with the musicians for advice.

While greater regional participation was one of my goals, I wanted to initiate cultural themes that would appeal to working-class audiences. In 2012, we were able to host a new opera called *The Forgotten*, which was about the 1932 event known as the Ford Hunger March, where thousands of unemployed auto workers marched against Ford Motor Company with the goal of getting jobs back and securing support for unemployment and health care, among other demands. Though it started peacefully, it ended violently. In the end, four workers were murdered by the police. Given the economic conditions in the county as a result of the Great Recession and the significance of the auto industry, I thought this would be of interest to the college and the community. We tried to promote this opera to many of the local unions in the county. *The Forgotten* performed to a sellout crowd at the Macomb Center for the Performing Arts, and I am sure many union members who attended had never been to an opera before.

When the Michigan Opera Company decided to perform *Frida*, an opera about the Mexican artist Frida Kahlo, the director of the opera selected our Performing Arts Center as one of the two sites to host a performance. He was a strong advocate of community participation and thought we could be a good site for the opera. We publicized the event regionally and attracted an audience from other parts of the Detroit area, surprising many of the traditional arts patrons from Oakland County with our programs. These activities refuted the widely held belief that cultural activities in the county were limited to bowling tournaments, karaoke bars, and mud wrestling. Our Performing Arts Center director, Christine Guarino, was making us a regional center for cultural activities.

In advocating for the ties with the regional Detroit cultural organizations, I had to be careful not to neglect our local poets, performers, and artists. There was a Macomb Symphony Orchestra that regularly performed at the Performing Arts Center. The Macomb Arts Center in Mt. Clemens played a role with the K–12 school districts in the county, and we tried to collaborate with these institutions as much as we could. These efforts were important internally at Macomb because, a few years before, the college terminated the theater program, leaving many staff assuming there was no role for the arts at the College.

I took some initial steps by encouraging the arts faculty to place student artwork all over each campus. I decorated my office with this artwork—regularly changing it—making one of the maintenance employees the "curator" of my collection, a role he took very seriously, often commenting on the artwork as he aligned the paintings on my office walls. I also discovered one of our college police officers was a local artist and I made sure his work was always displayed in my office. One of my former students M. L. Liebler was the poet laureate of St. Clair Shores. M. L. developed high school student poetry groups that integrated poems with music. His communication style and enthusiasm for students' work made him a great advocate for the arts. At my investiture, he created a special poem for the event. Every year I invited M. L. during National Poetry Week to perform at both major campuses. He always wanted to teach full-time at Macomb, but because his degree was not in English (his was in creative writing), some of the English faculty blocked his job application, maintaining he was unqualified. Even though I respected the union contract, in retrospect, I wondered if I should have forced this issue or found some way to get him hired full-time.

I also tried somewhat unsuccessfully to bridge a cultural gap concerning what was considered "art" within our institution. I wanted to develop a broader perspective that integrated some of our technical programs as "working class art." The digital design program at the college had for years produced exciting digital artwork and computer illustrations which were largely unknown outside of the technical complex on South Campus. To bring attention to these productions and highlight industrial art, I invited my friend Joe Blum, who spent almost ten years photographing the construction of the new East Span of the San Francisco-Oakland Bay Bridge to display his work at the college. Blum was a retired shipyard welder and his photographs (pictures often taken while he was climbing the bridge towers) revealed the beauty and grandeur of construction work. We enlarged his photographs and organized an exhibit in our Technical Complex at South Campus. These were displayed in large steel frames, appropriately made by our welding students. Joe came to our opening of the exhibition and spoke about the construction of the bridge to a community forum. This was an initial attempt to seek collaboration between fine art culture and technology art culture, but I was unable to get traction internally to continue this work.

I also highlighted some local history through an exhibition of an important private educational institution created within the auto industry. In 1916, Henry Ford developed his own educational institution—the Henry Ford Trade School. While the name suggests solely a vocational perspective, the instruction at the Trade School was much more. Students from low-income backgrounds, often orphans, were selected and given a broad education, including arts, sports, and cultural activities. Despite Ford's well-known antisemitic, racist, and anti-union views, they did not seep into the curriculum of the Trade School.[11]

In many ways, by integrating technical education with the liberal arts, the Henry Ford Trade School was a precursor to the modern community college. I had an opportunity to celebrate the Henry Ford Trade School because one of the oldest living graduates who founded a successful machine tool company lived in Macomb County. We put on an exhibition at our cultural center and honored his role and the role of the Trade School in the economic and cultural history of the Detroit region.

Despite these initial steps, my concept of working-class art was never developed sufficiently to win over any of the staff or local cultural institutions to initiate activities. Talent in the arts should never be seen as something distant or only the purview of the "professionals." It should be a part of everyday life, and the community college is a perfect place to establish this perspective.

Staff Contributions: Veterans Day

In addition to my initiatives, I wanted to respond to the interests of the staff, especially since my goal was to energize them into contributing to change at the college. In my first year as president, one of the information technology technicians, who provided computer support for me, asked why the college was not organizing any events for Veterans Day. He was a Vietnam War veteran and believed many others on the staff who served in the military would appreciate this recognition. While a Veterans Day celebration was not something I had considered, his suggestion made me realize we had never recognized the many veterans who were working at the college. I told him to form a committee of veterans to plan next year's Veterans Day celebration. Not only did the group put together an impressive ceremony with music and all branches of the armed forces represented by our staff veterans, resplendent with matching jackets, but they also initiated a brilliant new program to have staff veterans serve as mentors for the current student veterans returning from service in Iraq and Afghanistan.

I am certain that other staff had ideas for making the institution more responsive to the students and the community, but these never reached me. The idea for a Veterans Day celebration came because this individual had regular interactions with me and was not reluctant to voice his suggestions. Despite my belief that I was open to new ideas and suggestions, in retrospect, I probably had not sufficiently created that climate for staff to advance their ideas. One of the downsides of my attempts to implement my own programs is that I was not encouraging others enough to step up with their suggestions.

I continued a Macomb tradition of having lunch with all newly hired full-time college employees—whatever their role—once a semester. We also held regular staff recognition luncheons for all employees who had ten, twenty, and thirty years of seniority at the college. These events allowed me to interact with staff and speak directly about the significance of their efforts to the students and community. These luncheons helped me emphasize my message that everyone at the institution is important to the success of the students. Many of the faculty assumed they were the institution's center and that everyone else was less important. In reality, the clerical, technical, police, and maintenance workers play considerable roles in the institution and need to be acknowledged and recognized for their importance. In an organization of 2,000 employees spread over four campuses, continued successful communication of my agenda was important. I learned that repeating your vision, even utilizing the exact same language each time, was an important signal that we were going to be consistent in making sure our strategic plans would be followed.

While I do not regret my decision not to reorganize the college or substantially change the staff roles, I did underestimate the time it took to convince them of the need for change. In other areas not connected with the instructional process, but still critical to student success, we were able to initiate changes more quickly. We strengthened our financial aid system, reducing wait times for providing aid, and integrated those results into our registration process. We also clarified our data collection in these areas to obtain real-time statistics on enrollment processes and financial aid. We overhauled our human relations area and updated our hiring processes and medical insurance practices, which saved considerable money for the college. We also initiated a new education fund for any full-time Macomb employee who wished to advance their postsecondary degrees. We developed new approaches to internet access for students and staff. Our institutional researchers were able to work with fellow researchers from the University of Michigan and the Community College Research Center on important projects that resulted in redesigning some of our counseling and academic advising. All these projects were essential changes to our internal processes. Though they took months of work to develop and implement, overall, they resulted in Macomb becoming a more effective and efficient institution.

Delayed Opportunities

The activities discussed above were those I was able to at least start. I had other ideas I never implemented, but they may stimulate readers of this book to consider them in their efforts.

Our inability to offer more benefits to part-time faculty was a major concern for me. Many of these faculty, particularly in the liberal arts areas, were teaching at other colleges in the region. One of my long-term goals for part-time faculty was to convert them into "full-time" instructors by aggregating the teaching they did in the region. This could be accomplished if regional colleges could pool their part-time instructor lists, come up with a common set of fringe benefits and procedures for those who were teaching an equivalent of a full load, and then offer them to their eligible part-time teachers, so long as they remained teaching a full load. Establishing this would present some logistical challenges for the colleges, but it might help us recruit and retain a talented group of part-time instructors we could all share. I raised this collaborative approach to hire and support part-time instructors with my fellow presidents at one of our luncheons, but most other presidents thought it unworkable.

Another idea I considered to support the hiring of full time teachers was the adoption of a semi-apprenticeship system. Consistent with my belief that teaching was a skill learned within the context of the institution's goals and mission, Macomb would hire graduate students in specific disciplines as "teaching aides" for our full-time instructors. The specific disciplines targeted would be those where full-time faculty were close to retirement and enrollment was substantial. As paid "apprentices," they would work with our current instructors and become familiar with our instructional culture in preparation for potential full-time employment. When openings occurred in these areas, their participation as apprentices would give them a significant advantage in the selection process.

This approach had two major benefits. It would minimize one of the biggest wastes of time and effort for all postsecondary institutions, namely the faculty search process. Typically, this process takes months to complete and is often very costly. Many college resources are spent bringing in candidates, and searches require what seem like an endless number of meetings that tie up faculty and administrative time, representing many hours of effort that could and should be spent more productively by serving our students' needs. It also would provide far more relevant and real information on the abilities of candidates that go far beyond what curriculum vitae, teaching philosophies, interviews, and even teaching demonstrations can provide. The experience would benefit the apprentices as well, given that they would get a real feel for what we are like as a college and the students we serve to determine if we are a good fit for them. In short, as apprentices, they would really get to know the institution, and we would also get a fuller picture of their capabilities. While this concept seemed utopian, in a sense it would only legitimize what is already happening in many disciplines at the college: full-time hires typically started as part-time instructors. I did raise this concept with some administrators at Wayne State University to see if we could pilot the concept with their graduate programs, but we were never able to get past the talking stage. In addition, our full-time faculty union was apprehensive.

Building an Alumni Base

While large community colleges like Macomb have a significant number of graduates, we always struggled with how to maintain ties with them as alumni. There were over 150,000 Macomb alumni living within 25 miles of our campuses, many of whom were playing significant roles as employers or administrators of companies. While their financial contributions to our Foundation were always welcomed, their importance to our students' employment opportunities might be even more significant. I learned that in many occupational areas our students (with assistance from the faculty) formed their own networks to further their occupational career interests. Our veterinary tech instructor formed an association of alumni and current students from the vet tech program that would meet monthly with speakers to discuss their work and raise money for scholarships. Many of our autobody design students from their cooperative education experience formed their own organization that helped each other in searching for employment. Students in our information technology programs developed a specific computer laboratory for students with disabilities (which included many injured police officers or military veterans) to master IT skills to get them employment in sustainable-wage jobs. It was the relationship to occupational employment that created the bond between the students and the college.

Organizing students around their employment interests would also open up an unexplored area of community college work—alumni interactions with the college. Rarely do community colleges follow up with alumni in any organized fashion. Few business or community leaders mention their community college attendance in their biographies. Many elected officials who attended community colleges never mention their background unless it is on a community college campus. However, if community college completers were organized around their career aspirations, they might remain more attached to their institution and support our efforts at fundraising and securing employment for our students. As our alumni advance in their jobs, they can provide openings for other students. Many Macomb cooperative education program students were employed in companies by Macomb co-op alums who now held management positions.

Cultivating "good friends in low places" was essential for connecting the college to employers. Especially in careers that would retain students within the local and regional economy, it seems like a worthy investment for community colleges to maintain groups of alumni organized around their programs that lead to employment. This perspective would have taken the college into new ground by establishing a new linkage between the college and alumni. It would also have helped focus the institution on employment and extend our reach beyond completing a program. Unfortunately, while this was on my agenda, I was never able to provide the resources necessary to expand this new dimension of work.

What I Learned

After my first year, I gained more confidence in my organizational leadership skills. I had no formal education or training in management, but through my experience and education, I cobbled together some bits and pieces from eclectic sources that seemed to work. I was impressed as an undergraduate reading a book by Richard Neustadt titled *Presidential Power*, which argued that the president's power was not in the office's title or authority but in the power to persuade others to do what the president wanted. I always remembered this insight because it suggested that commanding something to happen was ineffective—the real power of leaders was to use their position to persuade others to support their perspective.[12] How well you understand your role as a "persuader" (and can organize your time and focus on it) is a critical element for a successful presidency.

Of course, the ability to persuade takes on particular importance in a unionized situation such as Macomb. It was important for me to make sure all the union leadership understood the career pathway approach; we always talked about it at our monthly meetings. My goal was to have at least the faculty unions support the initiative and have the other unions seek to understand the approach. Every year we had a Staff Development Day for the entire institution. I used that opportunity to make sure that our general approach to change at the institution was always emphasized. The regarded union support for these initiatives was important for their success. For me, this meant constantly attempting to motivate the college staff to increase their efforts at student success. Most people working at community colleges wanted students to succeed. They also took pride in their work, knowing that what the institution did mattered to the community. My task was to continue to persuade them that my strategies would help students and the community be successful. The biggest obstacle I often faced was their own underestimation of the value of the community college and their own work. Many staff, even those who had attended Macomb, believed our role was important but not as significant as a four-year institution or even other public institutions in their community, such as police and fire services. Many did not recognize how vital the work of community colleges is for not only the students' futures but for their communities. Part of this may be traced to their own background coming from working-class families. They didn't think what they were doing was that important. However, one of my primary tasks was to get the staff to recognize their own importance to Macomb County, and when working with other community colleges, their significance to the nation. Community college staff do not realize the importance of their work, and a major effort of any president should be to continually remind them of their own importance to the students and the community,

Finally, I tried a new approach to introducing the college to more cultural events by merging some of the classic formats of music and art with a more technical working-class perspective. My goal was to create within the college the perception that culture was not something alien to working-class life but an important aspect. By encouraging themes which I believed were relevant, I hoped to infuse a different perspective. Unfortunately, this remains a work in progress but a theme that community colleges should address in the future.

But there is also a limitation of being a leader when you are not connecting the dots between the programs you are initiating. Although I did not realize it at the time, my own strategy of creating many new projects simultaneously may not have been very helpful in achieving my overall goal of institutional change. In my first four years as president, I pushed too many specific initiatives and failed to develop a consistent thread in them. I had hoped that through the actions of the work some of the common elements would emerge. I believed this was the process of a total transformation, but for the staff, it appeared more as a blizzard of individual activities without a clear vision guiding them. This was an error. I depended too much on staff to instinctively put these pieces together and see the commonality of these activities. I should have been more intentional and linked the different activities together. Instead of viewing these developments as a new strategic vision for the college, they seemed to be many different programs independent from one another. In addition, many of these initiatives were short-lived or came off the rails when we could not continue the work because of a lack of resources or staff. I resisted going slower because I knew my tenure would be brief. In retrospect, I should have taken that road and very consciously found someone who could succeed me committed to the same general perspective. In retrospect, I also regret that I did not meet collectively with the campus leaders in many of these individual initiatives to have them collaborate and reinforce positive changes. A good college president should be able to link the activities together into a comprehensive vision and plan for the staff. They may not agree with all the activities, but they will at least see the relationship between them and the vision the college leader puts forth for the institution.

Despite these regrets, many of the activities I initiated are still embedded within the culture of the institution. In the past year, I was a consultant on a project regarding the community development efforts of rural community colleges. At one of the project conferences, there was a presentation made by a Macomb staff member on how the college dealt with financial issues affecting low-income students. The work was based on the S.O.S. program we launched in 2010. It made me proud that some of the things I initiated not only endured but grew and were recognized nationally as significant contributions to the work of community colleges.

Notes

1 Bailey et al.. In 2025, CCRC published a sequel to this work which builds upon this original work. See Davis Jenkins, Hana Lahr, John Fink, Serena C. Klempin, and Maggie P. Fay, *More Essential Than Ever: Community College Pathways to Educational and Career Success* (Harvard University Press, 2025).

2 Bailey et al., 81.

3 In CCRC's new book, *More Essential Than Ever*, the authors argue that community colleges, including those that have implemented aspects of guided pathways, continue to struggle to

effectively move the needle to support student success and close equity gaps (Jenkins et al., *More Essential Than Ever*). For the most up-to-date CCRC research on the pathway approach, visit https://ccrc.tc.columbia.edu/research/guided-pathways.html.

4   Data are from James Jacobs, Economic Forecast 2009, Macomb County, Michigan.

5   For a seminal work on the topic of student success and the college experience, see George D. Kuh, Jillian Kinzie, John H. Schuh, and Elizabeth J. Whitt, *Student Success in College: Creating Conditions that Matter* (Jossey-Bass, 2005).

6   One of the most revealing enrollment statistics we maintained at Macomb was the conversion rate; that is, the rate of students who submitted an application at Macomb and then actually went through the enrollment process. For white students, we were able to convert 55 percent of those who applied. For Black students, it was only 27 percent.

7   "Report on Diversity and Inclusion at Macomb Community College" (Macomb Community College, 2016).

8   An analysis of the student records of those who utilized the writing centers indicated, "The greater use of the RSW (Reading and Writing Studios), the greater the semester GPA." See Brett Griffiths, Randall Hickman, and Sebastian Zollner, "Institutional Assessment of a Genre-Analysis Approach to Writing Center Consultations," *Praxis: A Writing Center Journal* 15, no. 1 (2017): 5.

9   The concerns of part-time faculty are one of the major issues in all community colleges. See Susan Bickerstaff and Octaviano Chavarín, *Understanding the Needs of Part-Time Faculty at Six Community Colleges* (Community College Research Center, 2018).

10   Kelly Slay and Rebecca Christensen, *Adult Learners at Macomb: A Qualitative Analysis of Current and Prospective Students' Experiences* (Center for the Study of Higher and Postsecondary Education, School of Education, University of Michigan, 2015), 4.

11   For a discussion of Henry Ford Trade School and its curriculum see Samuel Gaft, "The History of the Henry Ford Trade School, 1916 to 1952" (EdD thesis, University of Michigan, 1998).

12   Richard E. Neustadt, *Presidential Power: The Politics of Leadership* (Science Editions, 1962).

9 The College in the Community

One major responsibility of a community college president is to promote the institution within the community. A defining characteristic of many American community colleges is their relationship to the specific jurisdictional areas that often provide local financial support. Unlike most four-year institutions that rarely are constrained by geographic boundaries, the relationship between a community college and its district is highly concentrated within a well-defined and popularly understood location. In Michigan, the governing authority of a community college (usually known as the Board of Trustees) is elected by citizens of the college district. In other states, board members are appointed by the governor, but their job is similar to elected boards—to ensure the college understands and aims to meet the needs of the community.

In general, citizens expect their community college not just to educate them but to play a role in their community. This can mean anything from holding community events at the facilities of the college; citizen use of the library, theater, and physical education facilities; college support for community activities, like food drives; becoming a site for disaster drills; and holding cultural events and exhibits for the community. In Michigan, property taxes are, in part, determined by what are called millage rates. Local services, such as libraries, parks, K–12 schools, and community colleges, rely on millages for much of their funding. Millage rates are determined directly by voters in each district. In my experience, it was clear that the presence of a local property millage to support a community college meant for many in the community that the community college was *their* institution. For example, I was regularly contacted by citizens who thought we should be more frequently mowing the lawns of the campus. One Macomb state representative would show up unannounced on campus to check on the cleanliness of our Student Activities Building. Anyone who seeks a presidency should anticipate spending a good part of their time at community meetings, events, and other activities. A successful president must feel comfortable within their community. Those who are out of sync with their communities will not be very effective or last long at the institution.

This close connection between the college and the community is even more pronounced in states like Michigan, where the institutions are governed exclusively by locally elected trustees. Boards of trustees have the power to set tuition, sign off on new college programs, and control institutional wages and working conditions. Since each Michigan community college was created through voter support of a local initiative and the boards are elected by the community, the twenty-eight community colleges in Michigan are under no formal regulation from the state. Other than receiving an annual state appropriation and support for major construction projects, community colleges in Michigan rely minimally on the state. That fact makes them some of the most independent and autonomous community colleges in the country.

The importance of community is especially significant in Macomb County, as the college continues to be its only local postsecondary institution. There is a strong presence of the college in the lives of Macomb citizens. Of the almost 800,000 residents in Macomb County, in 2008, we estimated about 30 percent of those over 18 had attended Macomb Community College. Virtually every family in the county had someone or knew someone who attended the college.

Especially in metropolitan areas, however, the de jure definition of educational institution's delivery area rarely matches the de facto reality of its impact in the community. Many citizens live and work in different places. Over 100,000 residents of Macomb County worked in Wayne or Oakland County. For the college to promote opportunity for our students, we needed to understand and sometimes play a role in the workforce and economic development of the region.

The Macomb Context

Given the specific history of the college, developing a regional role for Macomb Community College was particularly challenging. The college and the county grew up simultaneously in the 1960s, and they shared a common understanding of the mission of the institution and how it fit within the context of the community. Many educational leaders who founded the college were also leaders in the community during its significant demographic and economic growth. They wanted the college to be "theirs" and not be dependent upon any other institutions of higher learning in the region. Many believed the college would naturally evolve from a community college to a four-year institution. While the college admitted anyone who wanted to enroll, there were different tuition fees for "non-residents," that is, people not living within the service district area. Of course, as the racial dynamics of the region unfolded in the 1960s, there was even greater concern that Macomb County and the college maintain their separation from the rest of the region.

In dealing with the community, I had some significant advantages, but also some liabilities. I had spent over forty years in the community, so I knew it well and had already established ties with many of the leaders and important organizations. There was no need for a learning curve. On the other hand, I had spent forty years working, trying to get the college and students more involved in the region, and dealing with issues of income equality, opposing racism, and supporting collaboration across county lines. I used my Economic Forecast event to denounce local isolation and racist views as not helpful for regional activities and had clashed with some Macomb local leaders over their refusal to collaborate on regional activities, such as the development of a regional mass transportation system.

In addition, much of my earlier "relations with the community" activities were outside the institution, including organizing anti-war protests and encouraging youth activism at high schools, of which many of the senior Macomb leaders were undoubtedly aware but never brought up after I became president. Even my firing from the college was erased from local memory. When I was introduced at events, my earlier years were overlooked and what was emphasized was my involvement with the Industrial Technology Institute and the Community College Research Center. Instead of being a "radical," now I was bringing a certain "prestige" to the county with these associations. Even though I never hid my upbringing in Brooklyn, New York, or my current residence in Grosse Pointe, I was generally accepted as a "Macomb person." I was respected by the outside world and considered a proponent for the county, particularly because of the reputation of my annual Economic Forecast. I was a "go-to" person on most economic matters in Macomb County for the local media. I am sure many of the local leaders were unhappy with some of my statements to the media, but they also recognized my expertise and rarely contradicted me directly.

Now, as president of this important county institution, how was I going to both represent the interests of the county and stay true to my values and views on aligning the college with elements of change in the region? I knew there were signs the county was shedding some of its isolationist beliefs. Many of the older political leadership who had made an anti-Detroit ideology a fundamental part of their political beliefs had retired or passed away. The growing diversity of the Macomb County population, both with Black residents and new Americans from the Middle East, also helped to expose and curtail any overt racist beliefs—Macomb County was no longer an all-white county. Even my selection as president reflected a shift away from the isolationist perspective. Yet, how was I going to craft a strategy that could position the college to take advantage of these changes? How could I lead Macomb Community College to not only benefit our students but also benefit the community overall and shift the county forward?

Using the Economic Forecast

My initial thought was to continue the annual Economic Forecast as a means of informing and educating the county about the importance of the regional economy to the prosperity of Macomb County. They could not be viewed in isolation. Macomb's economic success was contingent on the success of the metropolitan Detroit area. One of my goals with the Economic Forecast was to paint a different picture of Macomb County than was often held by its leaders, as the numbers of non-white and immigrants continued to increase even during the Great Recession. I maintained a similar narrative about county issues, as discussed in an earlier chapter, but added a section that discussed the initiatives of Mark Hackel, the new County Executive, and his role as a regional leader.

In my Economic Forecast, I always started by defining the significance of the auto industry to Macomb County's future, and how any programs that wanted to support this sector had to be tied to a regional approach. Within that framework, I tried to deal with income inequalities, racism, and anti-Detroit sentiments. I focused on the need for county leadership to deal with the working poor and the significance of education as a gateway to opportunity. The view that the health and welfare of the county could be isolated from the rest of the region was simply untrue. Not only were there about 100,000 Macomb residents commuting to work outside of Macomb County, but every working day over 40,000 people commuted to jobs in Macomb County from Wayne County, and a great many of them were Detroit residents.

In addition, the county was given a new opportunity to play a leadership role in the region. As part of the settlement of the Detroit bankruptcy case, a regional water system was created, known as the Great Lakes Water Authority, which included Macomb County. Along with everyone else in the area, Macomb County representatives were now responsible for the regional water supply. There was no longer an easy means for Macomb politicians to beat up the city of Detroit for any issues with the water system. They were all responsible for the system.

Macomb County's population growth was largely young people with families. The two main sources of this growth were new immigrants to the county and young African American families from Detroit. Welcoming them into Macomb County, I argued, was not just a "nice" thing to do, but essential for the economic and social success of the community. Even though I knew this perspective was unsettling to many Macomb leaders, few openly disagreed with it.

New County and Regional Initiatives

As president, I also wanted to continue utilizing the college in the development of a civic culture in Macomb County. While many of Macomb's communities had local civic organizations, there were few organizations that spoke for the entire county. Clearly, Macomb County was not Detroit, but what were the cultural norms and attitudes that distinguished the county? How would new county leaders identify the strengths, opportunities, weaknesses, and threats to the future of Macomb County?

As one of the largest county-wide organizations, the college could play an important role in the development of a new Macomb County civic culture. Al Lorenzo recognized this, and he helped launch in the 1990s an organization called "Leadership Macomb," which was devoted to the development of young professionals who were living and working in the county. Each year, a "class" of young leaders was exposed to many aspects of Macomb life, including education, criminal justice, the economy, cultural activities, and government in a series of monthly meetings. Most were selected by the leaders of their companies, who paid their tuition to attend. Each year I spoke to them about the economic conditions in the county.[1]

When I became president, I continued to support Leadership Macomb, but along with others, also helped to organize a new group of business and civic leaders named "Advancing Macomb." This was an organization of Macomb leaders who were not elected officials but wanted to promote and support important community activities in the county. It was also designed to seek out new revenue sources from the Detroit area, including from foundations, to support these activities. Advancing Macomb became a much-needed organization that could gain regional visibility for Macomb County. In the past, Macomb County had received little outside support, in large part because non-profit organizations in the county rarely sought out funding. Advancing Macomb became an important collaborator with County Executive Mark Hackel to build recognition of Macomb County as an important part of the region deserving support for local activities.[2]

In the greater Detroit area, there were new coalitions formed between business and community colleges to promote training and education activities. The success of No Worker Left Behind (an initiative that launched in 2007 during the administration of Michigan's governor Jennifer

Granholm) ultimately motivated the Michigan business community to establish with the colleges in the region an organization that could respond to the employment needs of the private sector. This became known as the Workforce Intelligence Network. In addition, the Detroit Regional Chamber of Commerce became the home of "Detroit Drives Degrees," a coalition of four-year and two-year institutions that was designed to increase the number of students completing a four-year degree. Connected with this work, the Chamber had secured funding to launch the Detroit Promise, which provided full tuition for any Detroit Public School graduates at any community college in the region. These developments presented me with opportunities and challenges. Because of its origins, Macomb had always been an institution with significant ties in Macomb County. The college always had a strong and positive presence in the community. However, just as I was assuming the presidency, community involvement needed to be expanded beyond the county and across the region. These were new demands on my time, but they were welcomed because they fit nicely into my regional perspective for the institution.[3]

The Detroit Bankruptcy

Any efforts at developing a regional perspective were confronted with a new reality at that time. Despite the national recovery from the Great Recession, the city of Detroit remained in financial decline. Disinvestment of both residential and retail activities continued. In addition to the declining revenue for the city as a result of lower income and property taxes (a long-term trend since the 1960s), there was a significant growth in city worker pension costs. There were now twice as many pensioners as city employees, accumulating a shortfall of over $1.7 billion. To conserve funds, in 2008, the city had to lay off almost 25 percent of its workforce, resulting in a significant decline in city services. Over 40 percent of the streetlights were not functioning. There were 84,000 blighted homes (one house for every eight residents), and it was estimated that it would take $850 million to clear them away. The elimination of police and fire personnel resulted in Detroit having the poorest response times for first responders than in any other large American city. Finally, a complex financial arrangement negotiated by former mayor Kwame M. Kilpatrick to pay pensioners (which also gave Wall Street significantly high interest rates) was producing further strain on the city's budget.[4]

In 2015, the city was forced to declare bankruptcy—the largest municipality bankruptcy in the history of the United States. The consequences for the region were extremely significant. Just one example of one organization, the Detroit Institute of Arts, faced a major challenge to secure its collection from its creditors, who believed a sale of the collection would bring over $1.8 billion to help settle the bankruptcy. The DIA managed to escape the creditors only through the development of the "grand bargain" by which the DIA was forced to raise $100 million for the eventual settlement. I was on the Board of the DIA during this critical period, and the process of negotiations that produced this resolution was an extraordinary example of regional collaboration. Most leaders recognized the significance of this institution to the entire region.[5]

As mentioned earlier about the economic inter-reliability of the region, the college was affected by Detroit's bankruptcy. Some of our campus police officers were retired Detroit police officers who were now facing significant cuts in their Detroit pensions. The only unintended "positive" consequence of this financial crisis was the continued migration from the city of Black working-class residents to the county. This continued to undermine the racist myth that the suburbs were for white people, and the city would be the home of Black people. The 2020 Census revealed a startling development that almost half of the region's Black population were now residing in the suburbs. The white population in the city increased slightly as a trickle of white artists or cultural workers "discovered Detroit" as a place where housing was cheap, studios in abandoned buildings were plentiful, and enforcement of any city codes or ordinances was slight. Detroit began enjoying a reputation as an emerging cultural center. The college was not directly affected by the financial settlement of the bankruptcy, yet it provided us with a platform to implement real initiatives with our important constituencies to promote economic growth and prosperity for the region. All of these new initiatives were useful for maintaining the visibility of the college in the region, but what does a college do in its operations to promote community collaboration? What specific steps did I take?

Relationships with Other Educational Institutions

The first group I wanted to build relationships with was institutions from the same sector: educators. Traditionally, when educational administrators from different levels meet, the emphasis is usually on enrollment, budgets, and other internal organizational matters. There is often a deferential aspect to these discussions, the K–12 educators on the bottom of the status pecking order, followed by community colleges, the regional public universities, and lastly the major research institutions. There was little discussion of how well we could work together to serve our students who moved through many of these layers of Michigan education, and there was little discussion about better understanding our collective impact on the communities we served. Often, since the public institutions were in part funded by the state, any collaborative approaches to issues rapidly faded away when it came to competing for funding from the Michigan legislature.

I wanted more substantial discussions that focused on what we can do collaboratively to increase student success. Most citizens assume that educators on all levels regularly interact and work together, but that rarely happens. Due to my previous responsibilities with Tech Prep and School to Work programs, I already had some understanding of the issues faced by the K–12 public school districts. I was more empathetic about the difficult conditions they faced and, unconcerned about differences in status, I started to regularly attend the County Superintendents meetings. With their help and the input of the Macomb Intermediate School District, we created the dual enrollment program which became the largest one in Michigan. In addition to the dual enrollment program, we also tried to aid some of their districts with their major concerns of declining enrollment. Many of the older suburban districts adjacent to Detroit were attempting to market and attract Detroit students to their Macomb school districts. We developed specific scholarship programs with local employers to fund students from these districts to attend Macomb.

In dealing with the districts, I stressed that as public educators we all had something in common—the success of our students. I was careful never to initiate blame on their activities for poor test scores and rather aimed to understand and appreciate the difficult role they were playing trying to educate students in a period of significant economic inequality. Indeed, the K–12 districts had substantial interactions with families of their students, and I learned from them about the educational impact on students from families who had been evicted, or those who faced long-term unemployment due to work-related disabilities, or the impact of a divorce on the learning of students. I realized these issues don't suddenly stop when these students register for classes at Macomb, and we were probably less able to cope with them than the public schools. I tried to encourage our academic and occupational units to meet regularly with the K–12 educators. The goal was both to learn about these conditions as well as make sure the K–12 educators learned about our college policies on testing at admissions and changes in our requirements. In turn, we needed to keep up with the continual changes demanded of the K–12 school districts by the Michigan legislature.[6]

Relations with Four-Year Institutions

My relationship with the four-year institutions was somewhat easier because we were both involved in higher education but also complicated by a contentious issue that was initiated by the Michigan community colleges before I became president of Macomb. In 2006, the Michigan Community College Association asked the state legislature to allow community colleges to offer four-year degrees as a means of Increasing enrollment and expanding access to bachelor's degrees for communities, particularly for rural community colleges. One of the major concerns for the colleges was the need to offer four-year degrees in nursing. Because of the increasing hospital demand for nurses with four-year degrees, community colleges were worried their associate's degree programs were in jeopardy. I opposed these efforts and considered them a diversion from the primary task of community colleges, which was to promote student success for people who never thought college was an opportunity. Attempting to add four-year programs not only would subtract resources from this central mission (which no other public higher education entity had as its focus) but also lead us to unending conflict with university transfer partners, ultimately disrupting the transfer process for our students who sought four-year degrees.

My approach to the four-year colleges was to focus on how Macomb Community College could play a role in increasing the number of college graduates with four-year degrees in the Detroit region. I believed, along with many, that the key to success for the region relied heavily on increasing the number of people with bachelor's degrees. We partnered with the Detroit Chamber, Wayne State University, and the University of Michigan-Dearborn to help form an organization named Detroit Drives Degrees. This organization was committed to the development of more individuals with four-year degrees in the region. Instead of seeing ourselves as competitors to these institutions, we could play an important role as collaborators. Part of this process was for them to recognize our significance in encouraging younger students who were unsure or unprepared to be successful in college and serving adult students who needed a four-year degree to increase their opportunities at their current workplace or seek a different job. In these meetings, our partnership grew as we all focused on the development of higher education for the region and serving our students better.[7] In the process, we created a synergetic atmosphere where we discussed teaching and learning issues for our students as they moved from the community college to four-year education.

Regional Community College Activities

I utilized a different strategy to collaborate with the five community colleges in the Detroit metropolitan area. Here I was on more solid ground to urge direct collaborations. For example, a regional perspective would have benefited all of us by reducing our costs. Not all of us had to have expensive culinary arts programs or public service complexes to train police and firefighters. A regional approach would also help us coordinate tuition, enrollment processes, and hiring practices. Yet the presidents of the five institutions rarely, if ever, had gotten together to plan as a regional group. Exacerbating the lack of collaboration was that three of the colleges were located in Wayne County and often were in direct competition recruiting students well beyond their de jure district lines.

To attempt more direct collaboration, I initiated meetings between the presidents of Oakland, Schoolcraft, Henry Ford, and Wayne County Community Colleges. I advanced two specific areas. First, I wanted to see if we could agree to divide up expertise on some of the advanced technologies needed by the auto industry, so one college could specialize and devote resources and equipment that we could all utilize. Second, and as mentioned in an earlier chapter, I was interested in whether we could devise a plan to make the adjuncts we shared full-time employees, so they could qualify for medical and retirement benefits.

While there was some interest, our collaboration rarely went further than a few friendly lunches and some exchange of gossip. I realized that most presidents were attracted to a presidency in Michigan precisely because it allowed them to make decisions independent of any state interference. Institutional autonomy was seen as a plus for them, not a negative. Collaborations interfered with their desire to be independent actors. To be honest, the presidents were also reflecting their trustees. None of these boards, including Macomb, had made regional collaboration an important priority for their institutions.

While my initiatives with my colleagues failed to develop any commitment to regional activities, they did support a more collaborative regional approach to workforce issues through the creation of a new organization that included all the community colleges and the local workforce boards. The Workforce Intelligence Network (WIN) was a practitioner-focused organization of senior college administrators responsible for the workforce development activities at their institutions and the directors of the local workforce development boards. WIN continues to exist, and it effectively obtained large federal grants from the United States Department of Labor and other federal agencies that wanted to support regional efforts.[8]

Employers

Outside of the relations with other educators, the second most important external constituency for the college was employers in the community. Fortunately, my work at ITI and my experience as a board member of a community bank aided me in understanding how distinctly different the culture, language, and decision-making process of employers are compared to those in the higher education sector. I was not intimidated or unsure of myself in our interactions, despite the fact that we came at issues from a very different perspective. First, I recognized how diverse employers were and the need to deeply understand their specific conditions before suggesting working relationships. Our relations with employers were extremely varied, often depending on the market conditions they faced, the technologies they were adapting, and their history and internal organizational culture. It was also influenced by their previous relations with college training activities and their experiences with our students. In these relationships, the geographical location of the companies (i.e., whether they were in our service delivery area or not) was of little concern. We concentrated our outreach efforts at Macomb County employers, and we did have a partnership with the Macomb County Economic Development Department to aid in attracting firms into the county. But what was more critical than geographical closeness was the willingness of the company to take a collaborative approach to partner with us. Our goal was to be more than a training provider, but to seek the participation of the firm in college activities such as program advising, participation in advising parents and students about careers, and material support for our Foundation. And as a college, we wanted to do more than just educate or train students. We wanted to become a validator and supporter of these students as they entered the workplace. Our goal with employers was to develop what I called "relationship education." We wanted a long-term relationship that would be based on our shared interests to promote the community and the students. In some of the specialized areas of manufacturing and health care, we were able to fashion some long-term successful college-employer relationships.

The Welding Girl

Employers were not afraid of evaluating our programs by telling stories of the students who came to work for them. One of my favorites came from an employer who built large steel trailers. He hired workers through direct advertising by placing a sign in front of his shop looking for welders. A young woman applied to be a welder. She had completed a welding program at Macomb Community College. No woman had ever applied for a welding job at his company before, so he was skeptical about her abilities. He gave her a hands-on test of her welding abilities. She not only passed the test but became his very best welder. When I met her, she told me she liked welding and thought it was a great job as she continued her education to be a psychologist. She saw no disconnect between our present work and her future career choice. We immediately introduced "the welding girl" in our foundation fundraising and marketing efforts for our manufacturing program.

In these activities, the size of the company mattered. The college had a long and well-developed relationship with all the domestic OEMs with regular education and training activities. Many of these efforts concentrated on the joint union-management organizations established in the 1980s by collective bargaining between the UAW and domestic OEMs. Through the joint training funds, there were training programs for hourly workers, and the college continued to play a role in their apprenticeship programs. In these relationships, we were considered a valuable vendor to the companies, but we were rarely sought out as a partner for our advice on how they should pursue their training and education activities. The OEMs maintained large training and education departments, and most of their skills needs and educational requirements outside of the obligations within the union contracts were handled by them. The college played more of a supporting role on a contract basis initiated by the companies. In these situations, the training managers from a company were aware of our abilities and sought out partnerships, especially when state funds were available to subsidize the training. Otherwise, there was little other ongoing interaction outside of the customized training and apprenticeship activities.

Institutional relationships within the large companies varied considerably depending upon which part of their organization was involved. We have always had positive relations with the government affairs, corporate human resources, and executive units of the major firms. They expressed their respect for our work and a willingness to continue a general relationship. They attended college events and often were willing to speak to parents and students, but they provided little concrete information on skill need changes and future plans of the company. This information came from the plant managers and manufacturing engineers, and it was much harder to obtain and maintain. These were the people directly responsible for the products and had little time for helping us develop programs. When we did establish a relationship with these individuals, it was usually a short period as they were often rotated into different positions in the firm. However, when some of these people retired from the industry or were terminated because of their firm's downsizing efforts, we were able to hire them to manage our grant-funded projects. They were invaluable sources of concrete information and auto sector trends. In general, the growing competition within the industry was forcing them to lower costs and downsize their workforce, so their long-term training needs were not topics high on their agenda.

The "sweet spot" for us in developing long-term relations was the small and medium-sized manufacturing establishments. Many were owned by former Macomb students who graduated from our programs and maintained positive relationships with the college. They served on our advisory boards, made contributions to our Foundation, and not only hired our students but were able to provide us with invaluable insights into some of the future trends in the sector. They were also willing to donate equipment to our programs. Since they were embedded in the community and did not have the resources to conduct their own education and training programs, they were much more willing to partner with us. Some were attracted to the college because they knew we had access to state programs that provided funds for their training activities.

We were also a source for entry-level workers they could hire. Through our non-credit area, the college ran a six-week program "Orientation to Manufacturing" financed by the local workforce board. The program culminated in a "graduation" ceremony where some employers came to the event and hired workers on the spot. In general, the smaller firms were more willing to take advice from the college and connect with us as partners. We often learned from them what were some of the trends in manufacturing we needed to anticipate.

In contrast to the diverse response of manufacturers, the health-care sector aggressively sought ties with the college. Since most health-care occupations were regulated by public agencies external to the firms, these businesses were much more willing to utilize college expertise and support for their human resource plans. Among health-care providers in the county, there was an assumption that the college would be a valuable partner to produce trained workers, especially in areas such as nursing, physical therapy, and certified nursing assistants. Health care was an expanding employment sector and also faced significant staff turnover, so they were almost always hiring employees. In addition, the skills required in many of their occupations were highly regulated through state licensing requirements or through professional organization certifications. They looked to the college to provide these workers. The programs at Macomb were well-known by the local health-care providers, and many of the hospital administrative staff had started their careers at Macomb. These individuals were willing not only to play a role on the various advisory boards at the college, but they actively sought out college expertise for some emerging occupations. For example, they participated with the college on a federally funded grant concerning the skills needed by medical records technicians.

My experience in workforce activities provided me with a good background for dealing with the needs of employers. I was very conscious of the different cultures of education and employer leaders. Still, it was always surprising to me that despite all our marketing and outreach to them, few employers took advantage of the multiple college resources that could be utilized by their companies. For example, most companies maintained hiring preferences for veterans, yet very few accessed our Veterans Office for potential recruits. A few firms used our facilities for their staff meetings, and occasionally a local business owner would come to our cultural events or speakers. They did meet with me, if as president I reached out, and I always left the door open for them to communicate with me directly if they had any issues with the programs at the college. When they did express a demand for new workers, it usually was an immediate need, and it challenged our ability to react quickly.

But with employers who had a long-term relationship with the college, I did try to initiate discussions that would lead them into partnership where the college would become their source of future workers. I was especially interested in getting them to regularly hire our students and to help students succeed at the workplace. These conversations were always off the record, but very insightful for me. In some instances, I needed to confront them on their practices. When some company owners complained to me that their apprentices from the college were not completing their agreements and leaving for other jobs, I reminded them that their starting salary of $15 an hour was less than the $17 an hour a student could earn for completing a six-week robotic technical training program. I asked them what they would do

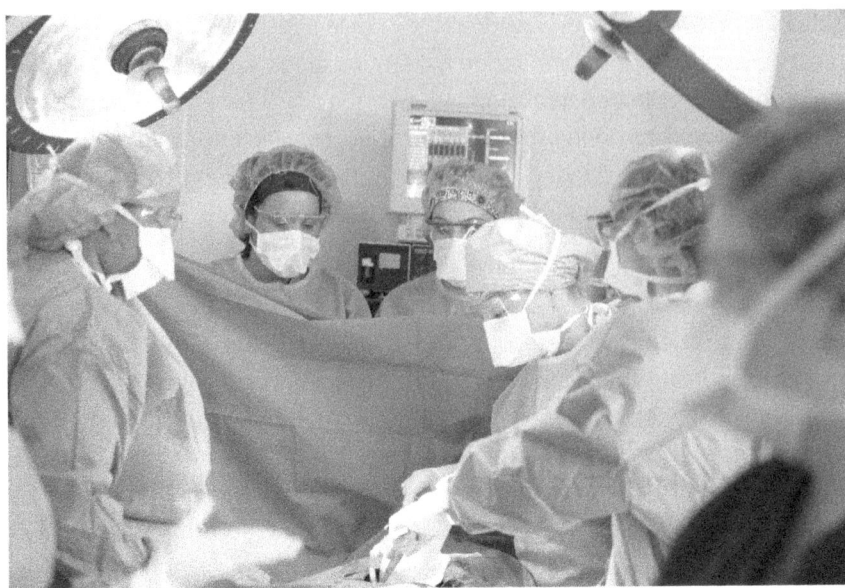

Figure 9.1 Our health-care programs are well-known and respected by local health-care providers. In this picture, Macomb students are engaged in learning at a clinical site. Image courtesy of Macomb Community College.

if they were in a similar position. In these conversations, I learned that local employers often made their wage determinations based on what their competitors paid, not on what students could earn in other jobs or the value a student or graduate could contribute to the firm.

In my dealings with employers, I tried to position the college as a strategic long-term partner and provider of their workforce needs. Most had never thought about all the capabilities we were able to provide. We wanted a long-term partnership, but at the same time, most employers were focused on short-term market conditions. While employers were not hostile to our efforts, many were not ready to make a longer-term commitment to us.

Relations to Community Organizations

There was always a close tie between the college and the community, so my task was to broaden it. Al Lorenzo had developed a list of important community groups in the community, and specific senior administrators were assigned to cover these organizations. These groups were associated with the local chambers, hospital advisory boards, and specific business organizations, such as the Lake St. Clair Boat Dealers Association. While it was important for the college to monitor and respond to their needs, I wanted to extend our involvement to community groups and those that could be connected with our strategic objectives.

For example, as president, I initiated closer ties with the Macomb Inter-Faith Center for Racial Justice, which held an annual MLK Day celebration. I encouraged our leadership team with union presidents and even some board members to attend. I tried to broaden the network by looking for ties with community organizations, especially in the low-income areas that could be connected to the college. These included Leaps and Bounds (a childcare center in Warren), Care of Southeast Michigan (an organization for low-income Macomb residents), Macomb Literacy Council (a county-wide literacy effort), and Turning Point (a shelter for women facing domestic violence). We made sure that these organizations were aware of Macomb College services. We also played a role in two specific organizations for new Americans: ACCESS (the Arab American community organization) and the Chaldean American Chamber of Commerce whose growing community (Christians from Iraq) was centered in Macomb County. The college provided language training classes for the organization, and we helped in the development of their cultural center.

In addition, I also used the resources of the college to bridge some of the most important regional organizations into the county. I tried to work with ACCESS in the development of funding for local Arab businesses in our community. In addition, we enjoyed a very positive relationship with one of the few public urban markets. The Detroit Eastern Market was led by CEO Dan Carmody, who created a significant outreach to local Macomb farmers. We served as a central location for him to organize the farmers in northern Macomb County to sell their produce at the Eastern Market. Also, in collaboration with the Eastern Market, we considered the development of a community kitchen that would provide a space for local residents who wanted to start their own cake-making or other culinary small businesses in the community.

Representing Macomb in the Region

Beyond our efforts with educational institutions, employers, and community organizations, we also needed to relate to regional organizations that had relevance to the college. As one of the few visible Macomb County "leaders" who participated regularly with regional organizations, I was often considered by regional leaders outside the county as the "spokesperson" for Macomb County. For years, much of the county leadership had not participated in regional activities in large part because they believed they were irrelevant to Macomb County.

I utilized three criteria to consider my active participation in regional organizations. First was whether participating in an organization would advance the strategic agenda of the college. For example, would my participation help us better understand the changing skill needs in the region? A second consideration was whether there were opportunities to interact with potential funders or resources that could benefit the college programs. The third criterion was the existence of activities that would help our students or the community in gaining employment or increasing their economic and social conditions.

If these criteria were present, even modestly, I would take almost every opportunity to participate in organizations that promoted a regional perspective. I knew that most Macomb County civic leaders put minimal emphasis on these relationships, so my willingness to participate was easily accepted by these organizations. I joined the Metropolitan Affairs Coalition, which consisted of many regional civic and political leaders. The committee was part of SEMCOG, the Southeast Michigan Council of Governments, a membership organization of cities, counties, and other public institutions that saw the future of the region as important to their organization. I also joined the Board of the United Way of Southeast Michigan, which raised significant funds from Macomb County employees through their workplace check-off programs, but invested little of their budget in support of any Macomb community-based organizations. Since many of our low-income students utilized bus transportation to get to our campuses, I worked with the Detroit Regional Chamber of Commerce on its mass transportation initiative. We hosted one of the few meetings held in Macomb County in support of a regional transportation system. Finally, because of the centrality of the auto industry, I joined the Board of the Center for Automotive Research (CAR), an important research organization that monitors trends in the industry. I tried to limit my membership in other boards or organizations and concentrate my focus on these.

However, there was one important exception that I discussed in earlier chapters of this book. The organization in which I played the most significant role in bringing to Macomb County was the Detroit Institute of Arts. The Detroit Institute of Arts (known as "the DIA") was founded in the early twentieth century as part of city government. As Detroit became the worldwide center of the auto industry, the DIA had significant public and private support and quickly became the fifth largest art museum in the nation. One of its most famous and controversial works embedded in the walls of the museum is the mural frescoes of the Ford Rouge factory painted by Diego Rivera. As an artist heavily influenced by socialism, this work celebrated the role of workers in auto production. While extremely controversial when completed in 1933, these murals attracted thousands of visitors and are one of Rivera's most famous works.[9]

As the domestic auto industry and financial status of Detroit both declined, the relationship between the DIA and the city government evolved. While the DIA was part of the city of Detroit, the museum operated with revenues generated from ticket sales and donations from wealthy supporters of the arts, often residing outside Detroit. To recognize this reality, the city established a governance system where it still maintained ownership of the museum, but board members were selected from all three counties in the region.

This arrangement maintained organizational control within the DIA but did not generate any new public revenues for the museum, nor did it insulate the museum from the financial troubles of the city. Other art museums, which originated as part of their municipal governments, had secured a regional status that allowed them to draw revenues from the entire community they served. At the same time, when I became president at Macomb, the DIA Board had decided to undertake a similar regional funding strategy and was planning to initiate a campaign for a ten-year millage within Macomb, Oakland, and Wayne Counties. To win the millage would require a yes vote from each county to support the proposal. If passed, it would also mean that there would be permanent county representation on the DIA Board. Entrance to the DIA would be free to residents of the three counties, and the DIA would provide free outreach programs for public schools in the counties that voted for the millage.

Before initiating this campaign, the DIA did extensive polling of the electorate that indicated the millage had support from voters in Oakland and Wayne County but would be defeated in Macomb County. This was not surprising. With the exception of the zoo millage, Macomb County voters had not supported any other regional initiatives. Thus, one of the strategic goals of the DIA leadership was to develop sustained ties with Macomb County in order to win the millage. They started their courtship of Macomb County through a program entitled "Inside|Out Art," where copies of famous DIA paintings would be displayed in various parts of Macomb County.

In 2008, they held their first-ever installation event in Macomb County, a copy of a Van Gogh painting selected to be displayed at a sports bar in St. Clair Shores. To further complicate this odd choice of location, the DIA held the opening reception on a fall Monday night, coinciding with the traditional NFL Monday night football game. I could never learn precisely how this venue was chosen, but seeing a small crowd of art supporters, including DIA Board members, competing for seats at the bar with NFL fans while the game was blasted on multiple TV screens was both amusing and symbolic of the large gap between the county and the art museum leadership. However, I attended the event and offered strong support for the museum, which was noted by the chair of the DIA Board at the time, Eugene A. Gargaro. He immediately connected my interests in having Macomb Community College play a more regional role in cultural activities and his goals of building a better relationship between the DIA and Macomb County. Not long after this initial meeting, he asked if I would like to join the DIA Board.

I joined the board in 2010 right before the millage campaign was initiated. The DIA planned the vote to occur during the 2010 Michigan August primary. They were adopting a millage strategy utilized by many school boards to select a time when there is low turnout and proceed to harvest the dedicated supporters for their proposal. However, to place the millage on the ballot required authorization by the Macomb County Board of Commissioners. At the meeting of the commission, I spoke in favor of the authorization of the millage vote. There was strong opposition from some of the commissioners, revealing both some of the classic Macomb opposition to anything Detroit as well as their misunderstanding of the significance of cultural institutions. Despite evidence that many K–12 Macomb school districts and the college took students to exhibits, some of the Macomb commissioners voiced their opinion that the DIA was unimportant to Macomb County residents. Others argued that since art was something for rich people, and Macomb County did not have many rich people, the other counties should pay for its activities. Another commissioner suggested, "Why don't you hold a fund raiser?" not understanding the institution's operating budget was over $30 million annually. It was appalling how little these commissioners considered the significance of a world-class art museum for Macomb County and for the region. Fortunately, through the efforts of David Flynn, the chair of the board and a DIA supporter, the commissioners finally agreed to allow for a county-wide vote on the millage.

Through my efforts, the college became involved in the campaign. As a public institution, we could not directly support the millage. Nevertheless, we did have students, staff, and alumni as volunteers working outside of work hours on the campaign. We took on the argument that nobody in Macomb County utilized the DIA by indicating the number of professors who regularly sent their class exhibits to the DIA. Through some hard work by a small group of supporters, amazingly the vote passed by a slim margin—less than 1,000 votes. Except for the Detroit Zoo millage, the election was the first time a metropolitan-initiated millage passed in Macomb County. For many on the DIA Board, the Macomb victory was mainly due to the efforts of the college. There was a strong sense of support among some residents, and the work of the many students and alumni made a real difference. But it also indicated how the old isolationist view was giving way to a new perspective which we helped foster. Many younger groups of voters, born and raised in the county who had no previous history with Detroit, saw a tie to the DIA as a positive development for the county.[10]

Learning About Macomb County

The unexpected win in Macomb County for the DIA millage startled many regional leaders and revealed how little they knew about the community. Very few of the regional decision-makers either came from Macomb County or had any direct experience in Macomb County. Even though a significant portion of the domestic auto industry is located in Macomb County, there were few CEOs or senior management living in the county. Most CEOs of Macomb County auto suppliers lived in the higher socioeconomic areas of Oakland County or the Grosse Pointes. Nor were many of the traditional decision-makers from civic organizations, non-profits, or media residents of the county.

The lack of participation by Macomb County leaders in regional activities meant the county was overlooked by philanthropic organizations. The United Way of Southeast Michigan, which was funded through regular donations of the hourly auto industry workforce for years, invested very little in the local Macomb County community agencies. Other local philanthropic organizations were unfamiliar with the county and its issues. When I became president, the Community Foundation of Southeast Michigan Board of Directors, an important local philanthropic foundation, had no members from Macomb County on its board. The Detroit Regional Chamber of Commerce did not maintain any collaborative activities with the six local Macomb chamber chapters. Part of my task was to rectify the lack of knowledge of Macomb County and bring resources from the Detroit region into Macomb County.

Reaching Out Nationally

While community colleges are products of their local communities, many of the issues they face cut across similar localities. There were many community college leaders who were attempting to transform their organization, and my work at CCRC made it clear to me that I had a great deal to learn from the practice of others. I was especially interested in how other progressive community college presidents took on issues of class and race at their institutions. So, in what time I could squeeze out of my schedule, I sought out relationships with other community college leaders who I had learned had attempted some progressive change within their institutions. As I expected, there were a variety of responses. Many of the non-white community college presidents, mainly representing non-white communities, had put together progressive programs with strong support from local leaders, including their own boards. Some presidents in rural areas were able to create important programs to deal with local economic inequalities. There were a few presidents with activist backgrounds from the

1960s like mine, and we communicated easily. There were also presidents (particularly in the "red" states) who may have agreed with my politics but did not want to risk possible board reactions, including discipline or firing, or put at risk obtaining any future presidencies by becoming too open with their progressive politics.

I also encountered presidents who came to their roles from a non-educator background as employers, politicians, and civic leaders who were able to offer a fresh perspective on issues affecting community colleges. In meeting with them at conferences or on specific projects, we talked about their personal and political perspectives. Nevertheless, in part because our jobs kept us so busy, we never got to a critical mass to undertake any efforts except for some individual bilateral projects between specific colleges with relatively narrowly defined goals. I wonder if I should have done more to organize a national network of these presidents. But I was new to my job, and hardly in a position to organize presidents with years more experience. Bringing together a group of progressive presidents is a task for others to take up, and I look forward to some of the future community college leaders to make this happen. The effort being made by *Education for All*, a group of college presidents in support of diversity and inclusion efforts, is an extremely positive step.[11]

Tensions in My Work

My participation in and support of organizations in the Detroit region created some challenges for me. I knew my presence in these regional organizations was primarily because of my title as president of the largest community college in the region. Since I was one of the few Macomb leaders who were proponent supporters of regional activities, I was an attractive addition to the boards of most of these organizations. However, most people on these regional boards knew little about my personal political background or, more importantly, my own attempts at changing Macomb Community College. In participating in these regional organizations, I faced significant inner tension. I had to be restrained in my personal views and remember that my goal was to advance the institution, not my own personal political agenda. My decision to represent the institution was particularly difficult in the regional organizations because of the stereotypical belief of Macomb County as an unwilling player in any regional activities. I was somewhat timid and not forthcoming enough because I was representing the institution and did not want my personal views to create issues for the college. I had to walk a line that helped demolish the stereotypical view of the county, but at the same time, not present views that I knew had little support within my own board or from county leadership. In retrospect, I should have tried more aggressively to educate my board about the significance of a regional perspective for the success of the college.

Working Inside Macomb County

I felt more confident within the county articulating my views. While I limited my membership to only Leadership Macomb and Advancing Macomb, I spent a good deal of time speaking at other organizations or planning events with them. I also participated in many Macomb delegations to major events, such as the Mackinaw Island Policy Conference sponsored by the Detroit Regional Chamber of Commerce. My perspectives on many issues were already well-known in the county, so it was easier to "fit in my skin." I could articulate issues of poverty, race, and class easily into my prospective strategy for college, and while my views may not have been widely shared, they did not automatically alienate me. Many leaders in Macomb County were familiar with my views, and some not only tolerated them but were supportive. We engaged in significant voter registration drives among our students and joined national student efforts to encourage voting and civic engagement. I always supported the efforts of non-profit community groups in the county, especially those that were dealing with issues in the poorer, southern end of the county. I developed a very positive relationship with a large African American church located in Warren whose leader originally was a Macomb graduate. I also promoted local environmental activist groups, including some very interesting attempts at hydroponics and support for local agriculture. With the support of Mark Hackel, we tried unsuccessfully to have the Michigan State Agricultural School establish a program for innovative crop growing methods at our Center Campus. I also supported the efforts of environmental groups to clean up Lake St. Clair, putting us in conflict with some of the commercial interests who saw the lake as primarily a resource for boat owners.

I still had to learn how to balance my role as president with my political agenda. I had to represent the institution at many events and deal with individuals that were not aligned with either my political perspective or the interests of the college. Celebrating the Michigan Defense Contractor Association's annual conference held at our South Campus, speaking to marina owners about demands for high-end yachts, or attending breakfasts with the County Association of Police Chiefs were examples of times when I had to be most mindful of the balance I needed to strike. If I had to speak at these events, I always tried to turn these into something positive, such as celebrating the importance of the local boating industry to Macomb County's identity or supporting the police activities in cybercrime and family abuse issues. Often my remarks were window dressing, and I needed to devote more time and effort to turn them into something worthwhile. But this was not always possible, so I concentrated on my priorities and tried not to burn these bridges within these constituencies which were important to people in the community. This issue is even of greater importance today, as the nation becomes more polarized. Presidents cannot duck major issues, especially when concepts of public education are being attacked. But how to take on these issues within the context of your community will be a major challenge for the community college leaders of the future.

What I Learned

Relations between a community college president and the community must be managed carefully. Any community college president is faced with more demands from the community for their time than they could possibly give; thus, a process of prioritization must happen. How to make decisions about what is most important, including what to participate in and how extensive the participation should be, needs to be based on some intentional process of determining what is important to the institution and to the community. In making these decisions, there is always a tension between what you believe in as an individual and what is important for the institution. Understanding how to resolve this tension is extremely important, particularly for presidents who are seeking to change the perception of their institutions within the community.

In the development of community relations, it is necessary to present a consistent approach that prioritizes the long-range goals of the institution. In this regard, it is necessary to understand that the staff of the college need to be supportive of your goals, or at least neutral. The staff should not see any community outreach as either a personal crusade or favoring a particular group or set of individuals within the institution. Controlling the speed of change is an important leadership trait that is difficult to learn and requires significant monitoring and continual adaptation to unanticipated changes within the institution to do well.

The external demands on a president's time are only increasing as community colleges become more significant in their communities. For many presidents who excel at internal administration and work with faculty and staff, community relations are often difficult to implement. It is important to recognize how different the cultural and decision-making processes are in non educational institutions when developing partnerships or training activities. Working with the community is a great lesson to understanding how isolated the language and the culture of educational institutions are within American society.

Notes

1 Leadership Macomb was originally based at the college and spun off in the early 2000s. Despite this reorganization, the college was a major contributor to its regular programs. Leadership Macomb is now in its thirty-fifth year of operation and most of the present civic leaders in Macomb County have attended its events. For more information visit its website at www .leadershipmacomb.org.

2 "About Us," Advancing Macomb, https://advancingmacomb.com/about-us/.

3 For information on these organizations, see the website of the Detroit Chamber of Commerce: www.detroitchamber.com.

4 Bomey and Gallagher.

5 There was an interest among the creditors and many art collectors in the DIA's paintings. During the judicial proceedings, any time a decision was made in favor of the creditors, demand for the DIA catalogue of holdings increased. For the best source of the DIA's involvement in the Detroit bankruptcy case, read: Bomey.

6 About 35 percent of all Macomb high school graduates enrolled at Macomb Community College. We regularly kept enrollment figures on each public high school in the county and their academic progress at the college. I shared these results with the Superintendents of each of the school districts. See Macomb Community College, *Macomb County 2012: Public High School Graduates* (Macomb Community College, 2012).

7   After a significant struggle, the Michigan community colleges secured a partial victory—some colleges were granted the right to offer degrees in very specific fields. The results of this effort were analyzed by the legislature five years later. See Perry Zielak, "Four-year Degree Offerings at Michigan Community Colleges," October 9, 2017, https://www.house.mi.gov/hfa/PDF/CommunityColleges/CC_FourYearDegrees_memo_Oct17.pdf.

8   WIN continues to play an important role in the region through its ability to win federal workforce grants that involve many of the colleges in the region. See "About WIN," *Workforce Intelligence Network*, retrieved October 14, 2024, from https://winintelligence.org/about_win/index.php.

9   Mark Rosenthal, *Diego Rivera & Frida Kahlo in Detroit* (Yale University Press, 2015), 102–3.

10 For a discussion of support and opposition to the millage in Macomb County, see Alan Stamm, "DIA Millage Proposal Creates List of Pros, Cons for Suburban Voters," *MI Patch*, July 3, 2012, accessed October 14, 2024, https://patch.com/michigan/macomb/dia-millage-proposal-creates-pro-con-list-for-suburba95bcb397de.

11 For information about Education for All, see Ben Austen, "How Trump's War on Higher Education Is Hitting Community Colleges," *The New York Times Magazine*, August 4, 2025, https://www.nytimes.com/2025/08/04/magazine/trump-community-college-anti-dei.html.

10 Wrapping It Up

As the Great Recession receded, by 2017 Macomb County was showing signs of recovery. The population of the county continued to increase as more families from the Middle East and the Balkans came to live in the county. Official unemployment decreased to 5 percent, and the actual number of Macomb citizens in the labor force increased for the first time since 2010. Manufacturing employment increased 23 percent since it hit bottom in 2010, and in 2016 the domestic auto companies announced new investments in the county totaling over $2 billion. Technical and information technology jobs were growing in the region, which was a sign of the ways in which the auto industry was becoming more reliant on computer technology. Housing sales rebounded, and there was a growth in new housing permits. The impact of the Affordable Care Act reduced the number of county residents without any medical insurance from 7 percent in 2010 to less than 3 percent in 2016. In addition to these numbers, the credit enrollment at Macomb Community College declined from 2012, a sign that more people were returning to work rather than enrolling in college. As a working-class suburb, the patterns of local economic activity were slowly returning to Macomb County.

Despite the clear signs of increased economic activity, recovery brought about a "new normal" that suggested the county still faced serious economic challenges. For example, in 2016, the per capita county income was 16 percent lower than it was in 2000. The number of manufacturing jobs had grown since the Great Recession, but compared to sixteen years earlier in 2000, those jobs were still only 60 percent of what they used to be. Though the county experienced growing employment in health care and hospitality at this time, many of those jobs paid less than manufacturing work. Employment increased, but families still struggled. The number of households served by Macomb Food Distribution actually increased in 2016 compared to 2010. Another indication of the changes the county was experiencing was that home builders were finally constructing new homes, but the homes were smaller and, therefore, more affordable, in response to the decreasing incomes in the community. Data also suggested that economic tensions were forcing significant changes in households. There was one very telling data point that highlighted just how different the new normal was compared to the past. A Census data statistic revealed that the number of women in the workforce with children under six years of age was quite different decades ago. In 1980, it was 35 percent; by 2011, this number had almost doubled to 57 percent.[1]

Ultimately, what was emerging was a community with a disappearing middle class and concentrations of income on both ends of the spectrum. Families who had two working parents in the auto, construction, or health-care industries were recovering and fueling local growth. At the same time, those who either lost their auto employment or were forced into service work, especially those who were single heads of household and/or new immigrants, were not experiencing as optimistic an economic future. These were the individuals (and their families) who could greatly benefit from attending a community college.

As my presidency progressed, I did perceive that my vision and the changes that were happening as a result were gaining traction inside at the college. College staff were adopting the messages of student success and the importance of dealing with low-income families in the county. Every year the college held an Institutional Development Day open to all staff. There is a planning committee that selects the theme for the event. By 2015, the committee, without any prodding from me, selected diversity as its theme and invited one of our adult students, an older returning citizen (who had been incarcerated earlier in life) and who enrolled in our "Orientation to Manufacturing" program. He shared how enrolling at Macomb Community College ultimately changed his life. The staff was internalizing some of the themes I initiated. Things seemed to be on the right track. I was already into my third three-year contract—and beginning to consider an exit strategy.

Relations with the Board

My major weakness throughout my presidency was my reluctance to develop a more effective relationship with the Board of Trustees. During these first few years of my presidency, my relations with the board were cordial, but I did not develop a clear vision for how I could involve the board in my strategies. I maintained a friendly conventional relationship with most members. I would introduce my projects to them first to make sure there was no hesitancy about them, and so that I knew there would be support for them when they were brought to a board meeting. I always returned phone calls if there were any issues and ensured board members were introduced at any public event. I accompanied them to the national meetings of the Association of Community College Trustees (ACCT) and would take them to dinner and encourage them to bring their spouses or partners. We also fulfilled any of their requests for tickets for programs at our Center for Performing Arts. Since board members were not compensated, these were the only "perks" permitted, and many of our trustees looked forward to them. Frankly, I was not very good at many of these activities, unsure of how much to engage in casual conversations or structure experiences to help them learn more about community colleges and develop their own vision on what Macomb should be doing for the students and the community. Several did attend my Economic Forecast event, and each year I tried to organize a planning retreat for them to articulate their views of what Macomb should be doing. However, they seemed to have only a few questions and were willing but not overly eager to have a deep discussion about what should be done.

Probably the most serious issue I faced with the board concerned my activities within the region. All the board members had a focus on the activities in the county, but few understood how regional activities enhanced the work and impact of the college. They did not oppose involvement in regional activities; however, they also didn't perceive them as important for the institution. It was always a struggle to get them to understand many regional activities, let alone have them see how critical a regional perspective is to our work at the college.

These were all well-intentioned people, and they were supportive of the college and my role. However, there was no annual formal review of my activities. The style of the Macomb Board was to hold an informal review session with me during a summer retreat, meet separately to discuss my work, and then the board chair would meet with me to privately discuss their evaluation. While this review seemed superficial in contrast to what I had heard other presidents went through, I was unwilling to probe further for more board input. One of the two board members who opposed my candidacy was always hostile to my efforts and verbally clashed with me at the meetings. However, he also had personal issues with other board members which produced some internal tensons. I knew the board needed some attention, but I was unsure how to intervene, so I probably took the easy way out—I did nothing.

In 2010, one of the board members who opposed my candidacy suddenly relocated out of the county, which gave me an opportunity to fill his position. With input from the board, we publicly sought nominations to fill the position and interviewed candidates through a board committee. One person who applied was an African American young man—a lawyer who worked at the Chrysler Corporation. He was an attractive candidate, and I believed he would bring new ideas and energy to the board, so I strongly supported him. Plus, he would be a board member who looked like some of our students, and he could serve as a role model for the institution's change agenda.

Fortunately, other board members on our nomination committee were also impressed with his candidacy, and we quickly appointed him as the first Black board member for the college. I also believe he was the first and only Black person holding a county-wide electoral position of any kind. His appointment was limited to fulfilling the remaining two-year term of the board member who left, and he would need to run for reelection. While I knew he would have an uphill climb in an election campaign, perhaps as an incumbent, he had a chance to win.

Organizational Setback One: The Bond Request

Every president suffers setbacks and is forced to adjust their plans. Defeats are even more likely when you are intentionally trying to change the direction of the institution. How someone responds to these setbacks becomes an essential means of judging both the quality of their leadership and the resilience of their vision. My two biggest "losses" occurred during the national election in 2012. Ironically, on the national level, the reelection of President Obama insured that the administration's programs supporting community colleges would continue to grow. This would be beneficial for the college. However, on the local level, the elections produced a significant setback for my activities and change efforts at the college.

In my first four years as president, I was able to do a great deal because the initial activities were funded through foundation grants and winning federal competitive awards. These infusions provided the seed money for many of the activities discussed in the earlier chapters, but to keep them in the annual budget of the institution would require additional funding. For example, the development of a college alumni association would require both technical resources and new personnel to successfully implement, and we did not have the existing resources we needed to achieve that goal.

Even before I became the president, the college's financial position was always tenuous as state support for community colleges steadily diminished. The traditional formula for community college finance, developed in the 1960s, called for community college revenue to originate equally from three major sources. One-third of the revenue would derive from student tuition, one-third from local support (usually from property taxes), and one-third from state appropriations. In the 1960s, Michigan was riding on the success of the domestic auto industry and flush with tax revenues. Back then, the state contribution to our budget exceeded 40 percent. However, by 2008, reflecting the decline of the domestic auto industry, the state contribution to the colleges decreased substantially. When I became president, the state of Michigan was contributing less than 24 percent to our budget. To achieve a balanced budget, the college was forced to increase student tuition.[2]

During the early 2000s, Al Lorenzo convinced the board to raise tuition annually, often utilizing the annual rate of inflation as both the justification and the measurement of the increase. However, several board members were increasingly unhappy with being put in the position each year of raising tuition. What saved the colleges from even larger tuition increases was the "third leg" of the funding stool—the local contribution of the millage property tax assessment. Macomb County had a growing population which resulted in new investments in housing, retail, and commercial enterprises. Property values continued to increase, bringing in more dollars, even though the original 1964 millage (the third lowest of any community college in the state) remained in effect.

However, the Great Recession in 2008 eroded the third leg of the funding stool. Not only were housing values significantly lowered and new housing starts truncated, but the shrinkage of the domestic auto industry also resulted in many large plant closures in Macomb County, affecting the tax revenue for school districts, local government, and Macomb Community College. By 2015, Macomb was receiving $11 million less in revenue derived from property taxes than in 2008. In addition, in response to the immediate impact of the Great Recession, I implemented a tuition freeze in 2008, which meant we were not getting our annual three to 4 percent increase in tuition for our budget.

During these difficult times, the most logical response would be to obtain from the state a commitment to restore their funding contribution to one-third of college revenues, as was originally designed. Even in good financial times, this was an almost impossible task. Nor would it be possible for one college to obtain greater state funding than the rest. As local institutions impacting a relatively small geographical base, our demands would be opposed by all the other community colleges and the legislators who represented their communities. Even banding together through a statewide organization (like the Michigan Community College Association) to ask for major new funding would be extremely difficult. We lacked electoral power compared to the over 1 million K–12 students enrolled in school districts or the political clout of the fifteen public four-year universities.

We tried to trim our budget as an initial response to the economic conditions imposed upon us by the Great Recession by reducing senior leadership and not filling positions when individuals retired. The state also helped with the initiation in 2010 of a "buy-out" incentive for high seniority employees at Michigan community colleges. This resulted in some long-term employees leaving the institution, and we were then able to fill positions with less senior (and therefore lower-paid) employees or simply leave the position unfilled. We also found some gains in our Employee Relations unit through a more rigorous examination of our medical costs and practices regarding medical insurance. But these actions were taken during a period when I was attempting to implement new programs, which were increasing the workload for faculty and staff. This combination—fewer staff alongside new initiatives—was producing some resistance. You cannot ask people "to do more with less" too many times. We needed a way to secure more funding, and there was one clear best way to do that. A successful millage or bond campaign would infuse new resources, renew the buildings, and provide funding for new programs.

Even though I knew this would divert time and energy away from changing the institution, the financial situation forced us to seek voter approval for an increase in revenue. There were essentially two options we could undertake: seek a millage increase or seek public support for a bond proposal. Support for a new millage increase would provide new revenues on an annual basis for a relatively long period of time. It was a preferred option because it brought new revenue to the college that could be used for any activity. Issuing bonds, on the other hand, was a one-time infusion of funds and had a specific limitation on their use (typically only capital improvements). Plus, bonds needed to be paid back. However, these funds could provide all the necessary renovation of facilities on our campuses and, therefore, free up money from our institutional budget to be used for new, innovative programs.

To implement either a millage or a bond proposal, Michigan law requires a public education institution to seek voter approval. There are two options possible. One option is to place the proposal on the ballot during a regularly scheduled election. This would mean our proposal would be on a ballot with political candidates running for offices, as well as other ballot initiatives. The second option is to hold a special election, which would mean our millage or bond proposal would be the only item on the ballot. The costs of a special election option had to be assumed by the educational institution. This meant paying the precinct workers, poll watchers, and staff to count the votes, but it did ensure your proposal was the only item for consideration. Many school districts choose the special election option, assuming if the election is held at odd times during the year, most voters will not pay attention to the process and not vote. In addition, since most school districts are relatively small, there may only be five to ten polls involved, making it relatively inexpensive. For the college, however, we would need to cover the entire county with hundreds of polling locations, incurring significant costs.

But the special election allows the relatively small number of college supporters to turn out and vote for the millage. My beliefs made me reluctant to utilize this strategy because it seemed to be anti-democratic. For a public institution to seek electoral support by intentionally implementing a strategy that tended to limit public participation was, in my view, unacceptable. Instead, I focused our efforts on the presidential election of 2012 for a revenue increase, precisely because this would ensure the highest turnout, and partly because, with President Obama up for re-election, I assumed there was a reasonable likelihood that poorer and working-class people would turn out for the election and that they would vote in support of the college.

So, in 2011, we began our planning for a millage election to increase our revenues. In initiating a ballot proposal, the college had to operate within Michigan's Byzantine rules for any public educational institution that wants to seek additional funding. These prohibitions were established by anti-tax groups whose goal was to make it difficult for public institutions to raise funds through the electoral process. For example, the college could not use institutional funds to advocate for any millage increase or bond proposal; all funds had to come from private sources. Nor could we ask other public educational institutions to support our efforts. We could inform the public about the specific proposal but not advocate for the proposal or be connected with any efforts to support the proposal. Nor could staff advocate for the proposal during work hours. Taken as a package, these rules meant the institution had to remain neutral on a measure that we introduced! This seemed like we were entering the electoral struggle with both hands tied behind our backs.

One positive feature in the rules was that public institutions were permitted, before the proposal was actually submitted, to research, refine, and determine the exact language of their ballot proposals. This allowed us to spend time and college resources to determine what sort of millage proposal language might have the best chance of winning. In order to lead this effort and plan the campaign, we hired a new Vice President for Community Relations. Casandra Ulbrich was an elected member of the State Board of Education and, therefore, had electoral experience. She was also a community college graduate and former staff member for Congressman David Bonior, which meant she was familiar with the electoral conditions we faced in Macomb County. We purposefully chose to hire a polling agency that was traditionally utilized by Republicans because we wanted to counter our own biases. By 2011, as the economy was recovering, our polling indicated slim support for the millage but much better support for a bond issue. This would permit the college to sell bonds and utilize the funds for capital construction projects and renovations. Since many of these activities had to be done anyway, by raising funds from a bond issue to pay for them, we were able to repurpose our budget funds for some of the new programs and activities we wanted to implement.

With the economy still weak and unstable, we focused on the bond issue as our best strategic bet. Running a bond campaign was demanding and typically fell on my time as the institution's leader. Because of the rules, I had to do this outside of my normal work schedule, which meant many evenings or weekends speaking with groups in the community. While the timing of the bond campaign was not ideal because it diverted momentum from some of the activities to induce change, I knew this was an important priority for the institution. Our initial surveys indicated we had a majority of voters supporting our efforts. In addition, there was little public opposition to the bond issue, typically mobilized by the anti-tax groups in Macomb County. Also, as an added benefit, we secured an agreement from both the Republican and Democratic local political party leadership to stay mute on the issue—which meant no candidate from either party would insert the bond issue as part of their electoral campaign.[3]

By spring 2012, given these well-developed preparations, we introduced our proposal to the community. Our polling data indicated support for the bond issue, and we were somewhat confident that it would pass. Then, the wheels came off our well-organized plans. What we failed to consider was that we would be sharing the ballot with four statewide propositions. These were strongly opposed by Michigan's Republican governor. He initiated a well-funded media campaign to encourage the rejection of all of them. All over the state, the message was clear: "vote no on all four." In Macomb County, our bond issue was the fifth proposition on the same ballot, so we became victims of collateral damage—the voters in Macomb County who voted no on the first four continued to vote no on our proposition. So, what appeared to be a relatively easy victory turned out to be a solid defeat. We lost the vote in almost all communities in the county.

I was extremely disappointed with the election's outcome, realizing that all our work and plans were upset by a chain of events that were totally out of our control. I also blamed myself for the loss. As an individual who knew about politics, I should have anticipated this possibility. In retrospect, it might have been better to organize our vote in a special election where voters could focus only on our ballot initiative. In any event, the loss would mean curtailing expansion plans and revising the budget, affecting all parts of the institution. The only positive consequence was, since we ran an informational public campaign, most of the college staff were well aware of our financial situation. It would come as no surprise to them that there would be changes in our programs and operations as the result of the loss.

I did not want the loss to penalize the staff, so I made it clear there would be no layoffs. This meant diverting resources from new initiatives to preserve the employment of people during the sharpest economic downturn in Macomb County since the Great Depression. While we never laid anyone off, when individuals retired, we did not fill their positions. This increased the workload of our staff, an unfortunate by-product of the loss. We also suspended or decreased the scope of some much-needed renovation projects.

These actions gave us financial stability from which we could move forward. For me, the defeat of the bond issue was another reason why we needed to change our public support for community colleges. Public higher education is a public good and needs consistent support to achieve its goals. It should not be at the mercy of economic market conditions or political winds. In addition, it was a leadership failure for me—I had misread the conditions we faced and selected a losing strategy. While in public I tried to be optimistic about the future and unfazed by the loss, it did undercut my confidence in advancing my leadership. It also meant a readjustment of my work, concentrating not on what innovative things could be done but rather on how to maintain our existing programs.

Organization Setback Number Two: Board Elections

The same elections of 2012 produced another issue for me to confront as president—a new difficult board member. Our first non-white trustee, Charley Jackson Jr., failed to win his election. I knew it would be difficult for a Black male to win in a county-wide election where the electorate was close to 90 percent white. I was disappointed but not surprised about his loss. However, I was not prepared for the candidate who won the position. He was a self-employed conservative lawyer and an "outsider" new to electoral politics who identified himself as a fixture in the Macomb Republican Party.

However, as often happens with new board members who lack experience in higher education, after winning the election, he announced that his first goal was to save money by decreasing the college payroll. He asked for vast amounts of data about the college hiring practices and budget, often misreading our financial condition and continually upsetting many of our agenda items with questions that often sidetracked our ability to initiate important board discussions. But what was worse, he also utilized his legal skills to file formal complaints with state authorities over our handling of financial and personal records, forcing us into legal confrontations with him, wasting even more college resources and time.

Fortunately, all of his legal efforts were defeated by our college attorney. Unfortunately, his antics at board meetings discouraged other board members from actively participating in our monthly meetings. As a result, we needed to carefully plan out the board meetings to make sure we had a quorum and enough votes to pass the necessary items, such as an institutional budget or the hiring of new staff, because he would often vote no in protest, regardless of the issues.

In many ways, our new trustee possessed the traits of a model board member. He always read the materials and was prepared with a barrage of questions, some of them very penetrating and worth considering. On the other hand, he did not understand that his role was to collaborate with his fellow board members and provide community input to the strategic direction of the institution. Instead, he became a one-person investigator of the internal operations of the institution, looking for mistakes and "wasteful" activities of our administration. A board member is not the boss of the college workforce. In fact, the only employee who reported directly to the board was me as the college president. He also interjected his brand of Republican politics into many discussions and did not seem to appreciate that in Michigan these board positions are legally non-partisan. His confrontational style antagonized other board members, so almost anything he tried to advocate, even sometimes useful suggestions, was immediately rejected by other board members.

He was a challenge for me, and given the loss of the bond issue, I had little appetite for dealing with a disruptive board member. Instead of developing a strategy for dealing with him, I took the easy way out of the situation. I ignored him, kept him isolated from the rest of the board (not a difficult task since his antics at the meetings made him extremely unpopular), and allowed the college attorney to handle his legal challenges. However, when another one of our board members (who had spent thirty years on the board) decided to retire, I was far more vigilant and implemented a strategy used so effectively by Al Lorenzo. I did not organize a board search committee but intentionally recruited a candidate from a local political family with a recognizable name to serve the remainder of the term and win reelection. I disliked playing this conventional political game, but this was a better alternative than passively adjusting to whomever wins the election.

Having to deal with the new instability of the board was an unanticipated issue for me. When my board chair, Nancy Falcone (who was my initial supporter and confidant), decided to retire, I knew there might be more conservative and overtly partisan candidates who were going to run. On the other hand, I was not facing an immediate crisis; I could continue my role and did get another very supportive board member, James Kelly, appointed as chair from 2012 to 2016. Nevertheless, it was clear I would need to spend a good deal more time and energy handling board issues.

Due to their structure and design, the governing boards of community colleges can make it challenging for their institutions to be innovative. In many states, including Michigan, community college governing boards do not function like most four-year institutions. They meet much more often than four-year boards, and their operating culture resembles K–12 school boards, which are often deeply involved in the functioning of their institution. Even the process of selecting community college boards is very similar to school board elections. Anyone with enough signatures can petition to get on the ballot. The result is that eight to ten candidates may be competing for two slots, making it relatively easy for candidates antagonistic to public education to win seats. In states where board members are elected, these positions often become the first step for anyone wanting to initiate a career in politics. Public institutions should have elected boards; community colleges are part of their communities. However, it would be useful to detach the process from the rest of the electoral process by making it a separate non-partisan contest that is not on a normal electoral ballot. I hope this would encourage people to seek board positions, not as stepping stones for careers in politics, but because they value civic engagement and want to contribute input to an important institution in their community.

The defeat of the bond issue forced me into a far more conventional administrative role within the college. I needed to make decisions with a greater concern for their financial impact. While I embraced my role as president because it allowed me to implement change and I thrived on creating new programs and initiatives, I was not well suited for focusing on the necessary day-to-day administrative decisions. I am not a detail-oriented person, and outside of mentoring people, I do not enjoy dealing with many of the daily human resources and financial issues that come up regularly in an organization of 2,000 people.

In addition, as president of a large organization, many of the difficult employee relations issues you often face are problems created by previous internal decisions made by other administrators. You are often faced with reversing a previous decision that might offend lower-level administrators whose support you need for other issues. Sometimes it is wise to tolerate a decision you know was incorrect if you can gain internal support for issues that you think are very important. There are presidents who can make these calculations easily, but I was not one of them.

My work with the bargaining units did produce an important financial saving, reinforcing my view that a unionized community college can play a positive role in an educational institution. Right after our loss of the bond issue, the governor, with state legislature approval, made Michigan a Right to Work State. This meant that as soon as our present contract agreements expired, individuals would be "free" to leave their union. However, with the assistance of David Hecker, president of the Michigan American Federation of Teachers (AFT), and the support of all the other unions, we agreed to extend the current union contracts for an additional five years. This gave us the ability to avoid the new Right to Work rules. As part of this extension, we consolidated all the separate negotiated medical plans into one medical master plan for all our employees. Not only did we eliminate a significant amount of administrative paperwork, but we were able to reduce medical costs by over $2 million. Given our financial situation, achieving those savings was an important financial improvement.

Considering Retirement

Administrating an institution such as a community college and remaining committed to change is a difficult balancing act. There is too little discussion of these issues within the community college leadership discourse. The tenure for most community college presidents is about four years, and I was entering my eighth year in 2016. While there was financial recovery underway in Macomb County, and the college's financial future was looking better, I was beginning to think about the timing of my retirement. I was over seventy, and while I was in good health, I was in the last year of my contract, which would normally be extended for another three years. However, I also knew the college's operating millage was up for renewal in 2020 and I would need to stay at least through 2021 to ensure the college would be on a good financial footing. In addition, a number of important staff were also considering retirement, and if I stayed on, I would be faced with the need to recruit new talent to the institution precisely at the point I would be leaving. Finally, my new board chair was not seeking reelection after 2016, and there was a strong possibility I would be faced with a board that would require even more attention on my part to gain support for my objectives. These factors influenced me to announce my retirement after my present contract expired in June 2017. This would leave the next president with enough time to prepare for the millage renewal, deal with hiring new staff, and hopefully continue the changes I implemented. So, in early 2016, I told the board I would not seek renewal of my contract, and they should prepare for the selection of a new president. While I wanted to give the board and the college time to prepare for a new president, I probably should have waited a little longer before announcing my retirement. Almost as soon as I made the announcement, I detected a change inside the institution and within the community in terms of how I was perceived.

Was It Worth It?

For the nine years as president, I often felt I was trying to steer a canoe inside a raging river. As president, you are faced with all sorts of conflicting currents and need to "paddle like hell," often unable to make a judgment if these activities are inducing positive results. In some cases, the data to judge our success or failure was simply unavailable. By the spring of 2017, I was ready to stop paddling. Still, the important question remained: Was all this effort worth it?

How did the college change as a result of my efforts? Did my activities improve the lives of students and the community? Personally, I enjoyed myself immensely, and I have lots of good anecdotes to indicate I was successful. But these were subjective impressions. Maybe all this activity produced lots of motion but made little difference in the lives of others. What was the evidence to assess my performance? And probably for me remained the most personal question: Could someone have done this without my kind of radical perspective?

To answer the question, it is necessary to examine the dynamics operating in the community and among the students. As described earlier in this chapter, in 2008 when I became president, Macomb County had already entered the Great Recession. The signs of downturn were well underway. Macomb County was already suffering an economic downturn from a significant decline in domestic auto sales in 2007, as well as the collapse of the local residential housing market. In January of 2008, Chrysler, the largest employer in Macomb County, laid off 10,000 workers as auto sales continued to decline. The average selling price of a home in 2008 was $20,000 less than 2007, and home sales were 17 percent lower. County unemployment was officially at 8 percent and increasing. The economic decline did not curtail the population growth of the county, however. By 2008, there were over 830,000 people living in the county, making it one of the few areas in the Detroit region to increase its population from 2000 to 2010. However, the increase in population was not coming from the traditional source of growth, which included citizens leaving Detroit and moving to Macomb County. For the first time, in 2008, the growing new immigrant population to the county was greater than those migrating from other parts of the Detroit region. These were the conditions in the county before the Great Recession financial crisis.

At the college in 2008, there were 22,500 students taking credit classes. The white student population, which was 81 percent of all credit students in 2004, had shrunk to 77 percent by 2017. The Black student population was 7 percent of the credit student body, with about an equal number of immigrant students (most of whom were from parts of the Middle East). Almost 25 percent of the student body was on some form of federal tuition financial assistance.

When I retired as president in 2017, Macomb County was recovering from the Great Recession. The official unemployment rate was 5 percent, down from a high point of 14.8 percent in the summer of 2010. Over 35 percent of the families in the county fit the ALICE definition of working poor. Economic recovery had come to the county, but the new normal was a poorer Macomb County family. The domestic auto industry continued to decline in its economic significance to the county, as new jobs were found in the health care, hospitality, and service sectors.

These broad economic and social trends of course affected Macomb Community College. Enrollment at the college in 2017 was beginning to level off at around 21,000 credit students. This decline reflected the improved economic conditions. In the height of the Great Recession, from 2011 to 2014, credit attendance remained at 24,000 students. And during this time, the diversity of the student body continued to increase. Enrollment of African Americans grew to 11 percent of the student body. About 20 percent of Macomb students spoke a language other than English at home. The number of students identifying as white continued to decline to 69 percent. About 40 percent of the students were on some form of financial aid, mainly Pell grants or student loans.[4]

Given these changes in the college and the community, what was the performance of the institution? What was the impact of our changes upon student success? With the assistance of Macomb's Institutional Research unit, I was able to create a table (Table 10.1) which gives some empirical measurements of the state of the college in 2008 (when I became president) and in 2017 (when I retired).

This snapshot indicates some important progress. Total enrollment in credit and non-credit programs declined 16 percent from 2008 to 2017, and the number of adult students decreased by more than 3 percent. This is not surprising. Traditionally, student enrollment (especially adult student enrollment) is almost always correlated with employment conditions. Despite the decline in enrollment, the number of graduates actually increased by an impressive 18 percent, indicating that students were completing their programs and receiving degrees at a higher rate than before. This was a major positive finding. It suggests that the college became more focused on student success and made changes to support students and help them achieve degrees, not just enroll in courses. What's more, not only were more students graduating, but they were more likely to transfer to four-year programs. The transfer rate increased from 25 to 31 percent. The retention rate and the number of courses taken remained much the same, and there was an increase in the number of students receiving Pell grants. The number of students in ESL programs significantly increased, suggesting we were drawing more new immigrants into the college. There was also an increase in students taking a remedial course.

Table 10.1 Macomb Community College Performance Metrics

Key Data Variables	2008	2017
Enrollment (credit and non-credit)	46,794	39,274
% of non-white students	23.8%	29.8%
Number (and %) of students in remediation	1,940 (8.7%)	2,049 (9.3%)
Number of graduates	3,230	3,837
% of transfer students	25%	31.5%
% of students over 24 years old	33.5%	29.8%
Retention rate from semester to semester	67%	67%
Average number of semester credits taken	8.2	8.3
% of students taking online courses exclusively	4%	11.2%
% of students receiving Pell awards	23%	27%
Number (and %) of students in ESL programs	686 (3%)	1,791 (8.2%)

In addition, over 10 percent of the students were taking only online classes, an important trend that hit a peak during the Covid pandemic crisis when all students had to shift to online classes. Obviously, the growth of online education has had important implications for current and future community college programs.

This data review indicates that our efforts improved student graduation and transfer rates. While these were modest increases, they happened within the context of a community becoming poorer, less white, and attracting more immigrants than in 2018. We did not collect data on whether there was an increase in first-generation students, but the correlated demographic data suggests this was the case. Unfortunately, while we had lots of anecdotal examples, we lacked any hard empirical data that there were better employment outcomes for our students. But from this review of the evidence, it is clear. Our efforts made a difference. Our focus on students led to students achieving more academic success.

Moreover, this data only indicates the immediate changes in students while I was president. The structural reforms I put into place hopefully will lead to greater student success in the future. For example, we launched a new registration and student tracking system, which should ensure better counseling. Our financial aid office reduced the wait times to less than one week. Our Foundation's annual fundraising for student scholarships increased from $859,000 in 2009 to over $2,221,000 by 2017. We were able to award over $1,909,000 in emergency grants and scholarships for students beyond their federal awards. We started new activities and programs to support student success thanks to our ability to earn over $38.7 million in competitive grants.

In addition, some of our internal programs should also continue to benefit employees. We initiated a staff tuition reimbursement plan for all employees (not just faculty), resulting in $210,000 of tuition reimbursement dollars given to forty-six employees. Collectively, they earned six bachelor's degrees, nine master's degrees, and six PhDs. Finally, we positioned ourselves well in the Detroit metropolitan area. We were now considered a part of most regional activities as the leading community college in workforce development. In 2015, we received a Trade Adjustment Assistance Community College and Career Training (TAACCT) grant of $24.9 million, at the time the largest the college ever received, to coordinate the development of a new manufacturing curriculum for Macomb and six other Michigan community colleges.

For me, however, one of the most gratifying indicators of positive change was noted by our accrediting body, the Higher Learning Commission, in its accreditation review in 2016. Ten years before in 2006, the Commission's site visit report indicated that there was a concern regarding the lack of diversity in the students, faculty, and staff at the college. Ten years later, in 2016, the Commission's site review found: "The college appears to have taken the [2006] feedback seriously as it has made diversity one of its six core values. While MCC serves an area that is predominantly white, per the Census Data, the college has made improvements in diversifying the student body as well as the faculty and staff."[5]

My efforts began to change the culture of the institution to be more welcoming and supportive of students, especially first-generation students. This was always my intention. At this point, I believe Macomb is positioned well to take on the challenges that are now confronting the community as it continues to grow poorer, more diverse, and in significant need of postsecondary education to provide the necessary economic development opportunities for its people. We made a difference, and from this perspective, I believed my efforts were worth it.

However, it is hard to know how much positive change can be attributed to my overall perspectives and leadership. I do believe my perspective for change did provide me with a broad roadmap for my work. I was not simply reacting to whatever came up. I did try to steer the college on a particular course focused on students and student success. I am sure the broad themes around dealing with racism, support for the unions, and taking a regional perspective were connected to these views and outcomes. But in a broader sense, my commitment to seeing the community college as a significant place for promoting change did reflect my perspective. And hopefully other leaders, both at Macomb and across the community colleges, believe the same and will continue the good work to be done.

What I Learned

There is always a point when a president must consider retirement or a need to move on to another post. In my case, it was a combination of age, an inability to develop more financial resources, and changes in the composition of my board that led to my decision to retire. While these were good reasons to seek retirement, in retrospect, it would have been better for me and the institution to be more deliberate and considerate when we made the announcement of my retirement and when we commenced the selection process of the next president. I was not able to even summarize my achievements and evaluate my failures before exiting the institution, which I think would be useful for the board, my successor, and the staff of the institution. It would also have established some benchmarks for the institution and built a context for the changes that the new leadership would bring. The leaving of a president is not widely considered in the research on community college leadership, yet in the long run, it might be more critical than the selection process. One of the major strengths of Macomb is long-term leadership stability. For the past forty-five years, Macomb has had only three presidents. This speaks to an important new dimension that community colleges now face as they mature. Institutions must recognize that new leadership will always bring change, but it will be built upon the successes and failures of the past.

Notes

1 James Jacobs, *2016 Economic Forecast for Macomb County*, January 15, 2016.

2 The trend of revenue sources for the college reveals the growing difficulties we were facing. The revenue from local property taxes declined between 2007 and 2012 by over $11.6 million, and state appropriations declined by almost $4 million during the same period. By 2012, tuition and fees accounted for 42.5 percent of the college's annual revenue. See Macomb Community College, *Report to the Community: 2012* (Macomb Community College, 2012).

3 To prepare for the bond issue, we also commissioned an economic study of the college's impact on the community by two economists from the Upjohn Institute. Their analysis found that the college contributed over $108 million to the local economy measured by increased wages as the result of degrees earned at the college. Macomb Community College, *Celebrating the Commitment: Recognizing Macomb Community College's Impact on the County* (Macomb Community College, 2012).

4 The economic and population data described here were gathered from the Economic Forecasts of 2008 and 2016 that I presented, both cited earlier.

5 Higher Learning Commission, *Comprehensive Evaluation of Macomb Community College: Re-Affirmation Report* (Higher Learning Commission, 2016), 21.

11 After the Presidency

My presidency ended in June 2017, six months into the first Trump administration. Although he visited the campus twice during the election campaign, these were political rallies paid for by the campaign, so I had no reason to interact with him. At best, from his few statements about community colleges, he thinks of us as vocational training institutions. He had little interest in or acceptance of the mission of the community colleges as outlined in the Truman Commission written over seventy years ago. This document envisioned community colleges as a public good that would help individuals understand their environment and their role within it. In a remarkable paragraph, the Commission articulated a role for community colleges that still holds true today:

> American colleges and universities must envision a much larger role for higher education in the national life. They can no longer consider themselves merely the instrument for producing an intellectual elite; they must become the means by which every citizen, youth, and adult is enabled and encouraged to carry his education, formal and informal, as far as his native capacities permit. This conception is the inevitable consequence of the democratic faith; universal education is indispensable to the full and living realization of the democratic ideal. No society can long remain free unless its members are freemen, and men are not free where ignorance prevails. No more in mind than in body can this Nation or any endure half slave, half free. Education that liberates and ennobles must be made equally available to all. Justice to the individual demands this; the safety and progress of the Nation depend upon it. America cannot afford to let any of its potential human resources go undiscovered and undeveloped. (*The Truman Commission Report, 1947*)[1]

Future Trends

Although I could not have anticipated it, my retirement in 2017 resulted in me missing one of the most important external events affecting community colleges and their future: the Covid pandemic crisis. The immediate response of the majority of community colleges to this major public health crisis was overwhelmingly positive. The years of built-in flexibility and adjustment, which were part of the DNA of community colleges, positioned them well to suspend their in-class operations and move to all online classes, all within a matter of days. Some institutions, such as Macomb, took less than a week to make the transition. In addition to moving instruction to a fully online modality, many community colleges were able to secure computer devices for their students. For those students without access to the internet, many colleges provided internet access by offering free Wi-Fi connections in their parking lots for their students to secure a signal. In many instances, the colleges also donated their health-care supplies to the local health-care providers, and when vaccinations became available, they served as sites for citizens in the community to obtain a shot.

While I was proud of the response of the colleges, I was also glad I did not face this disruption of college activities and plans. As enrollment plummeted, my successor Jim Sawyer was forced to lay off staff and curtail some operations of the college, simply to focus on a college response. Interactions between staff were conducted solely on Zoom, and, as a result, there was a loss of organizational unity and morale suffered. Even with recovery, many of the teaching staff are only teaching remotely, and it is unclear what the long-term impact will be on the institution.

Immediately, Covid had a significant impact on community college enrollment. In 2019, overall aggregate national enrollment in credit courses was 6.59 million students; two years later, it had dipped to 5.7 million students, an 18 percent decline. Even though Covid hit in 2020, many community college enrollments are still below 2019 levels. In Fall 2023, according to CCRC data, only 27 percent of community colleges returned to their 2019 enrollment levels.[2] Macomb's credit enrollment was still 20 percent less in 2023 than it was in 2019.

The decline in community college enrollments began before Covid (enrollment peaked in 2013 at 7.19 million), but it intensified dramatically, particularly among an important constituency. Most of the data from institutions indicated that students most affected by Covid and most likely to drop out of school during the 2020 Spring semester or fail to return in September were students from low-income backgrounds. While the specific reasons were varied (some got Covid, others had to take care of their families, others were without computer access), Covid disrupted the efforts of colleges to promote opportunities for these students. Even in 2025, while there are some signs students have returned, many have not chosen to return or enroll in college.[3]

The difficulty in colleges regaining enrollment points to the fragility of low-income students' relationship to higher education. Community colleges cannot assume students will return. To get students back, it will require some significant adjustments of programs and activities. Former positive features, such as low tuition and easy access, will not automatically draw significant numbers of students to them. The one growing market of students is high school students attending dual enrollment programs. In 2024, there was a 12.8 percent increase in dual enrollment students at community colleges.

These enrollment declines seem to contradict how Americans perceive community colleges. A recent national survey of attitudes toward higher education revealed that community colleges were the sector of higher education most people believed held the highest value. In addition, community colleges were perceived to be run wisely and more efficiently than any other sectors of American higher education. Over 60 percent of the respondents supported the concept of offering free tuition for community colleges.[4] This disconnect may be understood to mean the public considers community colleges a positive addition to higher education, but when it comes to enrollment choices, people believe community colleges are not an adequate gateway to obtain a four-year credential. If community colleges are to regain their enrollment, they must increase their abilities to move individuals, particularly those who experience economic and social barriers, into four-year degrees. Raising completion rates and developing more of a commitment to quality—and becoming clear about their mission—will be an even more vital part of the future agenda for community colleges. Colleges cannot rely on being low cost and close to home as the dominant reasons for enrollment. The emphasis on quality instruction and career pathways, coupled with a vigorous commitment to a completion agenda, presents important opportunities for the future of community colleges.[5]

The struggle to win back enrollment will be made even more difficult by the increasing "demographic cliff" that shows the United States is experiencing a slowdown in population growth. This trend will result in fewer young people graduating from high school, which means the one "growth" area of community college credit enrollment—high school students in dual enrollment programs—will also be threatened. In 2025, American high schools will graduate the highest number of seniors, and from then, demographers expect this group to continue declining through 2035. Even if significant numbers of new immigrants move to communities across the country, which in the short run under the Trump administration is highly unlikely, this will not make up the internal loss of students. While this is the macro picture, the impact is already being felt in many parts of the Northeast and Midwest, where the numbers of young people in high school declined considerably before Covid. In Midwest states such as Michigan, there are already 60,000 fewer students in the K–12 public education system compared to a decade ago.

While the demographic cliff should be a concern, there is nothing inevitable about its impact. Maintaining a culture of institutional flexibility and nimbleness can produce strategies to overcome possible enrollment declines. However, now is the time to start incremental changes. Perhaps the easiest approach is to intensify what many colleges have already begun in the past twenty years: continue to increase student success and degree attainment for the students who are in credit programs. This will be particularly important for low-income students who often drop out or fail to complete credit programs. An increase in the completion of programs could make up for the loss of student populations.

However, newer approaches to student success need to be developed. In the past few years, there has been an important emphasis on program design and classroom teaching, and many colleges have initiated important changes that have resulted in raising completion rates and course-taking success. Still, there needs to be more coordinated effort directed at alleviating the external barriers to successful learning. These barriers include the lack of health care, unemployment, inadequate housing, poverty, and several other "non-educational" issues which affect the success of all students, especially low-income students. Colleges need to coordinate their internal learning strategies alongside efforts to mitigate or resolve the external economic and social barriers to student success. They can't do that kind of work alone. Partnerships with organizations in the community are key. This will mean even greater community involvement in the future for American community colleges.

As mentioned earlier, the largest growing market of community college enrollment recently has been dual-enrolled high school students. There is much promise in dual enrollment, and hopefully those trends continue. However, there needs to be more attention paid to the significant number of working adults without any higher education credentials who could be attracted to attend colleges as well. Again, using Michigan as an example, while the state has lost over 60,000 young students from the public school system, Census data indicates there are

2.3 million Michigan adults without any postsecondary experience. If only 10 percent of those adults could be convinced to seek a degree, the issue of a demographic cliff would disappear.

Attracting more adults, however, is not simply a marketing issue. Many adults do not attend community colleges because the programs do not have enough relevance to their work or personal lives. Most companies, even those that offer tuition plans, rarely tie education requirements to potential career pathways within their workplaces. It will take a significant effort on behalf of community colleges to recast their programs and build closer ties with employers to win these students back. These efforts would intertwine community colleges closer into the fabric of their local economy and ensure they play a positive role in the economic development of their community. While most college leaders rhetorically connect their workforce courses and programs to the needs in the local economy, there is more intentional and strategic work to be done. The recent focus by many community colleges on artificial intelligence programs needs to be more than a knee-jerk response to the new occupational flavor of the day. Colleges need to undertake applied research with their business partners to understand specifically how this technology will be utilized by their local companies, in terms of both hiring practices and the advancement of current workers. Programs should not be started that get ahead of the technology implementation process. In addition, in their rush to be "relevant" and responsive to the latest technology, the colleges should not forget the impact of AI on many of their existing occupational programs.[6]

We have just begun to explore how to lead new efforts on the scale necessary to enroll more adults in community colleges. As colleges become more engaged in their communities, more efforts will commence to reform occupational programs using a career pathways approach. Combinations of work-based and classroom education will increase as well. Both of these trends have been on the agenda for most community colleges. They will require significant resources and leadership effort for many institutions. Most of the colleges have extended efforts in these directions already and there are many good examples for institutions to follow.

Let me suggest another dimension that could be unfolding which may provide the colleges with additional enrollment. The impact of technologies, such as artificial intelligence, is altering not only the skills individuals need to have but the learning process itself. The time is over when an earned degree or credential meant someone no longer needed additional education to be prepared for the workplace. As the nature of work is changing, there will continually be a need to upgrade skills and pursue additional education or training. While some of this new learning will be performed at the workplace, it is likely that the new learning will be a combination of workplace and formal education. In many cases, occupations that require licensing will require their workforce to pursue continual educational upgrades.

These changes will provide opportunities for community colleges in ways that have the possibility of changing the relationship between the institutions and the communities they serve. For example, in the area of health care, if community colleges have programs for occupational therapists, these individuals will be required to upgrade their skills throughout their careers through continual training and education. It would require the colleges to remain in close contact with their students over their working lifetimes. For students who have earned an accounting degree or who are machine tool apprentices, they will be faced with retooling their skills. It could be a combination of classroom and work-based learning. There is no reason why the colleges should not use their expertise in education to aid employers in their design of work-based learning experiences.

To take on these emerging education needs, colleges would need to maintain ties with their alumni in a far tighter and intentional way. It is conceivable to have community college alumni associations that continually interact with their graduates—not just to raise funds for their programs or to serve as mentors for current students, but to alert them about opportunities to increase their skills. It would also mean that colleges seek out ties with companies in ways that help them adjust to the new needs of the workplace and help them design training for their workforce. This will require a great deal more interaction between the colleges and the companies that encourage long-term partnerships. While many of the large multinational companies will have the resources and the skills to develop and implement their own work-based learning, the small- and medium-sized firms, often owned by former community college graduates, will be more likely to develop a long-term relationship. Obviously, the lessons learned by the institution in these interventions with adults can help them prepare and direct younger students into thriving career pathways in the future.

One area of concern is the evolving relationship of community colleges to other segments of the higher education sector. To serve our students well, it is important to have good ties with postsecondary institutions and encourage a common perspective on the student success of our transfer students. This should be the primary consideration of the colleges in terms of what strategies they utilize. In addition, since many community college students transfer to public four-year colleges in the same state, it would be advantageous for funding and policy purposes if elected officials in the state would see (and enable and incentivize) a close working bond between these institutions.

In light of these concerns, while some states allow community colleges to award baccalaureate degrees, this is an option that should be pursued with careful consideration. The community college baccalaureate degree has existed in a few states for almost twenty years and there has been a growing number of states that have granted the colleges permission to offer degrees. However, in many of those states, the number of students achieving bachelor's degrees at a community college is significantly small. Context matters considerably. In 2012, after an enormous struggle, Michigan community colleges finally received permission to offer bachelor's degrees but in only a few specific fields. Yet more than a decade later, there is just a handful of degree-earning students and little or no expansion of these programs. In addition, it is reasonable to believe that the demographic cliff will further intensify four-year concerns about enrollment and make them even more hostile toward community colleges. If these efforts result in creating more hostility between four-year colleges and community colleges, it will harm our ability to ensure that the students who want to transfer will be able to do so easily, seamlessly, and successfully. What is far more important than allowing community colleges to offer bachelor's degrees is to make sure community colleges and four-year schools are engaged collectively and collaboratively to ensure the success of their students.

Both the long-term impact of Covid and the demographic cliff are trends that community colleges have the ability to navigate and mitigate. As public institutions, they would benefit from sustained support from both state and federal governments. While the media attention is focused on the Trump administration's attack upon the elite colleges and universities, community colleges and their students are faced with huge financial challenges as public support is curtailed.[7] As the Truman Commission stated, higher education should be considered a public good, which is often the justification within the colleges to believe that a bipartisan approach is necessary for the support of the colleges. This view, however, should not reject an important role for any public institution: the continued support for democratic values. Moreover, as institutions embedded within their communities, it is striking to me how underutilized community colleges continue to be in promoting civic participation and engagement. After retirement, I consciously avoided involvement in any programs or activities at Macomb Community College as president emeritus. However, I did ask for the establishment of the James Jacobs Legacy Speaker Series. This activity outlined a role Macomb Community College might play to fulfill some of the goals of the Truman Commission.

Civic Participation: Legacy Project

It is now conventional wisdom to note that America is a divided nation unable to resolve major social and political issues because "each side" seems unwilling to listen, let alone compromise, to find solutions. Almost every week, another incident or event underscores the reality we face. Nevertheless, where are there potential solutions to national malaise? This will unlikely come from our leaders, individuals, organizations, or corporations. None seems to be held in high regard by the public. It appears more likely that other organizations will need to resolve this growing dilemma.

One of these organizations can be community colleges. There is long-standing recognition that community colleges are the backbone of their local community's workforce and economic development. With a comprehensive understanding of their communities, residents, and employers, community colleges can quickly adapt to evolving needs, creating new training that connects residents to jobs and employers to skilled workers. The reason this works is the local credibility of community colleges—they have earned the trust of their residents by serving their needs.

However, positive economic growth and sustainable employment alone do not make thriving communities. A vibrant civic culture must also exist, with residents engaging in civil discourse, debating, and making decisions based on their values. These elements are fundamental to democracy as well as prosperity. Communities with high economic growth are typically characterized by significant levels of civic engagement. With their deep local roots and legitimacy, community colleges are ideally positioned to help foster civic engagement—not just for their students and staff but for their entire community. As part of my "Legacy Project" at the college, I have developed this concept into a project that I hope others will build upon and improve.[8]

Programs such as these are critical to fostering and sustaining the civic culture of our communities, and they are also essential to addressing our current polarized environment. Creating an atmosphere of community learning, showcasing credible informational resources, and modeling thoughtful discussion and debate can help encourage individuals to be more discerning about where they get their information and how they engage with others on issues of importance. This is a natural progression for community colleges, often viewed as community conveners. It is my hope that other community colleges initiate these activities, and we collaborate on speakers and themes that we believe would encourage community engagement and civic participation.

Democracy and Community Colleges

To some, even within the community college circles, activities such as the Legacy Project may be considered too "political." Not wanting to be political has caused community college leaders to be reluctant to promote civic engagement. They are worried that being drawn into "one side" will harm their long-term view that they need to work with everyone—and "taking sides" harms the long-term future of their institutions. The recent controversies regarding student activism in support of the people in Gaza highlight the difficulties that higher education institutions face when dealing with major political issues.

Unfortunately, staying out of politics is not an option for any public education institution. A growing nihilism has captured part of the American population, and community colleges must be part of the response to these views. While it is easy to blame this development on President Trump and his supporters, in some ways, they are the product, not the cause, of this growing trend. For years, it was common in Macomb County that when describing something as "political" it meant it was dirty, valueless, and without merit. That viewpoint suggested that, in politics, facts and values don't matter. It assumes everyone lies, manipulates, and destroys institutions to obtain control or their desired goal. This view of politics as a malicious exercise may explain why fervent Trump supporters are unmoved by all that is discovered about his behavior—they assume this is what you can expect from anyone engaging in "politics." Given this understanding of politics, it is not difficult to view how Trump can say or do anything and his "base" will support him, no matter what.

Perhaps more important than Trump, however, is the threat of the anti-science theories that many social media sites advance about almost any issue. While some outlets focus on issues such as climate change, vaccines, or fluoride, why should we believe this kind of anti-science sentiment will not spread to discussions of airline maintenance procedures or highway safety rules? It is an extraordinary paradox that with all the recent focus on artificial intelligence, vast amounts of information are useless to confront the subjective anti-empirical thinking that is becoming firmly embedded in the culture. Too many Americans believe that if you say something long enough and loud enough, it will be "accepted" regardless of how dubious the claim is or whether there is any empirical basis for the claim. Community colleges need to confront these anti-factual subjective views.

Part of the anti-science strategy is to debunk anyone who believes in factual investigation, critical thinking, and research. Indeed, this mindset is motivating the attack on our colleges and universities. In this critical time, it is important for higher education in general, and community colleges specifically, to advance and defend a new understanding of "partisanship." As public educational institutions, empirical evidence and values remain the bedrock of any discussion of differences. Otherwise, there is no judgment or standard on which to view or to participate. Community colleges need to be part of bringing a new understanding of what is "non-partisan" and why it is essential to speak loud and clearly on behalf of public education and our students. You cannot live as a citizen in a democracy without this perspective—socialist, liberal, or conservative. The Greek word for civilized is πολιτισμένος (politismenos), the root of the word "politics." Developing a civic culture based on discussions within empirical thought and steadfast values should be part of every community college agenda. I would argue this is also a critical challenge that new leaders of community colleges will face: how to shape an understanding of politics which will encourage civil debate and lead to resolution that will move forward not only our institutions but also our society.

Notes

1 Cited in Patrick Sullivan, *Economic Inequality, Neoliberalism, and the American Community College* (Palgrave Macmillan, 2017), ix.

2 Clive Belfield, Thomas Brock, John Fink, and Davis Jenkins, *Aftershocks: How the Pandemic Affected Community College Finances* (Community College Research Center, 2024), https://ccrc.tc.columbia.edu/arccnetwork/2024/02/14/aftershocks-how-the-pandemic-affected-community-college-finances/.

3 CCRC has examined enrollment data indicating the impact of Covid on enrollment. See Clive Belfield and Thomas Brock, "Community Colleges and the COVID-19 Pandemic: Which States Have Been Hit Hardest by Enrollment Disruptions?" *Community College Research Center*, March 2, 2021, https://ccrc.tc.columbia.edu/easyblog/community-colleges-covid-19-states-hardest-hit.html.

4 Sophie Nguyen, Rachel Fishman, and Olivia Cheche, *Varying Degrees 2024: New America's Eighth Annual Survey on Higher Education* (New America, July 2024).

5 This point is one of the central themes of the newly released CCRC study which summarized ten years of research into the pathways approach. Jenkins et al.

6 Maria S. Cormier, Thomas Brock, James Jacobs, Richard Kazis, and Hayley Glatter, *Preparing for Tomorrow's Middle-Skill Jobs: How Community Colleges Are Responding to Technology Innovation in the Workplace* (Community College Research Center, Teachers College, Columbia University, 2022).

7 For a discussion of these challenges and the opposition launched by community college presidents, see Ben Austen, "How Trump's War on Higher Education Is Hitting Community Colleges," *The New York Times Magazine*, August 4, 2025, https://www.nytimes.com/2025/08/04/magazine/trump-community-college-anti-dei.html.

8 I was able to raise some money from foundations and, with support from the college, we initiated the program in March 2018 where national speakers could come to Macomb to speak to our students and also the community at an evening event. At our first session, we featured the

American economist Larry Summers, whose high-level roles have included serving as secretary of the US Department of the Treasury, director of the White House National Economic Council, and former president of Harvard University. Nearly 600 community members turned out to hear him discuss the topic "Economic Globalism vs. Nationalism and Its Effect on Macomb County" with David Wessel, a senior fellow in economic studies at the Brookings Institution and Pulitzer Prize-winning former writer and editor for the *Wall Street Journal*. Since then, the project has offered five additional programs at Macomb Community College, drawing over 1,700 community members. At a recent session held in March 2024, Carol Graham from the Brookings Institution spoke about "Elevating the Wellbeing of Communities such as Macomb." She was introduced by the Macomb County Executive and interacted with a panel of community leaders.

12 Epilogue

To complete this journey, I need to return to the original question posed by my reporter friend: In my time at Macomb, have I changed my political views? The answer on one level is obvious, of course. Indeed, I have changed. The conditions we face in 2025 are quite different from those in 1967 when I first started working at Macomb. The country has changed. In part because of what I and millions of others did, we moved America into a more progressive direction. Despite the incessant media attention on the antics of Trump, the conservatives on the Supreme Court, and the ultra-right capture of the Republican Party, there has been a steady growth of positive cultural change in the past fifty years, which will not be easily reversed. The Civil Rights Movement of the 1960s has morphed from dealing with de jure legal challenges so that people of color are treated equally to one where issues are now tied to economic and social equity. The Women's Movement has made substantial economic progress while fighting male supremacy and creating a space to express their creativity and identity. Abortions were illegal in the 1960s, and while the Supreme Court's recent ruling has again made it a contested terrain, the attempt to take away the right to abortion has energized a mass response. Gay and transgender rights are now more recognized when fifty years ago they were considered criminal behavior. Ecological issues are now considered so fundamental that all mainstream institutions must consider them. Even personal issues are now expressed in new social terms. The attacks by the current administration on many of these issues are not gaining popularity; indeed, there appears to be a growing opposition to these attempts to take America backward.

These issues are evolving and there is a long way to go. It is always fashionable among progressives to deplore the present conditions of American society. While it is correct to argue that we have a long struggle ahead to produce major changes, we should not fail to notice how far our efforts have taken us. Conditions are far from perfect, but they have improved continually in the last fifty years. It did not come easy; we did it through hard work and effort. This is not a linear struggle. There will be more setbacks beyond the ascendancy of Trump, for example, but the long-run progress is clear.

This does not mean radical right-wing leadership is inconsequential or that it is unnecessary to confront their ideas and activities, but only focusing on their activities belies the significance of the social changes brought about through the activities of millions. I was proud to be part of that struggle and believe in its significance. In this sense, I haven't changed. Instead, I have been very consistent from the days I started working for progressive changes in American society at Macomb.

To underscore how far we have come, within the context of Macomb County consider this development. In the 1970 Census, three years after I started teaching at South Campus, Warren, Michigan, was the third largest city in the state with 179,260 residents. Of them, 132 were Black (0.0007 percent of the population). Those 132 individuals lived in 28 households, 23 of which were military or federal housing. That means only five Black households resided in Warren. In

1967, an interracial family who bought a house in Warren was confronted by a white racist mob who threatened to blow up the house. Today, Warren's population is over 20 percent non-white, and the public schools are almost 40 percent non-white. In November 2023, there was a Black candidate elected to the Warren City Council. Part of the district is represented in Lansing by a representative from the Hmong community. It is conventional wisdom that the future of Warren and many institutions in Macomb County are now intimately tied to how well the county welcomes non-white and new immigrants into the social and economic fabric of the community.[1]

Nevertheless, at the same time, none of these positive social changes has halted the enormous accumulation of wealth at the top and a significant decline in the broad middle class. We are now in a new Gilded Age. Multimillionaires participate in politics as a new hobby. Supreme Court decisions allow them to spend millions of dollars on campaigns and more run for office. The disappearance of the middle class is an important loss that can lead to an unraveling of the above-mentioned progressive changes. There is a significant growth in the number of the working poor population. Trade unions represent a small fraction of the working class and are facing major challenges to increase membership. The various economic reforms of capitalism won through the New Deal and post-War period, such as retirement benefits, public housing, agricultural reform, public education, and public health, are being altered and narrowed through privatization strategies. Even significant changes, such as expanding medical care to individuals, can only occur through an inefficient and often ineffective trifecta of the private sector insurance industry, the private pharmaceutical sector, and a not-for-profit hospital system. The dominance of major corporations in the critical information technology sector and the rise of conspicuous consumption capitalists, such as Elon Musk or Jeff Bezos, have become essential features of our economy. There is a real threat to democracy and shared values that has unfolded within an economic system dominated by so few. In this regard, lots of work needs to be done.

A new populist movement, similar to what existed in nineteenth-century America, would be a refreshing change to our current political and economic alternatives. In assembling that movement for change, I would argue that community colleges will be central in the economic and political challenges we will face. These institutions can become important motivators to protect and extend the public space and the broad middle class. They were products of the broad middle-class era, originally designed to bring higher education to working adults and their children. Their goal was to utilize education to develop their skills for the economy of the future. In a real sense, they are the institutions of opportunity and equity, and it will be essential for them to confront and take on the growing class issues. However, they cannot do it alone. In the future, they must consider themselves part of a broader coalition with unions, community-based organizations, environmental groups, and the anti-racist and feminist movements. In that regard, they need to shed the widely held view that they are apolitical educational institutions that somehow stand outside of political debates into institutions that can promote democracy and equity.

Here I can agree with my reporter friend that I have changed. I was attracted to the community college to "organize" workers because they were the places where these people could be found. I failed to see how important it was to change the operations of these institutions. In that sense, Macomb Community College was a tremendous learning experience for me. By staying at Macomb and engaging in change, I shed my often-infantile views of how change occurs and recognized that changing the institution will more rapidly promote and effectively bring about what I desired.

Community colleges can be transformed to be a part of changing America. I hope my modest steps at Macomb were a small start and that others who follow will advance them. I wish I had discovered this dimension earlier, and I thank the Macomb staff, students, and the community for helping me finally understand how the transformation of institutions happens. Of course, this does not mean demonstrations, mass political activity, or elections are unimportant. However, there needs to be equal, if not greater, weight given to changing the present institutions directly through long-term commitment and practical steps guided by a vision that keeps this activity on course. You cannot do this outside of the confines of the institution, but to do it well, you need a compelling vision primarily developed externally.

What advice would I give to younger people, particularly former community college students who are completing their postsecondary education and are committed to change but unsure how to reconcile their political views and personal and economic future? I would urge you to take your talents and utilize them to change institutions that affect working people—wherever you are. You will be far more effective not to adopt the romantic view of an "organizer" who negates their education and class background so they can be "with the people." People can figure out the changes necessary; what they need are institutions that help them develop their agency. In this light, it is crucial to understand how your selected occupation or profession fits within working communities and how you can promote change within it. It may be through unionization. It may be through existing work teams. It may be through a book club of like-minded friends. The best tactics and strategies will emerge from your specific context. What is critical is to embed your vision within the practices of the institutions that matter to working people—whether in the public or private sector. By doing this, you will overcome the right-wing arguments of an "elitist" progressive culture that is antithetical to their interest in working people. It is time to take a step into America and influence change. If this book helped motivate you to make that decision, I think my effort to write it was worthwhile.

Note

1 Zack Stanton, "In 1967, a Black Man and a White Woman Bought a Home; American Politics Would Never Be the Same," *Politico*, December 2023, https://www.politico.com/news/magazine/2023/12/22/macomb-county-michigan-suburbs-american-politics-00131386."

Bibliography

Adelman, Clifford. 2000. *A Parallel Postsecondary Universe: The Certification System in Information Technology*. Office of Educational Research and Improvement, U.S. Department of Education.

American Association of Community and Junior Colleges. 1988. *Building Communities: A Vision for a New Century*. AACJC.

Bahr, Peter R., Yiren Chen, and Rooney Columbus. 2023. "Community College Skills Builders: Prevalence, Characteristics, Behavior, and Outcomes of Successful Non-completing Students across Four States." *Journal of Higher Education* 94 (1): 96–131. https://doi.org/10.1080/00221546.2022.2082782.

Bailey, Thomas R., and Clive R. Belfield. 2019. "The False Dichotomy between Academic Learning and Occupational Skills." *Daedalus* 148 (4): 164–78.

Bailey, Thomas R., and Jim Jacobs. 2009, November. "Can Community Colleges Rise to the Occasion?" *The American Prospect*, 18–20.

Bailey, Thomas R., Shanna Smith Jaggars, and Davis Jenkins. 2015. *Redesigning America's Community Colleges: A Clearer Path to Student Success*. Harvard University Press.

Bailey, Thomas R., Yukari Matsuzuka, James Jacobs, Vanessa Smith Morest, and Katherine L. Hughes. 2003. "Institutionalization and Sustainability of the National Science Foundation's Advanced Technological Education Program." Community College Research Center, Teachers College, Columbia University.

Belden, Russonello & Stewart. 2004. *Expanding Opportunity: Communicating about the Role of Community Colleges*. Douglas Gould and Company.

Belfield, Clive, and Thomas Brock. 2021. "Community Colleges and the COVID-19 Pandemic: Which States Have Been Hit Hardest by Enrollment Disruptions?" Community College Research Center, March 2. https://ccrc.tc.columbia.edu/easyblog/community-colleges-covid-19-states-hardest-hit.html.

Belfield, Clive, Thomas Brock, John Fink, and Davis Jenkins. 2024. "Aftershocks: How the Pandemic Affected Community College Finances." Community College Research Center. https://ccrc.tc.columbia.edu/arccnetwork/2024/02/14/aftershocks-how-the-pandemic-affected-community-college-finances/.

Bickerstaff, Susan, and Octaviano Chavarín. 2018. "Understanding the Needs of Part-Time Faculty at Six Community Colleges." Community College Research Center.

Bluestone, Barry, and Irving Bluestone. 1992. *Negotiating the Future: A Labor Perspective on American Business*. HarperCollins.

Bomey, Nathan. 2016. *Detroit Resurrected: To Bankruptcy and Back*. W.W. Norton & Company.

Bomey, Nathan, and John Gallagher. 2013, September 15. "How Detroit Went Broke." *Detroit Free Press*.

Bradley, Walter. n.d. "The Origins and Development of Macomb Community College 1952–1975." Unpublished manuscript.

Brick, Michael. 1963. *The American Association of Junior Colleges: Forum and Focus*. PhD diss., Teachers College, Columbia University.

Brint, Steven, and Jerome Karabel. 1989. *The Diverted Dream: Community Colleges and the Promise of Educational Opportunity in America, 1900–1985*. Oxford University Press.

Brown, Peter. 1991. *Minority Party: Why Democrats Face Defeat in 1982 and Beyond*. Regnery Gateway.

Center for Automotive Research. 2007. *Beyond the Big Leave: The Future of U.S. Automotive Human Resources*. Center for Automotive Research.

Center for Community Studies. 2003. *Macomb County: A County in Transition*. Macomb Community College.

Cohen, Arthur M., and Florence B. Brawer. 1996. *The American Community College*. 3rd ed. Jossey-Bass.

College Board. 1995. *Policy Recommendations for Educating Adults*. College Board.

College Board Advocacy & Policy Center. 2013. *Rethinking Pell Grants*. The College Board. https://secure-media.collegeboard.org/digitalServices/pdf/advocacy/policycenter/advocacy-rethinking-pell-grants-report.pdf.

Commission on Higher Education & Economic Growth. 2004. *Final Report of the Lt. Governor's Commission on Higher Education & Economic Growth*. State of Michigan.

Community College Research Center. 2008. "Bridges to Opportunity for Underprepared Adults: A State Policy Guide for Community College Leaders." Community College Research Center, Teachers College, Columbia University. https://ccrc.tc.columbia.edu/publications/underprepared-adults-state-policy-guide.html.

Community College Research Center. 2017. "Building Transfer Student Success at Macomb Community College: A Report on Transfer and Degree Completion." Teachers College, Columbia University, October. https://ccrc.tc.columbia.edu/publications/building-transfer-student-success-macomb-community-college-report-transfer-degree-completion.html.

Community College Research Center. 2024. "Understanding Dual Enrollment." https://ccrc.tc.columbia.edu/publications/understanding-dual-enrollment.html.

Community College Research Center. n.d. "Achieving the Dream: Community Colleges Count." https://ccrc.tc.columbia.edu/research-project/achieving-the-dream.html.

Community College Research Center. n.d. "Bridges to Opportunity Initiative." https://ccrc.tc.columbia.edu/research-project/bridges-to-opportunity.html.

Community College Research Center. n.d. "Our History." https://ccrc.tc.columbia.edu/ccrc-history.html.

Cormier, Maria S., Thomas Brock, James Jacobs, Richard Kazis, and Hayley Glatter. 2022. "Preparing for Tomorrow's Middle-Skill Jobs: How Community Colleges Are Responding to Technology Innovation in the Workplace." Community College Research Center, Teachers College, Columbia University.

Detroit Promise. "About Us." https://detroitpromise.com/about/.

Detroit Regional Chamber of Commerce. 2013. *Michigan Is Auto: Assets of the Motor State*. Regional Chamber.

Dougherty, Kevin J., and Marianne F. Bakia. 1999. *The New Economic Development Role of the Community College*. Community College Research Center, Columbia University, Teachers College.

Fasenfest, David, and James Jacobs. 2000. "Revival and Change in the Automobile Industry of Southeast Michigan." Paper presented at Uddevalla Symposium 2000: *Entrepreneurship, Firm Growth and Regional Development in the New Economic Geography*, Trollhattan, Sweden, June 15–17.

Fasenfest, David, and James Jacobs. 2003. "An Anatomy of Change and Transition: The Automobile Industry of Southeast Michigan." *Small Business Economics* 21 (2): 156.

Fink, John. 2019. "Acceleration for All? Mapping Racial Equity in Access to AP and Dual Enrollment." Community College Research Center, October 8. https://ccrc.tc.columbia.edu/easyblog/mapping -racial-equity-ap-dual-enrollment.html.

Fischer, Karin. 2009. "As the Auto Industry Shrinks, a Community College Retools." *The Chronicle of Higher Education*, May 8. https://www.chronicle.com/article/as-the-auto-industry-shrinks-a-community -college-retools/.

Floyd, Deborah L., and Michael L. Skolnik. 2019. "The Community College Baccalaureate." In *13 Ideas That Are Transforming the Community College World*, edited by Terry U. O'Banion, 103–27. Rowman & Littlefield.

Ford Motor Company Sociological Department & English School. n.d. The Henry Ford Museum of American Innovation. Accessed June 5, 2025. https://www.thehenryford.org/collections-and -research/digital-resources/popular-topics/sociological-department/.

Fuller, Joseph B., and Manjari Raman. 2022. *The Partnership Imperative: Community Colleges, Employers, and America's Chronic Skills Gap*. Harvard Business School.

Gaft, Samuel. 1998. "The History of the Henry Ford Trade School, 1916 to 1952." EdD thesis, University of Michigan.

Georgakas, Dan, and Marvin Surkin. 1975. *Detroit: I Do Mind Dying: A Study in Urban Revolution*. St. Martin's Press.

Gerstle, Gary. 2022. *The Rise and Fall of the Neoliberal Order*. Oxford University Press.

Geschwender, James A. 1977. *Class, Race, & Worker Insurgency: The League of Revolutionary Black Workers*. Cambridge University Press.

Gleazer, Edward J., Jr. 1980. *The Community College: Values, Vision, and Vitality*. American Association of Community and Junior Colleges.

Goldin, Claudia, and Lawrence F. Katz. 2008. *The Race Between Education and Technology*. Harvard University Press.

Goldman Sachs. "Program Details: 10,000 Small Businesses." https://10ksbapply.com/program-details/.

Gorelik, Daniel. n.d. "NYC's Spanish Civil War Volunteers: Biographies/Saul Wellman." https://scwnyc.stuy .edu/archive/Saul%20Wellman.html.

Grasgreen, Allie. 2015. "Community Colleges Lifted via Obama." *Politico*, May 18. https://www.politico .com/story/2015/05/community-colleges-lifted-via-obama-118077.

Griffiths, Brett, Randall Hickman, and Sebastian Zollner. 2017. "Institutional Assessment of a Genre-Analysis Approach to Writing Center Consultations." *Praxis: A Writing Center Journal* 15 (1): 5.

Grubb, W. Norton. 1999. *Honored but Invisible: An Inside Look at Teaching in Community Colleges*. Routledge.

Grubb, W. Norton, and Marvin Lazerson. 2004. *The Education Gospel: The Economic Power of Schooling*. Harvard University Press.

Grubb, W. Norton, Norena Badway, and Denise Bell. 1997. *Workforce, Economic and Community Development: The Changing Landscape of the Entrepreneurial Community College*. National Center for Research in Vocational Education.

Halperin, Samuel. 1998. *The Forgotten Half: American Youth and Young Families*. American Youth Policy Forum.

Hamlin, Michael. 2012. *A Black Revolutionary's Life in Labor: Black Workers Power in Detroit*. Tide Books.

Higher Learning Commission. 2016. *Comprehensive Evaluation of Macomb Community College: Re-Affirmation Report*. Higher Learning Commission.

Industrial Technology Institute. 1984. *An Investment in the Future of Manufacturing*. Industrial Technology Institute.

Jacobs, James. 1977. "The Conduct of Local Political Intelligence." PhD diss., Princeton University.

Jacobs, James. 1987. *Final Report: Training and Public Policy*. Industrial Technology Institute.

Jacobs, James 1987. *Liaison Office Newsletter*, vols. 1–4. Industrial Technology Institute.

Jacobs, James. 1989. "Training the Workforce of the Future." *Technology Review*, August–September, 66–72.

Jacobs, James. 1994. "The Role of Trustees in the Governance Process." In *Handbook of Community College Administration: A Human Resources Perspective*, edited by A. Hoffman. College and University Personnel Association Perspective.

Jacobs, James. 2002. "Community Colleges and the Workforce Investment Act: Promises and Problems of the New Vocationalism." In *The New Vocationalism in Community Colleges*, edited by Debra Bragg. Jossey-Bass.

Jacobs, James. 2008. "Economic Forecast for Macomb County." Presentation, January 22, 2008.

Jacobs, James. 2009. "Economic Forecast for Macomb County." Presentation, February 3, 2009.

Jacobs, James. 2016. "Economic Forecast for Macomb County." Presentation, January 15, 2016.

Jacobs, James. 2017. "Economic Forecast for Macomb County." Presentation, January 11, 2017.

Jacobs, James. 2023. "Student Centered Vision for Workforce Development." Community College Research Center, Teachers College, Columbia University. https://ccrc.tc.columbia.edu/easyblog/student-centered-vision-workplace-development.html.

Jacobs, James. "Build Upon the Strengths of America's Community College." *Brookings Institution*, Metropolitan Policy Program. https://www.brookings.edu/wp-content/uploads/2016/07/0927_great_lakes_community_college.pdf.

Jacobs, James, and W. Norton Grubb. 2006. "The Limits of 'Training for Now': Lessons from Information Technology Certification." In *Defending the Community College Equity Agenda*, edited by Thomas Bailey and Vanessa S. Morest, 132–54. Johns Hopkins University Press.

Jacobs, James, and George Harrison. 2000. *School-to-Work in Macomb*. Temple University.

Jacobs, James, and Roberta C. Teahen. 1997. "Shadow Colleges and NCA Accreditation: A Conceptual Framework." In *A Collection of Papers on Self-Study and Institutional Improvement*, 13–19. North Central Association of Colleges and Schools.

Jacobs, Jim, Ellen Ullman, and Tabitha Whissemore. 2011. "You've Got a Friend… in Industry." *Community College Journal* 82 (1): 22–7.

Jacobs, Jim. "Working Class Political Attitudes Through a Professor's Eyes." *Radicals in The Professions Newsletter*, Ann Arbor, vol. 1, no. 3. January 1968, 6–9.

Jenkins, Davis, John Fink, and Tatiana Velasco. "Which Community College Awards Are Likely to Prepare Students for Post-Completion Success?" Community College Research Center, Teachers College, Columbia University. https://ccrc.tc.columbia.edu/publications/community-college-awards-for-post-completion-success.html.

Jenkins, Davis, Hana Lahr, John Fink, Serena C. Klempin, and Maggie P. Fay. 2025. *More Essential Than Ever: Community College Pathways to Educational and Career Success*. Harvard University Press.

Karp, Melinda Mechur, Juan Carlos Calcagno, Katherine L. Hughes, Dong Wook Jeong, and Thomas Bailey. 2007. *The Postsecondary Achievement of Participants in Dual Enrollment: An Analysis of Student Outcomes in Two States*. New York: Community College Research Center, Teachers College, Columbia University.

Karp, Melinda Mechur, James Jacobs, and Katherine Hughes. 2002. *Credentials, Curriculum, and Access: The Debate Over Nursing Preparation*. Washington, DC: Community College Press.

Klug, Thomas A. 2017. "The Deindustrialization of Detroit." In *Detroit 1967*, edited by Joel Stone. Wayne State University Press.

Kuh, George D., Jillian Kinzie, John H. Schuh, and Elizabeth J. Whitt. 2005. *Student Success in College: Creating Conditions That Matter*. Jossey-Bass.

Levin, John S. 2007. *Nontraditional Students and Community Colleges: The Conflict of Justice and Neoliberalism*. Palgrave Macmillan.

Liebowitz, Marty, and Judith Combes Taylor. 2004. *Breaking Through: Helping Low-Skilled Adults Enter and Succeed in College and Careers*. Jobs for the Future.

Little, Jill. 2013. "Student Options for Success: Non-Academic Financial Support for Students in Need." Internal report. Macomb Community College.

Lorenzo, Albert L. 2005. "The University Center: A Collaborative Approach to Baccalaureate Degrees." In *The Community College Baccalaureate: Emerging Trends and Policy Issues*, edited by D.L. Floyd, M.L. Skolnik, and K.P. Walker, 73–93. Stylus Publishing.

Lorenzo, Albert L., and James J. Blanzy. 1988, January. *Mid-America Group: A Foundation for Renewal*. Macomb Community College.

Macomb Association of School Administrators. 1966. *A Citizens Report: Macomb Occupational Education Survey*. Michigan Department of Education, Division of Vocational Education.

Macomb Community College. 1954. *College Catalogue*.

Macomb Community College. 2007. *Self-Study Report*, February.

Macomb Community College. 2012. *Celebrating the Commitment: Recognizing Macomb Community College's Impact on the County*.

Macomb Community College. 2012. *Macomb County 2012: Public High School Graduates*.

Macomb Community College. 2012. *Report to the Community: 2012*.

Macomb Community College. 2016. *Macomb Community College Data Book*.

Macomb Community College. 2016. *Report on Diversity and Inclusion at Macomb Community College: A Report to President Jacobs*, June.

Macomb Community College. 2016. *Year One Report: Innovation Fund*.

Macomb Community College. 2024. *Transforming Lives and Communities: Macomb Community College at 70*.

Macomb Intermediate School District. 2024. "Early College at Macomb." https://ecmacomb.org/pdf /2023-2024/ECofM_brochure_2024_web_version_Accessible.pdf.

Meza, Elizabeth, and Ivy Love. 2023. "When Community Colleges Offer a Bachelor's Degree: A Literature Review on Student Access and Outcomes." New America, March 28. https://www.newamerica.org/ education-policy/reports/when-community-colleges-offer-a-bachelors-degree/.

Mirel, Jeffrey. 1999. *The Rise and Fall of An Urban School System: Detroit, 1907-81*, 2nd ed. University of Michigan Press.

MIT Task Force on the Work of the Future. 2021. *Mobility and the Work of the Future*. Massachusetts Institute of Technology.

National Advisory Committee on the Junior College. 1964. "A National Resource for Occupational Education." Association of American Junior Colleges.

Neil, Gerald L. 1971. *History of Warren, Michigan 1837-1970*.

Neustadt, Richard E. 1962. *Presidential Power: The Politics of Leadership*. Science Editions.

Nguyen, Sophie, Rachel Fishman, and Olivia Cheche. 2024. "Varying Degrees 2024: New America's Eighth Annual Survey on Higher Education." New America, July.

O'Banion, Terry. 2016. *Bread and Roses: Helping Students Make a Good Living and Live a Good Life*. League for Innovation.

Parnell, Dale, and Dan Hull. 1991. *Tech-Prep Associate Degree: A Win/Win Experience*. Center for Occupational Research and Development.

Phelps, Allen L., Dale C. Brandenburg, and James Jacobs. 1990. *The UAW Joint Funds: Opportunities and Dilemmas for Postsecondary Vocational Education*. National Center for Research in Vocational Education.

Pincus, F.L. 1980. "The False Promises of Community Colleges: Class Conflict and Vocational Education." *Harvard Educational Review* 50 (3): 30.

Piore, Michael J., and Charles F. Sabel. 1984. *The Second Industrial Divide*. Basic Books.

Ratledge, Alyssa, and Stanley Dai. 2022. *The Detroit Promise Path Evaluation: Outcomes After Four Years*. MDRC.

Riddle, Dave. 1998. "The Rise of the Reagan Democrats in Warren, Michigan 1964-1984." Ph.D. dissertation, Wayne State University.

Rosenfeld, Stuart A. 1992. *Competitive Manufacturing: New Strategies for Regional Development*. Rutgers University Press.

Rosenfeld, Stuart A. 1995. *New Technologies and New Skills: Two-Year Colleges at the Vanguard of Modernization*. Regional Technology Strategies.

Rosenthal, Jack. 1972. "50 Richest Counties Are in the Suburbs." *New York Times*, September 19.

Rosenthal, Mark. 2015. *Diego Rivera & Frida Kahlo in Detroit*. Yale University Press.

Rothschild, Emma. 1973. *Paradise Lost: The Decline of the Auto-Industrial Age*. Random House.

Rothstein, Richie. 1967. "Organizing in The Heart of America." *Radicals in The Professions Newsletter*, vol. 1, no. 2, December.

Roumell, George T., Jr. 2016. "'You Will Make a Difference:' George T. Roumell Jr.'s Fall 2015 Commencement Address to the MSU College of Law." *Michigan Bar Journal*, July.

Sale, Kirkpatrick. 1974. *SDS: The Rise and Development of the Students for a Democratic Society*. Vintage Books.

Schwartz, Robert, and Kerry McKittrick. 2024. "From Margins to Mainstream: Bringing Career-Connected Learning to Scale." *American Educator* 48: 4–11.

Secretary's Commission on Achieving Necessary Skills (SCANS). 1991. *What Work Requires of Schools: A SCANS Report for America 2000*. U.S. Department of Labor.

Serrin, William. 1973. *The Company and the Union*. Alfred A. Knopf.

Shore, Ira. 1980. *Critical Thinking and Everyday Life*. South End Press.

Slay, Kelly, and Rebecca Christensen. 2015. "Adult Learners at Macomb: A Qualitative Analysis of Current and Prospective Students' Experiences." Center for the Study of Higher and Postsecondary Education, School of Education, University of Michigan.

Stamm, Alan. 2012. "DIA Millage Proposal Creates List of Pros, Cons for Suburban Voters." *MI Patch*, July 3. https://patch.com/michigan/macomb/dia-millage-proposal-creates-pro-con-list-for-suburba95bcb397de.

Stanton, Zack. 2023. "In 1967, a Black Man and a White Woman Bought a Home; American Politics Would Never Be the Same," *Politico*, December. https://www.politico.com/news/magazine/2023/12/22/macomb-county-michigan-suburbs-american-politics-00131386.

Sugrue, Thomas J. 1996. *The Origins of the Urban Crisis: Race and Inequality in Postwar Detroit*. Princeton University Press.

Sullivan, Patrick. 2017. *Economic Inequality, Neoliberalism, and the American Community College*. Palgrave Macmillan.

Teles, Elizabeth J. 2012. "Curriculum and Teaching Strategies for STEM Technicians: The NSF Advanced Technological Education Program." In *Career Pathways for STEM Technicians*, edited by Dan Hull. CORD Publications.

The Modernization Forum. 1993. *Skills for Industrial Modernization*. Report of the Modernization Skills Commission.

The New York Times. 1996. *The Downsizing of America*. Random House.

The White House, Office of the Press Secretary. 2009. "Remarks by the President on the American Graduation Initiative in Warren, MI." July 14. https://obamawhitehouse.archives.gov/the-press-office/remarks-president-american-graduation-initiative-warren-mi.

Thompson, Heather Ann. 2001. *Whose Detroit? Politics, Labor, and Race in a Modern American City*. Cornell University Press.

Thorton, Kevin, and Dale Prentiss. 1995. *Tanks and Industry: The Detroit Arsenal, 1940-1954*. History Office U.S. Army Tank-Automotive and Armaments Command.

United For ALICE. 2023. "The State of ALICE in Michigan." https://www.UnitedForALICE.org/Michigan.

Van Noy, Michelle, James Jacobs, Suzanne Korey, Thomas Bailey, and Katherine L. Hughes. 2009. "The Landscape of Noncredit Workforce Education: State Policies and Community College Practices." Community College Research Center, Teachers College, Columbia University.

Vargas, Joel, Sarah Hooker, Michael Collins, and Ana Bertha Gutierrez. 2019. "Eliminating the Gap between High School and College." In *13 Ideas That Are Transforming the Community College World*, edited by Terry U. O'Banion, 191–212. Rowman & Littlefield.

Varty, James, and James Jacobs. 1983. "The Role of a Technical Institute/Community College in Supporting Economic Development." Paper presented at the Third International Conference on Cooperative Education, Melbourne, Australia.

Washington's Community and Technical Colleges. 2022, December. "Integrated Basic Education and Skills Training (I-BEST)." December. https://www.sbctc.edu/resources/documents/about/facts-pubs/i -best.pdf.

Wessel, David. 1999, May 28. "A Community College Hopes to Answer Call of the Global Economy." *Wall Street Journal.*

Womack, James P., Daniel T. Jones, and Daniel Roos. 1990. *The Machine That Changed the World.* Macmillan Books.

Wylie, Jeanie. 1990. *Poletown: Community Betrayed.* University of Illinois Press.

Wyner, Josh, and Davis Jenkins. 2024. "Eight Strategies to Strengthen the Value of Community College Credentials." The Aspen Institute College Excellence Program, November 19. https://highered .aspeninstitute.org/blog-posts/eight-strategies-strengthen-value-community-college-credentials.

Xu, Di, and Shanna Smith Jaggars. 2013. "Examining the Effectiveness of Online Learning Within a Community College System: An Instrumental Variable Approach." Community College Research Center, Teachers College, Columbia University, April. https://ccrc.tc.columbia.edu/publications/ examining-effectiveness-of-online-learning.html.

Zeidenberg, Matthew, Sung-Woo Cho, and Davis Jenkins. 2010. "Washington State's Integrated Basic Education and Skills Training Program (I-BEST): New Evidence of Effectiveness." CCRC Working Paper No. 20. Community College Research Center.

Zielak, Perry. 2017. "Four-year Degree Offerings at Michigan Community Colleges." October 9. https:// www.house.mi.gov/hfa/PDF/CommunityColleges/CC_FourYearDegrees_memo_Oct17.pdf.

Index

About the Author

James Jacobs served in various roles at Macomb Community College for more than forty years, including as its president from 2008 to 2017. Prior to becoming president, he concurrently served as the director for the Center for Workforce Development and Policy at Macomb Community College and as the associate director of the Community College Research Center (CCRC) at Teachers College, Columbia University. Jacobs earned his PhD from Princeton University. He specializes in the areas of workforce skills and technology, economic development, worker retraining, and community college workforce development, and is widely published in these areas of expertise. In addition, Jacobs has conducted research, developed programs, and consulted on workforce development and community college issues at the national, state, and local levels.

Jacobs is a past president of the National Council for Workforce Education, a national postsecondary organization of occupational education and workforce development specialists. Jacobs served on several local boards, including the Center for Automotive Research, Metropolitan Affairs Council, Detroit Institute of Arts, United Way for Southeastern Michigan, and Advancing Macomb. He is widely known for the Macomb County Economic Forecast, which he has presented annually for more than thirty years for the coalition of the county's chambers of commerce. Jacobs currently works as a consultant to national community research and action projects.